DANGEROUS SHALLOWS

In Search of the Ghost Ships of Cape Cod

ERIC TAKAKJIAN AND RANDALL PEFFER

D1595885

LYONS
PRESS

Guilford, Connecticut

An imprint of The Rowman & Littlefield Publishing Group, Inc.
4501 Forbes Blvd., Ste. 200
Lanham, MD 20706
www.rowman.com

Distributed by NATIONAL BOOK NETWORK

Copyright © 2020 Eric Takakjian and Randall Peffer

All rights reserved. No part of this book may be reproduced in any form or by any electronic or mechanical means, including information storage and retrieval systems, without written permission from the publisher, except by a reviewer who may quote passages in a review.

British Library Cataloguing in Publication Information available

Library of Congress Cataloging-in-Publication Data available

ISBN 978-1-4930-4230-2 (paperback)
ISBN 978-1-4930-4231-9 (e-book)

∞™ The paper used in this publication meets the minimum requirements of American National Standard for Information Sciences—Permanence of Paper for Printed Library Materials, ANSI/NISO Z39.48-1992.

It helps to have a screw or two loose to be a shipwreck guy.

—Anonymous Diver

Contents

Author's Note

This book is a mystery story, pure and complicated. And it's also a story about ghosts. Too many ghosts. It is also a story about collaboration at the most intense levels. It takes a team to find, explore, and analyze a shipwreck. A team to recover artifacts. It has also taken a team to write this book. The genesis for this project began with me, my research partner Tim Colman, and a small dedicated group of wreck divers. We are the detectives in this narrative. Our search to find the graves of legendary wrecks—to put names, faces, and stories on the remains of over a hundred ships that litter the seabed off southern New England—often began with a single sentence in an old periodical, a footnote in a book, or a rumor.

Our quest took us to libraries, archives, museums, organizations of mariners, and commercial fishermen to separate facts from fiction. Then, when we thought we had enough clues, we set out to sea, for days upon days of deep and challenging seafaring and diving. Beneath the sea we came face-to-face, time and again, with the bones of the past and the ghosts of frightening maritime disasters such as the sinking of the *City of Columbus*, a passenger ship that came to grief on Devil's Bridge off Martha's Vineyard with over one hundred fatalities.

Writer and professional mariner Randy Peffer joined this project to collaborate with me in undertaking additional research as well as in giving shape, focus, and articulation to the narrative.

The events, the actions of individual persons, and the dialogue in this book have been carefully reconstructed from first-hand experiences and observations as well as from the stories of the people involved, their families, and eyewitnesses. When necessary and appropriate we have also relied on an extensive collection of relevant books, websites, military records, and the established protocols of operation and communication onboard vessels of the type and vintage of the ghost ships in this book. As with almost all events with multiple witnesses, sometimes the stories about what happened diverge. When such discrepancies arose during our research, we went with the story for which there exists the most corroborating first-hand testimony and evidence.

To help readers keep track of time in the text, flashbacks related to the damage or loss of ships are in italics.

—Eric Takakjian, 2019

Prologue

Treasure of Le Magnifique

1989

My story starts with rumors. Of ghost ships. Of wrecks full of treasure. Of a passenger liner vanishing into the night. Of a rogue submarine captain on a reign of terror.

It's a sparkling May morning. At 8:30 a.m. in Provincetown, Massachusetts. Shank Painter Road is empty except for a couple of beer delivery trucks and a few bicyclists. A cold front has blown through overnight, keeping the local fishermen and other commercial mariners ashore. Inside Matt Costa's Dairy Queen restaurant, the air steams with freshly brewed coffee and the scent of pastries. Like most mornings when I'm not at sea as first mate on a tugboat, I'm huddling at a table with a bunch of guys our waitress calls "wreck hounds."

I'm young, just turning thirty; recently married; just out of the US Coast Guard (USCG) after four years of active duty and seven years of reserve time. Barely a nickel to my name. Trying to make my way as a commercial mariner and salvage diver. My breakfast gang is made up of more seasoned men, and I feel privileged to be included in their morning gatherings. They are salvagers and divers. Wreck hunters. Fishermen, like Dave Dutra with his long, braided, graying ponytail. Guys who make their living off the sea. Guys who are always trying to scrape together a few extra bucks from one maritime disaster or another.

Dave's fresh from a little detour he recently took from ground fishing aboard his dragger *Richard & Arnold*. He was part of a clutch of guys who located the wreck of a ship called *White Squall* that sunk off the outer edge of the Cape more than a hundred years ago with 125 tons of pure Malaysian tin. They got more than a ton up before greed and personality differences ripped apart their syndicate. Now the tin-salvaging operation seems a fading fantasy. But with wreck hounds like these guys, new hope comes daily with the sugar in their coffee, the ketchup on their eggs.

This morning they're at it as usual, spinning stories of undiscovered "virgin" wrecks off the coast of Massachusetts. I'm all ears.

"Any of you boys ever heard the story of *Le Magnifique*?" asks Dave.

"That old thing?" One of the guys groans. "You may as well hope to find the *Flying Dutchman*."

I've never heard of *Le Magnifique*, but if the wreck lives up to its name, it could be quite a discovery, I think. And any ship mentioned in the same breath as the *Flying Dutchman* . . . well, this is how legends start.

"I heard some guy just got a permit to look for it . . . again," says one of our gang. "Good luck. Like there's really treasure on that thing?"

"Hey, you never know," says Dave.

He has a point. People thought Mel Fisher was crazy until he found the Spanish treasure galleon *Atocha* and brought up millions in gold. And it looks to me like Barry Clifford has a cash cow in the *Wydah*. She's the wreck of the sixteenth-century pirate ship belonging to "Black Sam" Belamy that Barry found not far from here in 1984. *Le Magnifique*'s name is getting bantered around in my brain with some pretty illustrious company. My imagination is beginning to flood with images of shiny coins scattered over a reef. As a kid I devoured the *National Geographic* features about Fisher's discovery of the *Atocha*. Now my mind is already seething with questions and the promise of an adventure.

This is the late-1980s, pre-Internet, and pretty soon I find myself driving to Boston to start searching the public library for information about the *Le Magnifique* disaster. It's not long before I'm deep into the archives of the New England Historical Society. I'm stuffing myself with anything and everything related to the story of *Le Magnifique*. As it happens, my mother is an expert in eighteenth-century sailing warship construction and design. It's her interest in these ships that turned almost all of our family vacations during my childhood into pilgrimages to maritime museums such as Mystic Seaport.

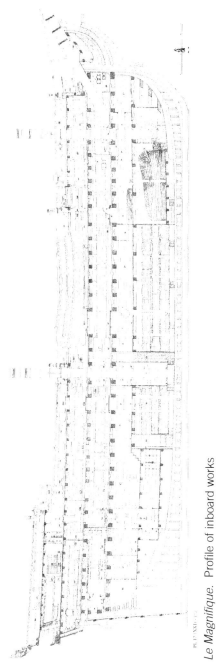

Le Magnifique. Profile of inboard works

DRAWN BY JEAN BOUDRIOT, PERSONAL COLLECTION OF ERIC TAKAKJIAN

How could her infatuation with ships like *Le Magnifique* not rub off on me? It was inevitable that I would learn to sail before I could ride a bike, inevitable that I would search for a life working on the water as well as plumbing the secrets beneath the waves. *Le Magnifique* is calling me back to my roots, back to a time before illness derailed my mother. This ship has quite a story.

In 1782 the French government sends Le Magnifique *from the West Indies to Boston to take part in celebrations of the US-French victory over the British in the American Revolution. She's a 74-gun, 176-foot man-o-war. As* Le Magnifique *sails past Lovell's Island in Boston Harbor, guided by an American harbor pilot, an unexpected wind shift pushes her onto a shoal. According to the New England Historical Society, "Historians have suggested that when she went to the bottom a small fortune in gold that the crew had recovered in the Caribbean was submerged with her."*

Though it seems that the French would remove any gold from the vessel during the hours that seamen spend trying to refloat their warship, the story of the treasure persists. The 1944 book The Romance of Boston Bay *by Edward Rowe Snow adds to the legend. Snow claims that in 1840, 1859, 1868, and 1869, salvagers attempt to locate the ship's treasure. They find timbers, cannonballs, and other artifacts, but no gold . . . until the 1920s. Snow writes that Charles H. Jennings, the local lighthouse keeper at the time, is digging on the island when he discovers coins in the sand. He washes them off and sets them aside. His temporary replacement soon arrives on the island to cover for the lighthouse keeper's scheduled leave. Jennings tells the man about his find and heads off to his vacation.*

Upon Jennings's return, the temporary keeper bolts off the island. Jennings soon discovers a large hole in the sand where he found the coins. "A few months later the assistant retired from the Lighthouse Service and lived in comfort for the rest of his life," Snow writes. "The reader may draw his own conclusions."

It takes more archival digging and plenty of phone calls, but by October 28, 1990, I'm part of a small team of divers who have come to Lovell's Island to search for *Le Magnifique*. Our leader—call him "Bob"—is not a diver. Bob's the guy who has acquired an exploration permit from the

Massachusetts Board of Underwater Archeological Resources to search the area around Lovell's Island for *Le Magnifique*. Bob's the guy who energizes wreck divers like me and Mark Stanton, the host of a cable TV show called "Divers Down." Bob has me, Mark, and several other experienced wreck divers fired up with his claims to have evidence that the French warship was carrying a secret cargo of gold when it wrecked on Lovell's Island.

Bob claims that under the guise of carrying wine to Boston for a dummy Spanish shipping company—a company set up to disguise the shipment of French war materiel to the American colonists during the Revolutionary War—*Le Magnifique* was actually smuggling gold species in wine casks. Bob says he's in possession of a letter from future First Lady of the United States Abigail Adams to George Washington, lamenting the loss of the "wine" after *Le Magnifique* wrecked. He says that the clear insinuation in the letter is that *wine* is code for *gold*.

Bob also produces a photocopy of a letter with the seal of the French National Maritime Museum. The letter is allegedly the typed, transcribed log entry from the captain of *Le Magnifique,* claiming that after the ship grounded off Lovell's Island some of the goods aboard, as well as the cannons, were salvaged, but not *le grand embarquement de monnaie a bord*—"the large shipment of money aboard." Mark Stanton, the other guys, and I are young and impressionable. We eat up Bob's pitch hook, line, and sinker. And so it is that we start looking for the wreck even before signing a contract with Bob.

Some of the divers were here at Lovell's a week ago while I was at sea working aboard a tug. They found a lot of contemporary debris, including junked refrigerators, pieces of old fishing boats, and some ship timbers. But who knows if any of the timbers relate to our French ship. Boston Harbor has been a mecca for illegal dumping and the scuttling of old boats for centuries. What I bring to the team is the mountain of lore I have gathered from my mother, her articles, and her books. I even have a 1- by 3-foot cutaway drawing of the construction details of *Le Magnifique* that shows every timber, the ship's magazines, and the cargo hold where the gold would have been stored. I'm the guy who everybody hopes will be able to see if any of this debris is our treasure ship.

It's late morning. I've just backed off the gray, gravelly beach where we have landed our small dive boat on the west side of Lovell's. My fins slap as I slip beneath the water of Boston Harbor. I'm wearing a dry suit with an aluminum "eighty" (cubic feet of gas) on my back. The air from my regulator hits my throat like a fresh gust of wind. I'm prone, just two or three feet off the bottom. The glass panes in my mask have not even fogged a little. Everything I see as I start to swim down the sloping edge of the island's shoal into deeper water looks magnified and sharp. The sun is high and bright today. Down here everything has a brilliant chartreuse cast.

Environmentalists say Boston Harbor is a cesspool, but today the visibility isn't too bad. I can see eight or ten feet. I'm swimming next to my dive buddy Mike Manfredi. He's slightly ahead of me, and from this angle his black dry suit reminds me of an astronaut's. He looks more like a spaceman than a merman. With each kick of my fins, I feel like I'm leaving the twentieth century and planet Earth, as we know it, farther behind.

This is not a deep, technical dive, so as I kick slowly with my fins my mind begins to wander to the historical significance of the wreck we're hunting. Gold or no gold, this is cool.

At the time of her loss, Le Magnifique *is forty years old. She has already exceeded the useful life of a wooden warship by at least ten years. And she's far from being in good shape. Records show that the French make extensive repairs to her hull before she leaves the West Indies for Boston. The other two ships sailing in company with her also run aground at Lovell's Island, but they're in top condition and are able to be refloated.* Le Magnifique's *hull is too weak and rotten to survive the grounding.*

The new US government's reaction and compensation for the loss is far out of proportion to the value of an old ship like Le Magnifique. *As punishment for the wreck, American pilot David Darling sailing aboard the French warship is drummed out of the pilot service, even though the wreck's not his fault. In addition, the United States presents the French with a spanking-new warship,* America, *just launched at Portsmouth, New Hampshire. John Paul Jones, the greatest American naval hero of the American Revolution has supervised the building of* America. *She's to be under his command and the first*

74-gun ship in the US Navy. After the United States gives America *to the French captain of* Le Magnifique, *Jones resigns his commission in the Navy as protest.*

Swimming north along the shoal in fifteen feet of water, I find myself wondering why the United States overreacted to the loss of *Le Magnifique*. Why does this country give up its newest and largest warship, as well as the services of its most famous naval hero, to compensate the French for their loss? Could the French really have lost a lot of gold down here?

Then I see the shadows. From ten feet away, they look like a series of four or five heavy spikes rising to uneven heights out of the gravel and muddy bottom. The highest one comes up about three feet. Moving closer, I see that they are wooden timbers, far too thick to be the bones of a fishing boat or even a nineteenth-century cargo schooner or clipper. The timbers are curved on an equal radius. I'm looking at the hull frames, "ribs," from the starboard side of a massively built wooden ship.

As I move in to lay a hand on one of these ribs, I can see Mike watching me. He's waiting to see if I think that we have struck it rich, whether what we're looking at here are the remains of a treasure ship.

I'm not sure until I see four-inch-thick planking connecting the frames. On the outer edge of the planking there's copper sheathing that wooden shipbuilders nailed to the bottoms of hulls to protect against marine growth, barnacles, and shipworms. This is looking promising. But how would we know this isn't a more recent wreck? I finger some of the sheathing and find that it has pulled away from the planking in places. Then I see small copper nails hanging in the sheathing. They're square-cut handmade nails like my mother said eighteenth-century shipbuilders used. This is it. This is *Le Magnifique*.

I'm on the verge of trying to catch Mike's eye and signal a thumbs up when he beckons to me with his waving hand and points into the haze to the north. Swimming closer, I see a mound of something on the bottom within the confines of the hull.

It's a large pile of iron cannonballs the size of large grapefruits. I picture my cutaway drawing of *Le Magnifique*. These cannonballs tell me exactly where we are on the wreck. This is the bottom of the ship's central magazine, just forward of the mainmast. Here's the ship's center of gravity, and it would be in the holds just forward and aft of the magazine that the crew stores anything heavy like gold.

Sometimes I just go into a "zone" when I'm on a dive and face to face with a wreck. For a few seconds I can picture being on the deck of *Le Magnifique.*

It's August 15, 1782, and the crew of 750 men are more than eager to land this ship in Boston and find a tavern where they can help the Americans celebrate their independence. I can hear Macarty Macteigne, the ship's captain, ordering the powder monkeys down into the magazine to bring up bags of gunpowder to load in the cannons to salute the American victory over England.

The ship's coasting through The Narrows when the sound of crackling canvas goes off like fireworks overhead. I feel the wind back suddenly southwest. Our sails are now set on the wrong side of the ship. The pilot and the captain order the watch to the sheets and braces to tack the yards and sails around to face the new wind. But hauling the yards and sails around on a full-rigged ship takes time, and before the braces can be let go and the sails tacked over, the wind drives Le Magnifique *out of the channel. Everything seems in slow motion as she grinds to a stop on a shoal and the sailing master starts swearing in French at the crew. No one yet knows that the voyage ends here.*

I take a deep breath. The hiss of the air in my regulator draws me back to the twentieth century. I run my gloved hands through the gravel, mud, and broken bits of clamshells forward of the cannonballs. Nothing. There's no sign of *le grand embarquement de monnaie a bord.*

But finding the wreck is like a blast of rocket fuel to my system. Stepping for a few short seconds onto the deck of a 74-gun French man-o-war as she sailed to her doom. What's that worth? Maybe more than gold. The ocean surrounding Massachusetts is a graveyard of ships. Approximately five thousand vessels have been lost here. Rumors of vast riches, ruthless betrayals, and needless deaths abound. But what's the truth? So many lost worlds call to me.

CHAPTER ONE

Descent to a Legend

The SS *Andrea Doria*

Rolling over with the funnel touching the water
US COAST GUARD PHOTO

1992

Diving the Italian passenger liner SS *Andrea Doria* for the first time is a major event for me, something I have been preparing for, and looking forward to, for a long time. Among scuba divers, the *Doria* is often called the Mt. Everest of wreck dives. It's big. It's beautiful. It's loaded with valuable artifacts. It's deep. And it's freaking dangerous. At least eighteen divers have died on the wreck.

My first trip to the *Doria* during the summer of 1992 is in the days before you could just write a check to the captain of a dive boat and join an expedition to the wreck as divers do now. It's the days before mixed breathing gases are available to recreational divers. Almost all of us are still risking deep dives using only compressed air in our tanks. Because of the danger there's only a very small group of people and only a few boats going to the *Doria* on a regular basis. These boats are *Wahoo*, *Seeker*, and *Sea Hunter III*.

To go to the *Doria* you have to be invited into the fold after doing a number of dives aboard one of these boats to shallower wrecks. The crew and passenger lists on all three boats read like a Who's Who of wreck diving at the time. I'm young and pretty much in awe of the people I'm with on the trip aboard *Wahoo* with Captain Steve Bielenda. My buddy Mike Manfredi and I are just about the only rookies among the twenty or so divers on the boat.

Just last week a diver died on the wreck, and now everyone aboard *Wahoo* is a little apprehensive about what lies ahead as Steve Bielenda gives us a briefing before the first dive. He tells the crew that on July 2 thirty-two-year-old Matthew G. Lawrence of Miami Lakes, Florida, died while diving on the *Doria* from *Seeker*. Lawrence died fourteen minutes into his dive. He succumbed from complications with the oxygen mixture in his tanks. When he died, he was trying to recover rosary beads inside the wreck.

"Heads up, gentlemen. There are a thousand ways to die down there," says Bielenda.

But he doesn't mention the stiff currents that can rise up out of nowhere and sweep you off into oblivion. He doesn't talk about the

Doria dive crew
ERIC TAKAKJIAN

trawler nets and the web of nearly invisible monofilament fishing line caught on the wreck and waiting to snare us. We already know about that.

I don't remember much about the fourteen-hour trip aboard the *Wahoo* from Jones Inlet on Long Island to the *Doria*. I just remember tossing in my berth all night in an area of the boat nicknamed the "spice rack" for its tiers of berths. I was trying not to inhale diesel fumes too deeply while my mind kept racing over the things I know about the ship. At home I have a half dozen books about the *Doria* and a large printout of the plans for each deck. Over years of looking at that printout and reading about the *Doria*, I have committed this ship and its ill-fated story to memory.

By any measurement SS *Andrea Doria* is an extraordinary ship of her day. She's a jewel among the last and greatest transatlantic passenger liners to travel between America and Europe in the years following WWII, before commercial air travel made ships like the *Andrea Doria*, RMS *Queen Mary*, RMS *Queen Elizabeth*, SS *United States*, and SS *Île de France* obsolete extravagances of a bygone era. With a home port of

Genoa, Italy, the *Doria* is a state-of-the-art passenger liner sailing for the Società di Navigazione Italia.

Launched on June 16, 1951, the ship takes her name from the sixteenth-century Genoese admiral Andrea Doria. She has a length of 697 feet, a beam of 90 feet, and a displacement of 29,100 gross tons. Sailing at full capacity she can carry about 1,200 passengers and 500 crew. Steam turbines power her twin screws and push the *Doria* to speeds of 23 to 26 knots.

Although the *Doria* is not the fastest or largest vessel in the transatlantic passenger fleet, she's known for her luxury. She's the first liner to feature three outdoor swimming pools. Her saloons are decorated with a million dollars' worth of furnishings, original art, and statuary. The SS *Andrea Doria* is a proud symbol of Italy's renaissance after the nightmare of WWII and the fascist rule of Benito Mussolini.

But things go to hell for the *Doria* on the night of July 25, 1956. The liner's closing with the New England coast bound for New York City on her one hundreth trouble-free ocean crossing. Traveling at high speed in thick fog, she collides with the eastbound Swedish-American liner MS *Stockholm* forty-five miles south of Nantucket Island. The smaller Swedish-American ship strikes the *Doria* in the starboard side, creating a gash that sets off unstoppable flooding and one of the most fabled commercial travel disasters and rescues of the twentieth century.

If not for the *Doria*'s double hull, more than a score of watertight compartments, improvements in maritime communications, and the quick assistance of the crew of *Stockholm* (whose bow is severely damaged) and other ships, the collision might have touched off a seafaring disaster as deadly as the sinking of the RMS *Titanic* in 1912. But thanks to the watertight doors and double hull, the *Doria* remains afloat for eleven hours until the morning of July 26, allowing the other ships to rescue 1,663 passengers and crew. Fifty-three people die. During the rescue ABC Radio commentator Edward P. Morgan broadcasts an account of the collision and rescue. Photos of the stricken ship and stories of the seaborne rescue flood magazines, TV, and cinematic newsreels around the world, creating a media and human interest sensation unlike anything

America will see again until the terrorist attacks on the World Trade Center in 2001 and the so-called "Miracle on the Hudson" in January 2009 when a US Airways passenger jet ditches in the river adjacent to Manhattan.

Lying in my berth aboard *Wahoo*, I hear the hiss of the bow wave against the hull and the low grumble of the twin diesels, but my mind is already in the *Doria*. I try to imagine how each deck, each cabin, each stairwell, and each corridor of the liner look to a diver trying to navigate the wreck.

The *Doria* rests on her starboard side. Everything is ninety degrees off-kilter. Walls look like floors. Floors look like walls. Stairwells are mazes of zigzag passageways, and passageways from one side of the ship to the other seem to be bottomless pits. If the stories of dead divers, the webs of fishing gear covering the *Doria*, and the twisted perspective of the wreck are not enough to illustrate why some divers call this ship a "haunted house," there are a couple of other creepy things. The wreck is loaded with eels that tend to slither up next to you and wrap themselves around your legs. And then there are the sharks. Often plenty of sharks.

Another element has recently added to the *Doria*'s eerie reputation. After decades of decay at the bottom of the ocean, the ship has become what divers call a "noisy wreck." You can hear it creak and moan as if it's trying to rise from a fitful nightmare. Some divers claim that when the current is running over and through the wreck, the *Doria* seems to sing a siren's song. It seduces you into foolish penetration dives to look for glittery trinkets like rosary beads. And then the *Doria* kills you.

July 10, 1992, comes clear and sunny. The North Atlantic looks like the proverbial millpond. Two hours after sunrise a golden haze shimmers above the water. We don't need to look at the LORAN coordinates in the wheelhouse of *Wahoo* to know that we're over the wreck. When Steve Bielenda cuts the engines back to idle, we can hear the screech and squawk of seabirds working the schools of baitfish that called the *Doria* home. One of the guys comes in from checking his gear on deck. It's the legendary wreck diver and author Gary Gentile. He sits down at the dinette table where a number of us are sipping coffee, guzzling bottles of water to keep hydrated for the dive, and nibbling on blueberry muffins. He says he has just seen a big-ass shark.

Hank Garvin and Gary Gilligan suit up and go into the water first. They're *Wahoo*'s dive mates. It's their job to tie our grappling hook anchor into the wreck so that the boat doesn't drift away. All of us know that the anchor line is our only certain route to safety. A lot of divers have died because they couldn't find the anchor line when their tanks started to get short of gas when it was time for them to head to the surface.

You need the anchor line to find your way back up to the boat, and you need it to provide way stations where you must pause for decompression intervals on you way back to the surface. The top of the *Doria* is 170 feet below the surface. The bottom is at 250 feet. You can't dive to such depths without making decompression stops before returning to the surface.

Air is 21 percent oxygen, 79 percent nitrogen. Oxygen fuels our tissues. Nitrogen, an inert gas, has basically no effect on the human body on Earth's surface. As we breathe, nitrogen travels in solution, like the gas in a bottle of seltzer water, through the bloodstream, and off-gases through the lungs when we exhale. But the deeper we dive below the surface of the water, the more nitrogen gets absorbed in the solution of the bloodstream because of increased pressure.

If we try to ascend to the surface too quickly, nitrogen comes out of solution and forms bubbles. The bubbles build up in tissue outside the blood. Depending where the nitrogen bubbles occur, they can cause anything from intense pain to blindness, paralysis, stroke, or death. Doctors call this condition "decompression sickness." Divers call it "getting bent" or the "bends."

To avoid the bends, deep-wreck divers must make decompression stops at intervals on their way back up the anchor line to the dive boat. As this is before the widespread use of dive computers in the mid-1990s, I carry laminated copies of the Canadian navy divers' decompression tables with me to tell me at what depth and for how long I have to stop and "hang" on the anchor line on my way back up to the surface.

The choice of what to carry while not burdening myself with excessive gear is something I've been mulling over for months. The water temperature is fifty-seven degrees on the surface but only in the mid-forties on the wreck, so I start the process of suiting up by putting on dive underwear, insulated long Johns. Then I zip myself into my dry suit and put my dive tables in a suit pocket.

I sit down on a bench at the back of the dive boat, and with Gary Gentile's help, I ease into a backpack harness holding two aluminum eighties. I also carry a spare tank with sixty cubic feet of oxygen for decompression. The two tanks on my back have two separate valves as part of an isolation manifold (which connects the tanks together). I have two separate regulators (one for primary use and one for backup) attached to the valves on the manifold. In case a regulator fails and starts to free flow, I can isolate the two tanks from each other to prevent the loss of all of my air, or I can shut down whichever regulator is having the problem and still access the gas in both tanks through the other regulator.

Among the other necessities that I carry are two handheld lights, a reel with five hundred feet of nylon safety line, a lift bag, fins, a dry suit hood, gloves, a mask, "Jon line" to tie myself off to the anchor line at deco (decompression) stops, and laminated decompression tables. I also have two dive timers to track my depth, bottom time, and decompression stop time.

Gentile helps me get my gloves on. Then he shakes my hand just before I jump in. *This is very cool*, I think. I feel like I have just been offered the chance to join a very small and select brotherhood of underwater adventurers. Gary wrote a book, *Andrea Doria Dive to an Era*, which I have recently read. I brought it along on the trip for him to sign.

With the *Doria* lying on her starboard side, Hank Garvin has tied us into the top of the wreck at the promenade deck on the port side of the ship, the second stanchion forward from the aft end of that deck. The visibility is great for New England water. I can see at least forty to fifty feet in all directions as I'm swimming down the anchor line. Still, it takes more than three minutes before the wreck starts to emerge as a dark presence below me.

The first things I see through the shadowy haze are lifeboat davits. They jut up from the top of the wreck like giant greenish fingers covered in barnacles, sponges, and anemones. The sun is high and strong this morning. Even without my dive light switched on, I can see to avoid the tangle of trawl nets and monofilament line hanging from the davits and waiting to snag me if I get careless or swept into them by currents.

Moving closer to the davits, I think about the crucial role they play in the sense of doom and urgency that sweeps over the ship on that horrible night in July 1956. *Andrea Doria* carries sixteen large steel lifeboats, eight on each side, that are meant to be launched from the davits in case of an order to abandon ship. If all sixteen lifeboats are filled to capacity, they're sufficient to carry the entire ship's company of about 1,700 passengers and crew to safety. But almost immediately after the collision, the *Doria* takes a severe twenty-eight-degree list to starboard, making it impossible to launch the eight lifeboats on the port side and difficult to load passengers into the starboard boats.

Although Captain Piero Calamai knows within half an hour of the collision that the *Doria's* doomed, he chooses not to give the order to abandon ship until help can arrive. He fears that the order and lack of enough lifeboats will cause a general panic among the people aboard. Meanwhile the *Doria's* crew races to lower the useable starboard boats and rig ropes or ladders for passengers and crews to board the boats.

As I start to swim forward along the promenade deck, I can almost hear voices of crewmen calling in Italian to each other. "*Minga*," shouts someone. It's Sicilian slang. It means "Piss." It means "This sucks, we're screwed." My neck and shoulders stiffen. I stop and look around.

The side of the ship is perfectly horizontal. The wreck is immense and bright up on the top, but dark over near the edges. Not just shadowy, but it feels dark to look down over the edges. It is by far the biggest wreck I've ever seen. Row after row of portholes run off to infinity in both directions. They have a patina of silt and marine growth clouding them, but something deep inside of me makes me stare at them as if at any second I expect to see faces appear beneath the portholes' glass. I'm awed by the sight.

Mike Manfredi is my dive partner. He gives me a look like, "This is cool. Let's go!" He obviously isn't hearing or seeing any ghosts. He's pumped to explore, to get on with our dive plan . . . so we turn and head for the promenade deck. We swim forward along the top of the wreck for a while. Cod and pollock, lots of pollock, rise out of the wreck—like silvery flashes in the gloom—and flee. They seem annoyed with the hiss and bubbles from our regulators, annoyed with our intrusion into their underworld. Suddenly I'm aware how cold it is down here. Even with all this gear on, even though I'm swimming, my fingers and arms tingle with the cold.

Avoiding the worst of the trawl nets and monofilament, we drop down to the promenade deck and continue to swim forward, continue to flush pollock from the broken cabin windows a few feet beneath us. Outer windows that used to enclose the seaside of the promenade deck have dropped out of their frames and are lying on the inboard bulkhead, which appears like a horizontal floor beneath us. We're using our dive lights now to probe the darkness.

Mike turns and points his light around behind us and then back toward me. There is just so much to see and take in; stuff is everywhere, way more than you can absorb in one dive. The light flashes in my direction. Its suddenness surprises me like a bolt of lightning.

This happens several times, and each bolt takes me further away from the here and now of this dive until I'm with Captain Calamai on the bridge of this ship.

It's just a couple of minutes after 11 p.m. on the night of July 25, 1956. About twenty minutes ago the second and third officers of the ship who are also on watch with Captain Calamai spotted a small blip on the radar screen about seventeen miles away. The fog is thick.

The liner is steaming at over 21 knots, and the bridge crew can't see the bow of the ship. If they were following the International Rules of the Road for shipping, they should be proceeding very slowly, so slowly that they should be able to stop the Doria *within the length of the ship, about 700 feet. Fat chance. At this speed it will take this liner about three miles and five minutes to come to a stop. The rules were made for another time, before ships were so big and carried so much momentum, before ships went this fast, before radar gave the bridge crew eyes in the fog and in the dark. Few ships slow down appreciably in the fog these days, especially liners . . . especially here in the Nantucket-Ambrose Traffic Lane. This is the main approach to New York City for ships coming to New York from Europe, like the* Andrea Doria.

Outbound ships from New York are moving at high speeds along the same route toward the Doria. *Everybody has a schedule to keep. There are two hundred longshoremen contracted to meet this liner tomorrow morning at the docks in Manhattan. After watching the rate at which we have been closing with the blip on the radar screen, the second and third officers are certain that the blip is speeding in our direction. Whatever it is, we will meet it head-on in the fog. It is only about five nautical miles away now, and we are converging with it at 40 knots. Every minute and a half we are a nautical mile closer. In about six minutes we will collide with that blip if we do not alter course.*

If this were 1992, the watch officer would hail the approaching ship on our VHF, ship-to-ship radio, when he first sees the blip. He would make a plan over channel thirteen, reserved for bridge-to-bridge communications, for how his liner will meet and pass the other vessel safely in the dark and fog. This is how we handle a "meet" on the oceangoing tugboat where I'm the first mate.

But right now on the bridge of the Doria, *it is 1956. Liners do not have VHF radios yet. Only the military has them. The* Andrea Doria's *radio room is not set up for communicating easily with another ship using its single sideband radio or Morse code. So the bridge crew counts on its alertness, its experience, the prudence of the crew on that unidentified blip, and the Rules of the Road to keep us safe from a collision.*

The Rules of the Road are unambiguous. According to centuries of international maritime traditions, ships meeting head-on should each give way with a clear and obvious turn to the right, and the ships should pass each other "port to port," left side to left side. The turn to the right should be accompanied by a single short blast of the horn. In common bridge usage we say we are meeting the other ship "on one whistle." When each ship follows this protocol, all will be well.

But tonight the second and third mates are nervous about the meet. For some reason Captain Calamai thinks the blip is a fishing vessel that is destined to turn left and head north for Nantucket Island, forty-five miles away, and the New England coast. Following this thinking, he has just now altered the Doria's *course to port by ordering the helmsman to turn the ship left four degrees.*

Calamai intends to pass the blip with an unconventional starboard-to-starboard meet. But how will the other ship know this? This subtle change of course to our left will be virtually imperceptible on the radarscope of the other ship. Jesus, somebody needs to speak up. Somebody has to tell the captain the liner needs to make an obvious change of course and signal that it is turning left with two blasts of the horn. The blip is only about two or three miles away now, and it will hear Doria's *horn loud and clear.*

This is bad. The skipper and the third officer are on the starboard wing of the bridge. They see the glow of light from the other ship through the fog. Curzio Franchini, the second officer, hears one of the officers on the bridge wing say that he sees light, and he leaves his post at the radarscope. Just as the Doria *is closing with the blip, he stops tracking the approaching ship's course to go out on the wing to see the lights for himself.*

I wish I could scream at him, "Don't leave the scope." The Doria *needs his eyes on that blip. The radar gives a much clearer picture of the two converging ships than the defuse glow of lights through fog. Only a man watching the radarscope can see how close the two ships are and their relative bearing to each other. The ships are only a mile apart on converging courses. And it seems that the other ship has not detected the* Doria's *subtle turn to port. It does not see that Captain Calamai intends to go against standard meeting protocol and pass starboard to starboard. The blip is holding its course.*

Minga. Two great ships are less than a minute and a half from plowing into each other, and the officers of the Doria *seem fixated on staring at the glow of light off the starboard bow.*

The Doria's *foghorn lets out a long, single bellow, signaling that it is running in restricted visibility. Why is the horn still functioning on this automatic sequence? Why has the captain not shifted the ship's horn to manual control and called for two short blasts to signal his intent to pass starboard to starboard?*

The phone on the bridge rings. Franchini answers on his way out to the wing where the captain and a third officer are still trying to make out the running lights of the approaching ship to gauge its course. It's the bow watch calling to say he sees lights off to starboard.

"That's alright," says Franchini in cool Italian. "We see them, too."

But things are far from alright, far from cool. The third officer, probing the fog with his binoculars, sees the two masthead lights of the approaching ship. She is less than a mile away and starting to show her red portside running light.

"She's turning. She's turning. She's coming at us."

Albeit, quite late in a meeting situation, the other ship is signaling with her change of course that she intends a normal port-to-port pass.

Just as there is a protocol in the Rules of the Road for meeting that makes passing port to port the standard, another protocol for a safe meeting says that you should not alter course to cross another vessel's bow, particularly in a head-on situation, particularly if the other vessel is seen off to starboard, as the blip is now.

"Tutto sinistra," Calamai orders the helmsman. "All left." The Andrea Doria is turning toward the oncoming vessel.

Minga. These two ships are less than a minute from a collision, and Calamai is overruling standard protocol again and ignoring the other ship's clear intention to pass port to port. The skipper is gambling that a hard left turn of the Doria will swing her away from the other ship.

But the Doria's not answering the helm, not turning. She has over 29,000 tons of forward momentum that cannot be quickly redirected even with her rudder hard to port.

At last, Franchini knows that he must do something. He realizes that his captain has made one too many unchallenged bad calls.

"Captain, the signal . . . the two whistles?" The second mate's voice is no longer cool or calm.

"Sí, sí." The captain is waking to a nightmare.

As Franchini sounds the two short blasts of the horn to signal that his ship is turning left, he realizes that the Doria is still charging toward a collision at full speed.

He challenges his commander again and asks about the engines.

Calamai tells him not to touch the engine telegraph that will tell the engine room to reduce speed. The ship turns better with her propellers spinning fast. The Doria's only hope now is to turn left faster than the approaching ship is turning right.

Everyone on the bridge can feel the ship leaning over to starboard as she skids forward instead of turning.

"Is she turning? Is she turning?" A third officer shouts at the helmsman who is holding the helm hard over to port with all the weight of his body as he stares at the gyrocompass and prays.

"Now," he grunts after a pause. "She's beginning to turn."

But it's too late. The sharp bow of the other ship is surging straight for the starboard wing of the Doria's bridge. Huge black letters seem to scream the name Stockholm as the Swedish-American passenger liner buries its heavily reinforced steel prow into the side of the Andrea Doria.

The rest is history.

Mike's dive light flashes my way again. He's shining it on brass numbers imbedded in the teak promenade deck to our left. Each number is the size of my gloved hand. They are in a box drawn with brass strapping on the deck. The eight is next to the one, which is next to the six. The lack of numerical order strikes me. The sequence is fractured like time has been for me on this dive. I want those numbers. I want to take a chisel or a screwdriver and pry them out of the teak deck to put in my goodie bag, souvenirs to remind me of this dive to the *Doria*. Artifacts to remind me of the way that time has broken open for me on this wreck.

My mind has been shuffling among events. Things that happened long ago, things that I have only read about or imagined, are breaking through into the present and happening again. It's as if linear time is an illusion, a simplification of experience to give order, meaning, and a sense of peaceful inevitability to our days. But here on the *Doria* at the bottom of the North Atlantic, the truth is more complex and darker. Here we live with ghosts. Sometimes things past become things present. Maybe things future. Events loop back into themselves. Endlessly it seems. The fifty-three dead of the *Andrea Doria* are gathering at the portholes; dead divers like Matthew Lawrence are rising from the wreck. They are calling to Captain Calamai and me, "Why?"

We have no answer, except to say that the ocean is a hostile environment. Careful preparation and constant vigilance are your best survival

Author and Mike after recovering shuffleboard court numbers from the *Andrea Doria*
ERIC TAKAKJIAN

tools. And sometimes they are inadequate. The sea is hungry. It takes what it can.

A piercing chill begins to creep into my body. Cold starts to numb my cheeks, lips, and hands. This is the land of the dead. I check my timer. If I stay here any longer, I will overrun my bottom time. I will be short of air for my decompression stops. I, too, will be a ghost. And that shark Gary Gentile saw? It can hardly wait to feed.

The next day on a second dive to the wreck, I recover some of those shuffleboard numbers, using a screwdriver. It feels like a small victory. We spend three days diving the wreck. The *Doria* is an amazing wreck. I'm elated to have dived it and can't wait to come back again next year. This is by far the coolest wreck I've ever dived since I started wreck diving.

Looking at those numbers, I think about the hours after the collision when the *Doria* is on the verge of capsizing and sinking as the sea overwhelms her watertight compartments. The hero of the day is the liner SS *Île de France*. Headed to Europe, forty-five miles east of the *Doria* and *Stockholm* collision, the French ship's captain turns around after hearing distress calls from the two damaged ships and comes back at full speed. Three hours after the collision, when the massive *Île*, one of the world's largest liners of the time, pulls up alongside the *Doria* with all of lights blazing, it gives everyone on the *Doria* a great feeling of encouragement and support knowing the other liner is lowering its own lifeboats to help.

Other ships respond as well. The first responders are the crew of the *Stockholm*. Even with the bow demolished and five dead, the Swedish ship begins rescuing *Doria* passengers while struggling to keep afloat. Eleven hours after the collision, SS *Andrea Doria* rolls on her starboard side and sinks. She's about to start her new career as the most famous shipwreck in America.

CHAPTER TWO

Big Ship, Big Sharks

The MV *Regal Sword*

1993

AFTER DIVING THE *ANDREA DORIA* DURING THE SUMMER OF 1992, I'M
stoked to find a deep wreck to dive that no one has ever seen. For years
I've been hearing fishermen talk about MV *Regal Sword*. The *Sword* sinks
after colliding with the tanker *Exxon Chester* southeast of Chatham on
the elbow of the Cape in June 1979. There's a photo in William Quinn's
book, *Shipwrecks Around New England*, of the bow of the *Exxon Chester*
stove-in and mangled as she's coming into Boston after the collision. The
picture haunts me. It has an eerie similarity to photos of the bow of *Stockholm* after it hits the *Doria*. The location of the *Regal Sword*'s collision
also takes me back to the loss of the Italian passenger liner. Both ships are
ghosts of Nantucket Shoals. But the *Sword* is a virgin wreck.

On her final voyage *Regal Sword* departs Portsmouth, New Hampshire, on June 18, 1979, with a partial load of three thousand tons of scrap
metal, mostly crushed cars. Launched in Sweden during 1961, *Regal
Sword* is a modern bulk carrier, measuring 575 feet long, 75 feet abeam,
and 16,450 gross tons. She's sailing under a Liberian flag for Hector
Marine Corporation and bound for Philadelphia, nearly empty, to load
more scrap. On board is a crew of thirty-three plus three of the officers'
wives. Captain Ioannis Ypsilantis has his wife and young daughter on
board as well, bringing the total ship's company to thirty-eight. Most of
the seamen are from Greece, the Philippines, or Sri Lanka.

Regal Sword in port
ERIC TAKAKJIAN

After leaving Portsmouth, Captain Ypsilantis shapes a course east of Cape Cod. The ship's 8,100-horsepower 6-cylinder MAN diesel engine quickly brings the *Sword* up to a speed of 14 knots. The voyage proceeds normally as the crew settles into its at-sea routine. As the freighter passes east of Highland Light at Truro on the backside of the Cape, fog begins to appear, patchy in spots, and then thick. This is typical weather for early June off Cape Cod in the vicinity of the lightship at Nantucket Shoals. Scores of ships pass this way every day in such conditions coming and going from New York and Boston. It's usually no big deal. But things are starting to unravel in the shipping lanes east of the lightship in the late afternoon of June 18, 1979.

I ended my active duty as coxswain on USCG rescue vessels in 1982. But I did my USCG Reserve duty at the USCG station in Chatham until 1989, and have come to know several of Chatham's local commercial fishermen. One is Captain Bill Amaru. Most ground fishermen like Bill are quite familiar with the wrecks in the areas they fish, and Bill has been fishing a long time. So I call him one day and ask about *Regal Sword*.

"Good luck trying to dive into that mess," he says. Then he shares the LORAN C coordinates of the wreck with me and tells me, "Heads up. Be freaking careful. The current can run like all hell out there, and the wreck is loaded with nets."

His caution excites me more than scares me. I pride myself in being careful at everything I do, whether it's running a tugboat, diving, or rebuilding an old sailboat. Here's a chance to put my meticulousness to the test. And then there's the adrenalin rush. Not even the possibility of recovering treasure gets me more pumped than diving a virgin wreck.

In my years of wreck diving, I've discovered I'm not alone. Many divers take extreme risks to be the first humans on a wreck. For them the treasure hunt is in finding the artifacts from the wreck that they collect in their goody bags, float to the surface with air-inflated lift bags, or haul aboard dive boats with cables and cranes. I admit to spending a lot of money to restore salvaged items like a ship's wheel, a brass engine telegraph, or a Chelsea ship's clock. Virgin wrecks are often undisturbed troves of this stuff.

Every wreck diver I know has at least one "artifacts room" in his or her house displaying his or her booty. Often we lend the things we have recovered to museums and display them at dive shows or clinics around the country. As long as the wreck was once a commercial ship like the *Doria*, salvaging artifacts is usually fair game in the United States. According to maritime law, recreational divers can't touch anything on a ship that belonged to the US or a foreign government. Often such wrecks are designated war graves, and touching anything at a war grave is taboo.

But wreck diving is about more than trophies. When we found the bones of *Le Magnifique*, I realized that almost nothing is as exciting to me as the opportunity to bear witness to the time capsule that is a ship-wreck. I love the challenge of the search above and below the water. For me the preparation and planning—the thoughts about what I might find hundreds of feet below the sea—are as exciting as a deep and dangerous dive. It sounds a little crazy, but my dive buddies and I even relish the long and sometimes rough boat rides to a wreck site that may be in the middle of nowhere a hundred or more miles from land.

Diving on a wreck gives you the opportunity to tangibly interact with history, which to me is the most compelling aspect of the whole endeavor. Wrecks can show you the past through a new lens. A diver gets to see the devastation of the past regenerating through a moldering wreck's interface with all manner of fish, lobsters, sea turtles, rays, dolphins, whales, and sharks. To wreck divers like me, the broken hulk of a bombed-out, sunken German submarine like *U-853* off the coast of Rhode Island is not just a reminder of the horror of war. With all the marine organisms the wreck hosts, it becomes a lush and unexpected symbol of life's renewal and beauty. The underwater photography of my friend and wreck diver Brad Sheard captures these transformations on wrecks in his photo book, *Lost Voyages*.

After reading Jon Krakauer's book *Into Thin Air*, about climbing Mount Everest, my dive buddies and I thought, "Wow we know that rush." I can hardly put into words the feelings that rock you in the moments when you know that you are one of the few or—better yet—the first person on the planet to see something like a ship's hull still standing tall above the seafloor. A ship that vanished, lost to time, without a trace a hundred or more years ago. It's like landing on the dark side of the moon. After such moments, after you surface from such a dive, totally stoked and wanting to share the discovery with everyone, you want to shout, "Hey you wouldn't believe what's down there!"

Not everyone is so lucky, and not everyone comes back. Each of my deep-wreck diving buddies and I have our own personal collection of almost-died stories, and we all have known and seen divers who didn't make it. But I've always been confident of my ability in the water. Before my dive to *Regal Sword*, I thought the sea was my playground. Afterwards I realized I had a lot more to learn. I had not yet nearly died in a wreck.

Tuesday, June 8, 1993. The day breaks calm, clear. The sea east of Cape Cod is flat as an iron. I'm aboard my new thirty-six-foot dive boat *Grey Eagle* with my wife Lori. We met at the USCG station in Chatham in the early spring of 1988. At the time, I was working on a tug for Zapata Gulf Marine towing container barges from the US to Puerto Rico, but I was still living in Provincetown and serving my monthly USCG Reserve duty at the station in Chatham.

Lori was the new girl at the station, and we met on the mess deck over coffee one weekend. When we got to talking, I learned that she had just recently joined the USCG after growing up as a surfer girl in Southern California and then working aboard supply, research, and party fishing vessels out of Port Hueneme. It was a strange coincidence because we discovered that when I was working on a tug out of Port Hueneme, my tug and her party boat had rafted alongside each other . . . but we had never met then.

As the saying goes, one thing led to another, and in May 1989 we married. After Lori mustered out of the USCG, she joined me as the co-captain of the *Grey Eagle*. She has great boat handling skills, and, although she is also a scuba diver, she quite often remains on the surface as the boat keeper when I'm diving on a deep wreck.

On this trip in search of the *Regal Sword*, we have our dive buddies Brian Skerry, Butch Amaral, Dave Morton, and Pat Morton along. After four hours of steaming, we arrive at the LORAN coordinates for the *Regal Sword* late in the morning. The wreck comes up huge on the depth sounder. I've never seen such a spike on a bottom recorder before. The wreck is deep. At 270 feet maximum depth, it's twenty feet deeper than the *Doria*. The top of the wreck spikes up to about 140 feet, giving the wreck 130 feet of relief. The *Sword*, must be resting upright on her bottom.

I've made a graph of LORAN lines for plotting out how the wreck lies on the bottom. To fill in the graph, we make a number of passes over the *Sword*, recording the LORAN positions and depths at different points. Then we transfer this data to the plotting sheet. This gives us a good feel for the wreck. It sits facing southeast, almost along the course it was traveling when the *Exon Chester* hit it.

At this point in my diving career, none of us has ever done any diving southeast of the elbow of Cape Cod. We're not sure what to expect for conditions. We know the visibility should be good. But as far as the ocean currents are concerned, we have little idea beyond Bill Amaru's warning, and no idea how to time the brief window of "slack water" when the current is calm between the changing of the tide. And then, of course, there's at least one other unknown—nets.

Our plan is to try hooking into the highest point on the wreck to make our trip down as easy and short as possible. We try to drop a "shot line." It's a 5/8-inch nylon line attached at the bottom to a 50-pound weight. The length of the shot line is 300 feet with beckets (loops) spliced into it for attaching buoys at 50-foot intervals. At the end of the line is an additional 20 feet of 3/8-inch chain. We set the line up with small lobster buoys at the 150-, 200-, and 250-foot marks. At the end is a large, orange inflated ball like tuna fishermen use to attach to their catch. With no current running, this setup will hold the line nearly vertical; the more current present at the site, the more the foam lobster buoys will submerge. A shot line will give us the most direct route down to the wreck, much shorter in distance than an anchor line that is hooked into a wreck.

When we first drop the shot line, all looks good. The small buoy at the 150 feet mark on the line is still on the surface . . . but not for long. Almost immediately we see that the current's running pretty hard. It starts dragging the small buoys underwater one by one. Soon the shot line is totally underwater except for the big, orange tuna ball at 300 feet . . . and it's starting to go under as well.

"Wow," says Butch in his understated way.

Freaking current, I'm thinking.

We decide to wait before trying again with the shot line or an anchor line. Our best guess is that the current will go slack about fifteen minutes after high water in Boston. So we consult the current tables in *Eldridge Tide and Pilot Book* for the time of the tide change at Boston. While we were waiting, a Chatham gill net boat shows up and asks us what we were doing. When we tell him we're waiting to dive the wreck, he asks us to retrieve the gill net he lost here last week, "if we get a chance." Not likely! Gill nets are a menace to divers, difficult to see, and easy to get tangled up in. Large wrecks tend to be loaded in what we call "ghost nets." Depending on the wreck's location, the type of ghost gear on the wreck will vary based on the type of fishing done in the vicinity.

When the current seems slack, we try snagging the wreck with a grappling hook on the end of our anchor line. We drop the grapple on the highest part of the wreck, and the hook grabs right away. It's probably caught on a net. Finally time to go diving. But things are far from safe until we can tie in the anchor line to the wreck.

Brian, Butch, and I suit up. Dave and Pat decide not to dive. They don't like not knowing where we are hooked in on the wreck. Lori runs the boat. We make a rough dive plan based on the unknown location and depth of the hook, the current, and our air supply. The plan is that we will swim and pull ourselves down the anchor line. All of us will be diving on air and carrying one stage bottle of oxygen for our decompression stops. After fifteen minutes or at 200 feet, if we don't see the wreck, we will turn around and come up in order to limit our decompression obligation on the way back to the surface. If we're on the wreck in less than fifteen minutes, we will spend a maximum of twenty minutes exploring before starting back up.

It's three in the afternoon when Brian, Butch, and I jump in the water. The sea is very clear and very blue. As we head down, the white line seems to run off in front of us into infinity. The visibility is probably more than fifty feet. As we start down the line the current seems light. But the deeper we go, the more it increases. There's a lot of scope in the anchor line, so we're going down at a shallow angle, which makes pulling against the current more and more difficult as the three of us descend deeper. I have it easy compared to Brian and Butch, who are towing large camera setups.

The deeper we go, the harder the current tries to tug us backward off the anchor line. It takes us a full fifteen minutes to hand-over-hand ourselves down to two hundred feet. When we get to this point on the line, we're hanging from the line like three flags in a stiff breeze. All I can see is the white anchor line going down into the abyss. It's like the wreck doesn't exist.

Yet as I hang onto the anchor line like a human pennant, like shark bait, I can picture the giant ship below. But not a sunken wreck.

The Regal Sword *is darting in and out of the fog banks at 10 knots on June 18, 1979. It's about 4:30 in the afternoon. But the fog is so thick the air seems dark, as if sunset is just a few minutes away.*

In the fog the Sword *seems like something strange, alive. The starboard running light looks like an eye. The bellowing of the foghorn is a bestial growl. The ship's riding high with nearly empty holds so her kingposts and derricks loom overhead—massive, disembodied arms. And although her crew thinks she's running on a course of 155 degrees, four miles east of the Boston shipping lanes, she is actually west of her plotted course and steaming outbound in the inbound Boston shipping lane. She's like a wrong-way driver on a fogbound highway . . . hurtling blindly toward Boston's inbound traffic.*

That inbound ship is the tanker SS Exxon Chester. *Exxon Oil Company owns the ship. With her crew of forty, the* Exxon Chester *left Bayway, New Jersey, during the afternoon of June 17 loaded with a cargo of hot asphalt, bound for Boston. The ship has been running in fog all day on June 18 at a reduced speed of 10 knots. Since 4:00 this afternoon, the* Chester *has been traveling at 333 degrees in the inbound Boston traffic lane.*

Built in 1952, the Exxon Chester *is near the end of her useful life, but she has modern navigation equipment, including three LORAN receivers for pinpoint position fixes and two radars. One of the radars is the new Sperry CAS (collision avoidance system). The* Chester *is 628 feet long, 82.7 feet abeam, and 17,327 gross tons displacement. Her steam turbines produce 12,500 brake horsepower for propulsion. Today she is fully loaded with 172,000 barrels of asphalt simmering at 300 to 325 degrees.*

In my time moving large oil barges with tugboats up and down the East Coast, I have often loaded where the Exxon Chester *took on her asphalt at Bayway. And I have made the run from New York to Boston like the* Chester *dozens of times. Made it all too often in the fog like this . . . with the dampness creeping into your clothes, slicking your hair. The air around you seems to grow blacker by the second as the fog fumes and swirls deeper and deeper around your ship.*

I can relate to her third mate. He's Bill Kenefick, just a few months out of Maine Maritime Academy. Years later we will meet, and he will share his memories of June 18, 1979.

This job on the Exxon Chester *is his first job as a deck officer. This is not the kind of trip a recently frocked deck officer ever forgets even if everything goes well. No deck officer forgets the hypersensitivity that comes with his first time running through thick fog with a massive, dangerous load in an area of dense ship traffic. And the* Exxon Chester's *load is absolutely dangerous. If any kind of accident aboard the tanker exposes that extremely hot asphalt to water, the resulting steam will blow the tanker up like a bomb. It's a weight on a deck officer's mind.*

Kenefick's not alone on the tanker's bridge. It's fully staffed with the captain, the second mate, an AB (able-bodied seaman), and an OS (ordinary seaman). The Chester *also has a bow lookout posted. Her foghorn is bleating at regular intervals as a warning to nearby ships. Kenefick has just come up to relieve the second mate while the man eats his dinner. At 4:47 p.m., the second mate tells Captain Edmund J. Sabowski and Kenefick that he sees a target 9 nautical miles ahead, 10 degrees to port on the Sperry CAS. Then he heads off the bridge for his meal.*

After deviating 22 degrees to starboard from its course to pass two stopped radar targets assumed to be fishing vessels, the ship turns back to port at 4:58 p.m. to its original course of 333 degrees. Kenefick observes that the target that is the Sword *has closed the distance between it and the tanker. The* Regal Sword *is now 6 miles ahead, bearing 5 degrees to port with a PAD (predicted area of danger) to port.*

At 5:00 p.m., Kenefick goes into the chart room and gets a position fix with the ship's LORAN receivers. They verify the tanker is on course in the inbound traffic lane to Boston. At the same time, Captain Sabowski observes the approaching target on the radar. The Regal Sword *seems to be on a course of 150 degrees at 4 1/2 miles ahead.*

Kenefick returns to the bridge from the chart room at 5:04 p.m. He can hear the groan of the Sword's *foghorn as he reports that the target is now between 3 and 4 miles ahead, bearing 5 degrees to port. The* Exxon Chester *and* Regal Sword *are on nearly reciprocal courses, but the target bearing on the Sperry CAS is opening between them. If this situation holds, the two ships should pass safely with an ordinary port-to-port meeting.*

But this is not how the bridge crew of the Sword *sees it.*

At 4:45 p.m., the officers on the bridge of the Regal Sword *spot a single blip that is the* Exxon Chester *on their radars bearing 7 degrees to starboard at a distance of 8 miles. Captain Ypsilantis still believes that he's at least 4 miles east of the Boston traffic lanes and all set up to pass the oncoming ship on his starboard side as long as it remains in the traffic lane. The* Regal Sword *is running in fog with visibility reduced to as little as 600 feet, yet no bow watch has been posted.*

Because of the fog, Ypsilantis has reduced his ship's speed to about 10 knots. He's navigating his vessel himself and maintaining the navigational plot. From this plot he estimates a distance of 1 mile as his closest point of approach with the oncoming target. According to his plot he should safely pass the unknown ship starboard-to-starboard. The chief mate's on watch on the starboard wing with the second mate. An AB's on the port wing. The foghorn's bellowing. Running lights are on.

To make sure that a starboard-to-starboard pass will go safely, Ypsilantis tells his helmsman to change course 5 degrees to port. When the Chester *is 6 miles ahead, Ypsilantis orders an additional change of course 5 degrees to port when the two ships are just 4 miles apart. Then he calls for yet another 5-degree turn to port to assure a safe passing distance between his ship and the target.*

At 5:01 p.m., he hails the approaching target on the VHF radio's distress channel 16 and the bridge-to-bridge channel 13, "Vessel in my head coming from Nantucket to Cape Cod."

No answer.

When the ships are only about 2 miles apart at 5:08 p.m., Ypsilantis is beginning to worry. He makes another radio call. "Vessel to my starboard side coming northbound, this is the Regal Sword. *Please pass starboard-to-starboard."*

Still no answer.

The freighter's captain goes out onto the starboard wing of the bridge to look visually for his traffic. He orders the foghorn sounded more frequently. Then he hears a foghorn to starboard. It sounds really close.

Although Ypsilantis doesn't know it, he has made the same two mistakes as the captain of the Andrea Doria *when it collided with the* Stockholm. *He has decided to make an irregular starboard-to-starboard pass in limited visibility without consent from the approaching vessel, and he has ignored Rule Eight of the International Rules of the Road, which states in part,*

Any alteration of course and/or speed to avoid collision shall, if the cir-cumstances of the case admit, be large enough to be readily apparent to another vessel observing visually or by radar; a succession of small alterations of course and/or speed should be avoided.

But the Greek skipper is not the only one making mistakes. Not only does the captain of the Chester *not notice the changes in the* Sword's *course, he does not recognize or acknowledge Ypsilantis's VHF calls. Maybe the radio calls are too vague about the caller's location. Maybe Ypsilantis's Greek accent makes him hard to understand. Maybe the officers of the* Exxon Chester *think they are just hearing a fishing boat hailing another fishing boat. There's often a lot of chatter on the VHF around Nantucket Shoals. For whatever reason no one on the bridge of the* Exxon Chester *picks up the mic on the VHF and answers the* Regal Sword.

With the vessels within 3 miles of each other, tanker Captain Sabowski orders the Chester *to turn right to 355 degrees to signal a port-to-port pass. As the two ships draw within 2 miles, the bridge crew on the tanker believe that their change of course has opened the closest point of approach considerably and that the* Sword *now bears 20 degrees to port.*

At 5:08 p.m., the target that is the Regal Sword *disappears at 3/4 mile in the snowy-looking static known as "sea clutter" on the tanker's radar displays. Now without any VHF communication, radar contact, or a visual sighting of the* Sword, *Sabowski makes a split decision. Still assuming a port-to-port pass, he orders his helmsman to turn to starboard another 15 degrees. Unknowingly he has turned right toward the* Sword, *which suddenly emerges from the fog between 400 and 1200 feet forward of the tanker.*

"It's like a wall of steel," says Bill Kenefick. As the Sword *starts across the bow of the* Exxon Chester, *the master orders the helm put over hard left in an attempt to steer astern of the freighter. Then he picks up the telephone and tells the man on bow watch to run for his life.*

At 5:13 p.m., the tanker strikes the Regal Sword *at a 60-degree angle, T-boning the starboard side of the freighter and penetrating the number 5 and number 6 cargo holds as well as the engine room. Kenefick will never forget the sound of the grinding and crushing of the steel, the shaking and vibration rippling through the tanker, as the two ships collide. The bow of the tanker impales the freighter, and the two giant ships fuse together. The only good news is that the bow watchman on the* Chester *has dodged the crushing blow and the engine room crew of the* Sword *escapes their fast-flooding compartment.*

A sharp sense of doom runs through Kenefick's chest as he considers what happens if the forward collision bulkhead on the Chester *has been breached*

Foredeck of the *Exxon Chester* with deckhouse and bridge of the *Regal Sword* in background
BILL KENEFICK

and seawater begins hitting the hot asphalt in tank number 1 and turning to steam. It could be only a matter of minutes before something blows. Sabowski sends a damage control party forward to assess the destruction. In short order he hears that the collision bulkhead on the tanker has held, but there's another problem. The weight of the flooding freighter is putting so much pressure on the bow of the Exxon Chester *that the hull is beginning to deform. This is an old ship. It could rupture.*

"Astern half," Sabowski tells the man on the engine telegraph. "We have to get out of this mess."

It's about this time that Kenefick hears the VHF radio crackle and a voice with a thick accent calling, "Mayday, Mayday. United Sates Coast Guard. This is the MV Regal Sword. *We have collided with another ship, and we are sinking fast. We need immediate assistance."*

When the Chester *backs away from the* Sword *with the screeching of tearing steel, Kenefick sees a hole 150 feet long in the side of the freighter. He can see the crushed automobiles inside the* Sword. *Water is pouring in over those cars. The freighter is already starting to list to starboard and sink by the stern. As the tanker continues to back away, the* Sword *fades into the fog. The last thing Kenefick sees is the bow of the freighter rising into the air as the stern of the* Regal Sword *loses buoyancy.*

Damn, he thinks. She's going down. Never in his all his dreams of a career as a merchant mariner did he expect to see something like this.

Over the VHF radio, he hears the captain of the Sword *report that all thirty-eight souls on the freighter are abandoning the ship, but he can see nothing because of the fog.*

The Regal Sword *sinks beneath the waves at 5:24 p.m., a mere eleven minutes after the collision. By now all the officers of the tanker are on the bridge. They are talking to the USCG on the radio, assessing the condition of their ship and its dangerous cargo, and deciding their next move. It's at this moment that the captain orders third mate Tom Lawton to launch a lifeboat. Somewhere out there in the fog are thirty-eight scared people, including women and a little girl needing immediate help. A USCG vessel will not be here for hours, and it's too foggy for a rescue helicopter to do any good.*

This is on us, Kenefick thinks.

"We're launching a lifeboat and standing by," Captain Sabowski tells the USCG.

At 6:35 p.m., the rescue boat from the tanker finds the lifeboat from the Regal Sword *and tows it to the tanker where the crew helps the castaways climb a rope "Jacob's ladder" up to the deck of the* Exxon Chester. *To Kenefick's way of thinking, his fellow third mate Tom Lawton is the hero of the day. Finding the* Sword's *lifeboat in the fog and then getting back to the* Chester *is no easy mission. When everyone from the sunken freighter is aboard, and the* Chester *has recovered her own lifeboat, the tanker radios the USCG that it is proceeding to Boston. The ship's dangerous cargo needs to be unloaded before it cools and causes more problems.*

More problems are exactly what Butch, Brian, and I are going to have if we don't turn around right now and head toward the surface. It's time to get back to the dive plan. We have used up fifteen minutes fighting our way down this anchor line, and this current is hell. I know if we stay any longer or go any deeper—as much as we would love to see this wreck— we will pay severely during the deco. Our air supply is limited and the thought of getting swept off the line with a deco obligation toward the end of the day is not something I want to contemplate. I turn to my partners and tap my wrist. It's the universal diver's signal for "time's up." My buddies give me thumbs up, and we start up the line. At least we haven't seen any sharks. Yet.

We're back aboard the *Grey Eagle* and heading for home when Lori stands up from her seat at the helm and says, "Hey, look, basking sharks!"

Off to starboard we see no fewer than ten huge fins. The dark shapes beneath the fins seem as long and wide as the *Grey Eagle*. As Lori slows the boat, the creatures are all around us. One of the guys can't resist putting his own spin on the classic line from the movie *Jaws*, "We're going to need a bigger boat."

The sharks are swimming in a school, loafing along on the surface at a speed of about 2 knots.

"Oh, wow," says Brian. "We should try and get some images."

These gentle giants are filter feeders. They are cruising the surface gorging themselves on a massive patch of little animals called copepods that have been drawn into these waters by a Gulf Stream eddy. The sharks are so intent on feeding they pay no notice to us tagging along with them. All of us grab cameras and start snapping pictures.

Then Dave asks, "Who's up for a swim?"

Everyone is pumped for the chance to get in the water with the sharks. We pull on our dry suits, masks, fins, and gloves. Lori runs the *Grey Eagle* out in front of the school a short way so as not to destroy the strange, rare, and majestic parade of the second-largest species of fish in the sea. After we slide into the water, Brian and Butch get great still and video images as the sharks start to swim past us. They look to be the size of whales. Brian grabs one by the dorsal fin and tries to hang on for a ride . . . but soon slips off.

The sharks don't look to be swimming fast until we try and keep up with them in the water. It's totally impossible. So we end up just floating there in the middle of the ocean and watching them parade by. Their huge mouths are wide open, lower jaws dropping about four feet below their heads as they plow through the copepods that look like tiny jellyfish. A basking shark "ram feeding" like this, filters about 450 tons of water per hour.

"Just when we thought this trip was going to be a blow out," says Butch once we are back aboard the *Grey Eagle*, "we get these cool basking sharks."

He speaks for us all.

Dive trips are always about coming face-to-face with the unknown and the unexpected. Sometimes what stops your breath in absolute terror, wonder, or amazement has nothing to do with a shipwreck, nothing to do with finding an artifact or even reliving a lost moment on a forgotten ship. Sometimes it's an immense shark. But whatever it is, it always reminds you that you are just a short-time visitor to the deep blue.

CHAPTER THREE

Fire & Treachery

The *Baleen*

STEVEN LANG

1994

A SHIPBOARD FIRE RANKS RIGHT UP THERE WITH A HURRICANE IN THE minds of most mariners when they think of the most terrifying things they might have to face at sea. Two experiences to be avoided at all costs. But a year after going in search of the *Regal Sword*, I find myself plunging into a fiery nightmare of sorts. Willingly . . . at first.

In the early 1990s I'm working as a mate aboard the tug *Jean Ture-camo* in New York Harbor. One afternoon when I have some spare time off watch on the tug, I'm plotting hang numbers on a chart of Massachusetts Bay. The chief engineer, Fred Robinson, is looking over my shoulder and asks what I'm doing. I launch into my shipwreck spiel and tell Fred I'm a diver with a thing for shipwrecks. In my spare time I collect hang numbers from fishermen in my quest to track down wrecks.

Fred has been going to sea for a long time and has lots of experiences to relate, including being shipwrecked once himself. He was aboard the tug *Mount Hope* when it struck a ledge in Narragansett Bay and sank. Fred says he managed to save the steam whistle just before jumping into the lifeboat. That's grace under pressure.

As Fred and I are talking, he notices I'm plotting what fishermen call "hang numbers" or simply "hangs" on a chart of Massachusetts Bay. Commercial fishermen keep logs of hang numbers to alert them to rocks and debris on the bottom of the ocean where they have had fishing gear hang up and be lost. During my years of searching for wrecks, I will spend decades walking the docks in New Bedford with my chart and a legal pad to collect hang numbers from fishing boat captains. Eventually Tim Coleman and I will accumulate a file containing approximately 35,000 hang numbers. Before the advent of GPS, mariners use the LORAN navigation system, which gives positions according to the intersection of two series of numbers known as TDs. Having a list of TDs from fishermen's hang logs really helps in pinpointing wrecks, because a lot of those hangs could be sunken ships.

"Hey, you know Boston Fuel lost two tugs back in the 70s," he says.

My mind clicks. I'm switched on. This is the first I have heard of these wrecks.

Fred says the two tugs were the *Brian C* and the *Baleen*. The *Brian C* sank on its delivery voyage to a new owner while somewhere off the coast of New Jersey. The *Baleen* caught fire and sank off Boston.

This is all I need to hear. The *Brian C* is a wreck for my dive buddies in New Jersey to investigate, but the *Baleen*'s close to home. What's especially intriguing is that the *Baleen* is not a wreck people are diving. It's a virgin wreck.

The *Baleen* had a long life for a tugboat, fifty-two years. But what I will always remember is her scary and unlucky demise. In a sense she died twice. Maybe I should have taken her disturbing end as an omen, a sign to leave her be . . . lost to the world of men on the bottom of Massachusetts Bay. But in the early 1990s I can't yet imagine the troubles and betrayals to come. And I'm spellbound when it comes to stories of virgin wrecks.

Built as the *John E Meyer* in 1923, at Manitowoc Shipbuilding Corp, in Manitowoc, Wisconsin, the tug that will become the *Baleen* has a 750-horsepower Hews & Phillips triple-expansion steam engine and a coal-fired boiler. Her heavy-plate steel hull has a registered gross tonnage of 205 and measures 102.8 feet in length, 24.1 feet abeam, 13.9 feet in draft. She spends a large part of her life in the Great Lakes, where she works for a variety of towing companies and is renamed the *Jesse James*.

In 1967 a towing company in Tampa, Florida, buys, rebuilds, and repowers her with a turbocharged sixteen-cylinder EMD diesel engine of 3,000 horsepower. In 1970 she's renamed the *Baleen* and purchased by the Reinauer Transportation Company of Wyckoff, New Jersey. Her new home port is Bath, Maine. It's at this point that the *Baleen* begins towing oil barges up and down the New England coast.

On October 30th, 1975, working for the Reinauer subsidiary Boston Fuel Transportation, Baleen *is on a voyage from Linden, New Jersey, to Boston. She's towing a barge loaded with 45,000 barrels of home heating oil. Around 1:30 in the afternoon* Baleen *finishes pushing her barge east through the Cape Cod Canal and puts the barge on "the wire," the towing hawser. The weather's stormy with gale-force winds blowing out of the northwest at over thirty miles per hour. Seas are running eight to twelve feet in steep chop.* Baleen's *taking a pounding, but the old tug and her barge labor on toward Boston.*

Tom Blom's one of the tug's six crewmen. In his words he's "nineteen years old, young, and stupid." He doesn't know enough yet about seafaring to be scared.

At about 2:45 in the afternoon, the tug's bashing against steep head seas about two miles off Manomet Point, in Plymouth. Blom and the mate are on watch in the wheelhouse when they hear a loud bang.

Blom thinks that one of the chief engineer's toolboxes has gone over in the engine room. The mate sends him below to find the chief and get him to clean up the mess. But when Blom goes into the engine room on his way to find the engineer, he sees the whole upper deck of the engine room's on fire with jetting flames. The turbocharger on the main engine has blown, spraying fuel and igniting it. The fire's spreading.

Blom screams out. "Fire." Then he, the captain, and the chief attack the blaze with CO2 bottles.

But the fire keeps spreading. Hit by hot metal fragments of the exploding supercharger, the solvents, paint, and gear stored in the upper engine room have caught fire.

Blom's reaction is short and to the point. "It's friggin' hot in there."

After ten minutes of trying to fight the fire, the skipper says, "We got to abandon ship."

The crew launch the large, fully-stocked deep ocean life raft on the port side. But as soon as the raft inflates, the men can see they have a problem. The northwest wind's pinning the raft to the side of the tug.

It probably takes them ten minutes to work the raft around to the lee side of the tug . . . but it seems like forever. The crew has to lower the chief down a rope at the bow to get in the raft and push it out from under the fenders. He gets a snoot-full of water.

While the captain's making a mayday call to the USCG, Blom and another crewman go below, passing through the burning engine room to find the cook who's drunk in his berth.

"This is madness," Blom says. But he's six-foot six, pumped on adrenalin, and he thinks he's bullet proof. He and a shipmate push through the smoke and flames and carry Cookie out of there.

Then the crew climbs into the life raft, curl up underneath its canopy, and begin to drift.

Blum will never forget that raft. It's fully stocked with food and drink. He cracks open a can of water and breaks out the chocolate bars. Then he find a copy of Moby Dick *someone has packed in the raft. He would like to have saved that.*

But this isn't the moment for reading or collecting souvenirs.

Some of the guys are in bad shape. The chief's having a hard time breathing because of all the water and the smoke he has inhaled. The skipper tells Blom to give the guy mouth-to-mouth. Blom's not excited by the prospect.

"Let me put it this way," he will say decades later. "We called the guy 'Hoggy' so you can guess how good he was at personal hygiene. Like no way was I putting my mouth on those lips."

Fortunately for the chief a USCG helicopter comes to the rescue, recovers two tankermen from the oil barge, and airlifts Blom, the chief, and the rest of the crew off a USCG patrol boat that has arrived to help.

Looking back on the fire and rescue, Blom says, "I was too young and too stupid to know how bad things were. It was just a big adventure. I only wish I hadn't left my three hundred–dollar leather jacket and my high school ring in Baleen.*"*

Meanwhile the 180-foot buoy tender/cutter USCGC Hornbeam *arrives on scene along with the commercial tug* Chicopee. *Their crews commence firefighting efforts with foam fire suppressant. Another commercial tug shows up a short time after the* Chicopee. *The strong winds and rough seas hamper the firefighting efforts, and for a while the firefighters fear that the tug might drift alongside the fuel barge and ignite it.*

The idea of a fully loaded fuel barge going up in flames and drifting toward the beaches and cottages of Cape Cod makes the firefighters ramp up their efforts despite the gale conditions. But they don't fully extinguish the flames shooting out of Baleen *until the next morning when the weather abates. Eventually winds settle down to about 10 knots and seas subside to two feet. Gutted by fire, and listing to port with decks still too hot to walk on, the old tug's a mess. But she's still afloat. At the moment.*

I love a mystery, and here's one right on my doorstep in Massachusetts Bay. Where's *Baleen*, and why did she sink?

The second question turns out to be easier to answer . . . at least partially. For a time in the early 1990s, I worked on the *Chicopee*, whose engineer was aboard the day the *Baleen* sank. Chief engineer Leroy Tolentino says he remembers the day well. When *Chicopee* arrived on scene, the *Hornbeam* was already trying to smother the blaze with firefighting foam. Once the fire was out the next morning, the *Chicopee*'s crew released the *Baleen*'s towing wire, shackled in their own towing hawser, and got underway for Boston with the loaded fuel barge.

With the *Baleen* disconnected from the barge, the *Hornbeam* was able to head for Boston towing the burned-out tug. For reasons that nobody seems to know, the *Hornbeam* decided to tow the *Baleen* stern first. Tugs generally do not have a lot of freeboard aft, and the *Baleen* was riding low in the water due to all the water poured into her to fight the fire. So why the USCG decided to tow her stern-first— when she was so vulnerable to shipping more water—is anyone's guess. Probably towing the *Baleen* became untenable as she continued to fill with water. Then the crew of the *Hornbeam* likely cut the tug loose when she was on the verge of sinking or endangering USCG cutter. However, only the crew of the *Hornbeam* knows what happened for sure.

During my research into the wreck, my inquiries to the USCG and the National Archives in search of the logs of the *Hornbeam* come up empty-handed. In response to my request for information, USCG Commander T. J. Flannagan wrote:

I regret to inform you that we have been unable to retrieve the deck logs for the United States Coast Guard Cutter Hornbeam *(WLB 394) for the period 30 October 1975 through 02 November 1975. A record search of the* Hornbeam, *the National Records Center, the Federal Records Center for the* Hornbeam's *homeport during the requested timeframe, and the National Archives Center failed to locate the logs.*

With no logs to help us pinpoint the location of the wreck, my research partner Tim Coleman and I start looking at potential hangs east of Boston. At the time, Tim is an avid sport fisherman and editor of *The New England Fisherman* magazine. He shares my interest in shipwrecks and does a lot of wreck fishing both in the Northeast and in the Florida Keys. He's always interested in finding new wrecks that make great fishing spots. Over the years to come, the two of us will work to unravel mysteries and track down shipwrecks all across New England waters.

In search of the *Baleen*, we begin sifting through our list of hangs gathered from fishermen, sorting out the known wrecks from the unknown hangs. This is early in our research of Massachusetts Bay, and we are a long way from having the full picture of what's on the bottom.

During this time Lori's and my dive boat the *Grey Eagle* is beginning to build a reputation as a deep-wreck dive boat for charter. We are carrying divers to the *Coyote*, a large WWI wooden hull freighter lying off of Boston at a depth of 170 feet, and to the "bone wreck," a former schooner cut down to a barge. It has the skeleton of a full-size whale on deck.

Each time we bring the boat to Scituate to dive these wrecks during the summer of 1994, we spend a few hours checking hang numbers in search of the *Baleen*. We go to those hang numbers and crisscross the area while watching for spikes on the depth sounder display that look like they could indicate a wreck and not just a rock pile dropped by a receding glacier. Sometimes we dedicate a day before or after the weekend to our search. Over the years Tim and I spend a lot of time doing this.

Because of technical advances like the use of mixed breathing gases and better training in recreational diving in the early 1990s, deep-wreck diving is becoming more and more popular. The *Grey Eagle* is at the forefront of this trend, and the boat is the first in New England to offer deep-wreck charters on a regular basis. But competition's heating up, and more boats are starting to appear on the scene. So discovering a fresh dive site with a virgin wreck like the *Baleen* would no doubt add to the *Grey Eagle's* reputation.

Searching for the *Baleen* to promote the dive charter business is a convenient excuse for me to solve a maritime mystery. As I've said before, the hunt for virgin wrecks is an addiction. It's so compelling that it prompted my friend, the attorney Joe Mazraani, to buy his own dive boat to search for a WWII German U-boat lost somewhere south of Nantucket. And look at the millions of dollars Mel Fisher spent to find the Spanish galleon *Atocha*.

I've always had a real respect for the ocean and a graphic understanding that a diver can take nothing for granted. Anyone of us could check out at any time on a dive. I've never felt that I could spit in death's eye, that's just not me. And after the *Regal Sword* dive, I have realized that I have a lot more to learn about the waters east of Cape Cod and south of Nantucket and Martha's Vineyard. Maybe finding and diving the *Baleen* will be a step in that direction . . . I hope.

During the summers of 1992, 1993, and 1994, the *Grey Eagle* covers a wide area looking for the *Baleen*. Some reports locate the site of the sinking off Farnham Rock near the town of Hull. Others say the sinking occurred northeast of Boston Light. The only thing Tim and I know for sure is that the wreck lies beneath a hundred feet or more of water. We check a lot of hangs. In the process we come across numerous rock piles, as well as wrecks. They are mainly fishing boats and wooden schooners. But by late summer in 1994, Tim and I have come up with a short list of promising hangs to dive.

On September 17 we head out into Massachusetts Bay with two locations to check. The first location is a deep wreck that we refer to as the "Bionic," due to the amount of fish swarming over it. This wreck's in 260 feet of water. My dive buddy Brian Skerry and I have two sets of doubles (tanks) each, one with air and the other with mixed gas. Basically we're ready for anything, and if the Bionic looks promising, we will dive it first.

When we arrive at the wreck site, the wreck shows right up on the sounder. But in terms of height off the bottom and length, the Bionic just does not look like much to me—it only rises a few feet off the ocean floor, definitely not what I would expect the *Baleen* to look like. So scratching this site we head to the second hang. Here the object on the bottom comes up close to thirty feet off the sand on the depth sounder display. It does not look like a rock pile to me but like a large wreck. There are indentations on each side of the spike on the sounder display where the spike meets the bottom. Rocks generally don't show up with these indentations.

Dave and Pat Morton, along with a diver I'll call "Fredo," get into their gear in a flash. We drop a shot line on the target and circle around.

Then the three of them jump in. A few minutes later Styrofoam cups surface as a signal from the divers below that they have tied the anchor line into a wreck. Moments later a bright-orange lift bag pops to the surface. The bag has a large bronze foghorn hanging under it.

Brian and I hit the water as soon as we can get into our gear. It doesn't take us long to reach the bottom. We land on the wreck roughly amidships on the port side. Visibility's good, at least twenty-five feet or more, and I can see immediately that this is the wreck of a large tug, sitting upright in the sand. I'm drawn to the pilothouse. The windows are blown out, and when I poke my head in, I can see that the interior looks scorched and gutted by fire. All the fittings like the helm and engine telegraph have either burned or melted.

As Brian flashes his dive light around inside the pilothouse, I have another one of those moments when I come adrift in time.

It's January 1985. I'm working for Seahorse Marine out of Morgan City, Louisiana. I'm a mate aboard the anchor-handling tug and supply vessel Explorer Seahorse, *doing a rig move in the Gulf of Mexico. At 215 feet long and 6,000 horsepower the* Explorer Seahorse *is a big boat and relatively new, maybe four years old. Aboard the tug is the regular crew as well as a relief captain and men called an "anchor crew." The anchor crew is a specialized group of riggers who do most of the deck work. Once we start handling anchors, the rig move operation proceeds around the clock. You can't stop once you begin to move an oil rig.*

Aboard the Explorer Seahorse *we have been turning and burning for about a day and a half. The captain's on watch running the boat. The relief captain and I are sleeping in the same stateroom. Around 0300 someone wakes us up.*

"Get up. There's a fire in the paint locker."

I rub my eyes open with the palms of my hands. I'm smelling acrid, petroleum-based smoke as I pull on my clothes and head for the deck. Even with all the boat's lights glowing, everything—bulkheads, doors, the deck—look blurry in the smoke.

The room below the starboard stack is burning. It's loaded with cans of paint and solvents used for vessel maintenance. Now those things are on fire.

Paint's curling and melting off the bulkhead and watertight door to the stack room. Thick black smoke's pouring out around the door. There's a fire station nearby on the side of the winch. One of the crew and I pull off the hose and nozzle and open the hydrant valve. But the main fire system isn't charged, so we don't have water yet.

The captain yells to the chief engineer to get the freaking fire pump online. It seems like forever before the system pressurizes. I can feel the sweat pouring out of my forehead and cheeks. Luckily we're not hooked into an anchor or the oil rig. The tug has just finished passing an anchor to the rig and is on its way to lift another of the rig's anchors when the fire starts.

Once we have water to the hose, I'm on the nozzle. A seaman's backing me up on the hose. The heat is so intense my skin's starting to bake, but I'm able to cool the door down with high velocity fog. Another crewman goes up on the catwalk above the door to the burning stack room and loosens the door dogs with a boat hook.

The seaman and I are staying low, knowing the brunt of the heat and toxic smoke will be high up in the compartment once we open the door. With the dogs loose, we approach the door and open it. I stick the nozzle inside the door, swirling it around, bouncing the fog off the bulkheads inside the compartment. The stack room is flaming like the inside of a furnace, but the high velocity fog pattern from the navy all-purpose nozzle starts knocking down the flames.

After a couple of minutes we're able to open the door the rest of the way and get inside the compartment. Once inside I blast everything in sight with the fog pattern and then go to a straight stream of water to break up the piles of burning stuff on the cabin sole. By then the compartment is starting to cool down from all the water. Once we have the fire out, we assess the damage and clean up the mess. Damage is limited to the stack room. The boat's still operational, so the crew gets right back to work. We still have anchors to pull and a rig to move.

The cause of the fire turns out to be missing lagging insulation on the bow thruster exhaust pipe running up through the stack room. The bow thruster has been in almost constant use for the past day and a half, and the exposed exhaust pipe got red hot. With the stack room being used as a paint locker, there was no shortage of fuel for the hot pipe to ignite. We should never have been using that compartment to store paint, and the missing exhaust lagging was something we should have caught and rectified. Bottom line: We were lucky. An alert crewman noticed the fire soon after it started, we had a good firefighting system, and we got the flames under control before the fire spread. The crew of the Baleen *was not as lucky. It must have been scary as all hell in the pilothouse of this old tug on the afternoon of October 30, 1975, with a fully loaded fuel barge on the wire, the wind blowing a gale, and the sea raging.*

I'm still imagining the fire as I hover outside the wreck's charred pilothouse and peer in. The fire has melted the massive Sperry helm stand and wheel to an indistinguishable lump of metal on the pilothouse deck. I force myself to take slow sips of air from my regulator to shake off images and memories of fires at sea. When Brian and I swim to the stern, I spot the large towing winch. This one has an unusual feature. The wire is underwrapped on the winch drum as opposed to being overwrapped as on most winches. In photos I have collected of the *Baleen*, you can see that the winch is underwrapped.

I flash Brian a big thumbs up. After years of searching, we have found the *Baleen*. This is going to be a great wreck to dive. It's loaded with features to see and artifacts like bronze portholes for recovery. It's also reasonably close to shore, so it'll be reachable and we'll be able to dive it in small windows of good weather. Deep? Yes, but not too deep for competent, entry-level technical divers. The wreck's maximum depth is 170 feet. I'm sure the *Baleen* will be a hit with our charter clients and aspiring deep-wreck divers. Little do I know the drama surrounding this wreck is just getting started.

But there's an ugly postscript to the *Baleen* story. By the mid-1990s the *Grey Eagle* has a solid base of regular clients, including a couple of dive shops and clubs that are booking dive charters regularly. But the competition for charters is definitely increasing. More and more dive boats are showing up in Massachusetts and Rhode Island waters promising deep-wreck dives. Offering to take divers to a virgin wreck like the *Baleen* is a big draw for the *Grey Eagle*'s business. It also gives me the opportunity to make a presentation about our discovery at the annual Boston Sea Rovers underwater clinic, an event attended by thousands of diving enthusiasts each March. I wanted to have a presentation about finding the *Baleen* ready for the upcoming Boston Sea Rovers clinic in

After a *Baleen* dive, L to R, Mark Blackwell, Pat Morton, Dave Morton, Lori Takakjian, author, Tom Mulloy
ERIC TAKAKJIAN

March of 1995. But we're not able to get back to the wreck that year, and we're a little short of underwater images for a presentation.

During the summer of 1995, we dive the wreck a lot. The *Baleen* proves to be really popular with charter clients, and Brian Skerry is able to get quite a few nice underwater photos of the tug. The next spring at the annual Sea Rovers dive clinic, I give a presentation titled "Quest for the *Baleen*" at the Copley Plaza Hotel in downtown Boston to an audience of about five hundred people. It's my first presentation at Sea Rovers, and it goes over well.

People are interested in the wreck. A lot of the clinic's attendees want to extend their horizons in diving. Deep wrecks and technical diving offer a path in that direction. The timing of this Sea Rovers clinic is such that it's right when people are starting to get ready for the upcoming dive season. Plenty of divers want to talk with me about making a trip to the *Baleen* as soon as we get settled spring and summer weather.

Bow of *Baleen* with diver in background
HEATHER KNOWLES

The new dive season gets off to a fast start for the *Grey Eagle* with us doing trips into Rhode Island Sound and to the wrecks off Scituate. Charter bookings are solid, but it's becoming tougher to fill the *Grey Eagle* with paying clients, as more and more boats are showing up on the Northeast wreck-diving scene. The *Baleen* and the Bone Wreck are very popular dives with our diving clientele. For dive boat operators, safeguarding the locations of these secret and pristine wrecks is as important as writers, musicians, and filmmakers safeguarding the copyrights on their intellectual property. We're like gold prospectors who want to keep the locations of our claims secret.

But when a gold rush is on, there are claim jumpers and false friends looking to steal your secrets. Some of the *Grey Eagle*'s charter clients could be spies. We first get wind of this when a diver on a trip with Lori and me tells us that one of his dive buddies instructed him to record the steaming time and course from the Scituate breakwater to the *Baleen*.

Our client has the moral fiber to tell his buddy he will not do it. He's not a thief.

The claim jumpers are persistent. Sometimes we get buzzed by private boats after the *Grey Eagle* ties in on a wreck and can't move. They come right up to us, record our LORAN position, and zoom off, knowing there's nothing we can do.

Then there's the diver I've nicknamed "Fredo," who was on the *Baleen* discovery trip. He has been a regular client, an aspiring technical diver, and a friend we have taken into our confidence and brought along on numerous search missions. Unknown to us, Fredo and one of his dive buddies are coming into the wheelhouse of the *Grey Eagle* while we're anchored on the *Baleen* and casually eyeballing the display on the LORAN navigation radio. He memorizes one TD position line on the display, and his buddy memorizes the other. With those LORAN TDs, any boat with a LORAN receiver can find the *Baleen*.

I don't realize what's going on at the time, but when I get ashore from work on my tug, Lori tells me that someone has gotten the LORAN numbers and that private boats have been out there stripping the wreck of the *Baleen*. To say I feel betrayed is an understatement. I feel the knife twisting in my back.

On our next trip out to the *Baleen*, when we pull up to the wreck, we find a mooring on it. It's made of lightweight lobster pot warp with a foam buoy attached on the surface. We send our own line down and pull the foam buoy up on deck. When I dive down to tie in our line, I find a Tide detergent bottle attached to a small chain on the mooring. There's a note sealed in laminated plastic film, attached to the outside of the detergent bottle. The note's addressed to me, and it says, "If you cut this line, we will publish the numbers."

At this point the TD numbers are as good as published anyway. I can't get my knife out fast enough. I still have the buoy to this day as a reminder to watch my back.

Once I have the story from several reliable sources as to how it all went down, I make phone calls to four individuals to tell them they're no longer welcome on my boat. All four are members of the same Boston-area dive club, and, of course, this causes a flap. If I want to continue

Threatening note to author on *Baleen* mooring
taped to a detergent bottle
ERIC TAKAKJIAN

to do business with this club, I'm going to have to attend a kangaroo court session with club officers to make my case.

The meeting's at a Dunkin' Donuts coffee shop in Buzzards Bay. I get there first. I'm drinking my coffee with the Tide jug and threatening note sitting on the table in front of me when the delegation from the Boston club shows up. In the end the three delegates from the club decide I can still do business with them. The fact that their members have committed a theft of intellectual property seems not to have much bearing on the subject, nor do they seem to care.

After the 1996 season ends, Lori and I make the decision to exit the charter business. We've had quite enough drama with the *Baleen* and dive charters in general. At the end of each season, we have had little to show for all our efforts. Owning and maintaining a dive charter boat is expensive, and we end up owing money to take people diving, instead of making money. It's time for a change.

Wreck of *Baleen* with a diver in background
HEATHER KNOWLES

Stern of *Baleen* with towing cable extending out to starboard
HEATHER KNOWLES

CHAPTER FOUR

A Killer Sub

U-853

1995

THERE ARE LEGENDARY WRECKS FIFTY OR MORE MILES OFFSHORE THAT Tim, Lori, and I have heard about. But to find them will require much longer trips and deeper, more dangerous dives. I don't have the boat, the high-tech gear, or the money for such expeditions yet. But guys can dream. So Tim and I spend a lot of hours, a lot of days, researching these wrecks, sorting through hang numbers south and east of Nantucket in an area called the Great South Channel.

Little by little we start to fill in the picture of what's lying on the seabed out there. In the past the only wreck diving that had been done in this patch of ocean was to the *Andrea Doria* and two unsuccessful expeditions to search for gold on the RMS *Republic*, a White Star liner that sunk fifty miles south of Nantucket after a collision in 1909. But through our research we are finding that these two wrecks are just the tip of an iceberg in a totally unexplored region. There is much, much more to be found.

We really want to go out there and start searching. But we're not ready for such a big and costly expedition, on a lot of different levels. So in the spring of 1995, Lori and I make plans to get back to one of my favorite dives, the wreck of *U-853*, a WWII German submarine that sunk in Rhode Island Sound in what has been called the Battle of Point

Judith. In my mind this is going to be just a fun, easy dive to kick off the summer diving season. Fat chance. German U-boats have a well-deserved lethal reputation among merchant sailors, their own crews, and divers. This sub is no exception.

My interest in submarines goes back to watching *Voyage to the Bottom of the Sea* on television as a child. When I became a diver in the mid-1970s, I heard stories about divers exploring the wrecks of Germany's *U-85* and *U-352* off the coast of North Carolina. Later I learned about *U-853* off Block Island. I've been collecting books since a very early age, most related to maritime and naval history. Many are submarine books with a focus on WWII. I love reading about both the US submarine operations in the Pacific and the Battle of the Atlantic. By the late 1980s I was reading everything I could get my hands on regarding the Battle of the Atlantic and German U-boat operations. Learning about the loss of *U-853* off Block Island during the very last days of WWII made my guts tighten. It's a deeply ironic story about unnecessary combat, death, and destruction.

U-853 is a Type IXC/40 U-boat, developed by the German Kriegsmarine as a long-range cruiser. The shipyard of Deschimag AG Weser of Bremen laid her keel on August 21, 1942. The Kriegsmarine commissions her in June of the same year. Her crew calls her *der Seiltänzer*, "the Tightrope Walker." She's 252 feet long, about 23 feet abeam. She displaces 1,100 long tons and has a range of over 11,000 nautical miles. She's capable of crossing the Atlantic from Europe to America, patrolling the US East Coast for weeks, and returning to Europe without refueling.

Unlike the well-known but smaller Type VII attack U-boats, *853* and many of her Type IX sisters do not usually work in wolf packs. As WWII approaches its end in Europe during 1944 and the spring of 1945, the head of Hitler's Kriegsmarine, Admiral Karl Dönitz, is sending Type IXs on lone-wolf missions to disrupt shipping off the Atlantic coast of the United States. Such is the case with *U-853*.

In the eyes of most of the men who serve in these U-boats in 1944, they're on suicide missions. The submarines are iron coffins. The best they can hope for is to be captured by the Americans and made POWs. But given the destruction of over 2,700 ships and the loss of over 50,000

Allied merchant sailors during WWII, mostly by U-boats, there's little hope the Americans will be so charitable.

Even though the U-bootwaffe has equipped some of the Type IXs like *U-853* with state-of-the-art T5 acoustic torpedoes, and fitted the submarines with snorkels so that the U-boats can travel for days underwater without surfacing, *U-853* is already obsolete for fighting a modern war by the time of her launching. Her design derives from a U-boat called the Type 1A, conceived in the early 1930s. And since 1943, advances in Allied radar and sonar detection, deployment of long-distance antisubmarine aircraft, development of high-speed convoys, and the US Navy's construction of hundreds of new hunter-killer escort destroyers—combined with the British breaking the German naval ciphers—make it nearly impossible for U-boats to complete their combat missions. During the final year and a half of the Battle of the Atlantic, only one in five U-boats is coming home safely from combat. During WWII about 39,000 men serve in U-boats. Fewer than 12,000 survive. The German U-Bootwaffe in WWII has the highest casualty rate of any military service in modern times.

U-853, with her crew of fifty-four, sorties from Stavenger, Norway, on February 24, 1945, with twenty-four-year-old Oberleutnant zur See Helmut Frömsdorf in command. Born on March 26, 1921, he hails from Schimmelwitz, Silesia, the border area between Germany and Poland. It's a region where ethnic Germans and ethnic Poles have long struggled over their national allegiances. But Frömsdorf and his family feel strong bonds to Germany, and just weeks after Germany's invasion of Poland in September 1939, Frömsdorf enlists as an officer candidate in the Kriegsmarine. He's not a member of the Nazi party, but he's a loyal and patriotic German who wants to do his duty for the Fatherland.

It doesn't take him long to earn his commission and apply for submarine service. He's attracted to the glamorous and elite aura surrounding the men of the U-bootwaffe during the so-called "Happy Time," when U-boats ruled the North Atlantic in the first three years of WWII. But at six feet five inches tall, Frömsdorf's too tall for the low ceilings and short berths aboard U-boats. The Kriegsmarine keeps him out of submarine service for more than two years.

Finally, because of the devastating loss of U-boats and their crews beginning in 1943, Frömsdorf gains an assignment as a watch officer in a combat-ready, veteran U-boat, U-853. *Eventually, in September of 1944, he takes command of the boat.*

After becoming the captain, he writes to his parents. "I am lucky in these difficult days of my Fatherland to have the honor of commanding this submarine, and it is my duty to accept . . . I'm not very good at last words, so goodbye for now, and give my sister my love."

U-853 *reaches the US East Coast and the Gulf of Maine in April 1945, after a slow passage across the Atlantic. The young captain's eager to prove himself. On April 23 he torpedoes the USS* Eagle Boat 56. *It isn't much of a challenge. His victim is stopped dead in the water when he fires on her. Far from a modern, combat-ready warship,* 56 *is a WWI-era patrol boat, used to tow targets for a US Navy dive-bomber training exercise off Portland, Maine. The torpedo from* 853 *sinks the US ship almost instantly and takes at least fifty-four of the sixty-seven American sailors to the bottom with her.*

If Frömsdorf were one for introspection, he might consider that now each man in his submarine carries the death of another sailor on his shoulders. But the U-boat skipper is too busy trying to survive. The destroyer USS Selfridge *tries to chase down* 853 *and drops nine depth charges on her; the German* unterseeboot *escapes. The very next day Frömsdorf eludes the frigate USS* Muskegon.

On April 30, Adolph Hitler commits suicide. Germany's remaining leaders moved quickly toward an unconditional surrender. To this end Germany's Admiral Dönitz, who is appointed president of the Third Reich after Adolph Hitler's death, sends out a radio message on May 4, 1945. He orders all the U-boats at sea to cease hostilities against Allied shipping and return home. Germany's official surrender is just three days away.

It seems that Helmut Frömsdorf never gets the message . . . or he craves one more chance to strike a blow for Germany. He's right off the coast of Rhode Island and in an excellent position to inflict major damage on any US Navy warships transiting Rhode Island Sound bound in or out of the naval bases at Newport and New London. But no military targets appear. Instead, during the afternoon of May 5, U-853 *spots the 369-foot collier SS* Black Point *steaming northeast off Point Judith, Rhode Island, with a load of 7,000 tons of coal for a power plant in Boston. The collier's on the final leg of her trip from Norfolk, Virginia. She left her convoy while passing New York and is steaming unescorted just four miles off the Rhode Island coast through seemingly safe waters.*

At 5:40 in the afternoon off Point Judith, Frömsdorf programs an attack solution into his torpedoes and fires on the Black Point. *A torpedo strikes the collier near the stern, shearing off the aft fifty feet of the vessel. According to eyewitnesses at the Point Judith Light USCG station, the* Black Point *begins to settle by the stern and list as sailors scramble to abandon ship. The* Black Point *sends a distress signal, then rolls over and slips beneath the waves within minutes. Forty-one merchant sailors survive. Twelve perish.*

The Yugoslav freighter SS Kamen, *steaming nearby, witnesses the attack and begins sending out distress messages while picking up survivors from the sinking collier. The* Black Point *is the last victim of a German U-boat in US waters.*

Just two minutes after the attack, the USCG-manned frigate Moberly *hears the SOS calls from the* Black Point *and the* Kamen. *The frigate, along with the Navy destroyer escorts* Amick *and* Atherton, *is about thirty miles away, heading for Boston. At the news of the attack, the three warships begin steaming at full speed toward Point Judith.*

Instead of fleeing the scene, Frömsdorf choses to remain in the area after his attack, hugging the bottom only eight miles from where he torpedoed the Black Point. *Within two hours of the attack, eight other US Navy and Coast Guard warships join the* Moberly, Amick, *and* Atherton. *Some set up a perimeter to fence in the U-boat, while others begin a coordinated sonar sweep of the area. At 8:14 in the evening, as daylight's fading,* Atherton's *sonar operators locate 853 near the bottom, moving due east. Slowly. Silently. Just before 8:30 p.m., the ship drops thirteen depth charges on the sonar target, then attacks with hedgehogs. But the sub continues to move.* Atherton *loses contact with it.*

By this time the destroyer USS Ericsson *has arrived on the scene and takes command of the search for 853. At almost midnight, after three hours of searching and false alarms,* Atherton *finds the U-boat lying one hundred feet beneath the surface of Rhode Island Sound only four thousand yards east of her previous position. During the rest of the night the U-boat and the warships play cat and mouse, with the ships dropping about two hundred depth charges and making repeated hedgehog attacks on* 853.

As dawn breaks, the Americans spot pools of oil and air bubbles rising to the surface along with the Germans' white life jackets, pieces of wood, and escape lungs. But Atherton, Moberly, *and* Ericsson *continue their attack. Two Navy blimps from Lakehurst, New Jersey, are on scene hovering over the stricken submarine, too. Shortly after they drop a sonobuoy to pick up under-water sounds, the sonar operators on both blimps hear "a rhythmic hammering on a metal surface." Then they hear "a long shrill shriek." As the seas calm over,* U-853, *a Kriegsmarine officer's black cap, and a chart table float to the surface.*

At about noon a Navy hard hat diver, Ed Bockelman, from the submarine rescue vessel USS Penguin *goes down to survey the wreckage. He finds* 853, *her hull torn open in two places. Beneath the conning tower hatch, the diver*

USS *Ericsson* DD-440 dropping depth charges on *U-853*
US NAVAL HISTORY AND HERITAGE COMMAND

sees the tower packed with the bodies of German sailors wearing escape gear. At last the biggest and most complex naval battle in history, the five-year Battle of the Atlantic, is over. Fifty-four Germans and twelve merchant mariners have died here because of a missed radio message or a misguided sense of duty.

By the late 1950s the wreck has become popular with recreational divers. But too many go just to see the bones of dead men. Then in 1960 a diver named Burton Mason, head of Submarine Research Associates in Trumbull, Connecticut, recovers a skeleton from the wreck; makes a show of giving the bones a military funeral in Newport, Rhode Island; and proceeds with plans to refloat the wreck and use it as a tourist attraction. Following protests from local clerics, two US Navy admirals, and the West German government, Mason finally gives up his salvage plans. U-853 *is designated a war grave under interna-*

tional maritime law, and divers are prohibited from taking anything from the wreck. She lies about seven miles east of Block Island in 130 feet of water.

My first trip to *U-853* comes over Labor Day weekend of 1990. When the *Grey Eagle*, with Lori at the helm as usual, arrives over the wreck, there's already a buoyed mooring line tied into the top of the conning tower. Swimming down the line as the wreck comes into view, I have no doubt that I'm looking at a German U-boat for the first time in my life. The visibility is exceptional at over 60 feet. This is the stuff I've dreamed about since I was a kid. It's lean, sleek, and over 250 feet long.

Butch Amaral and I are diving together. We swim up to the bow first and then back to the aft torpedo-loading hatch before returning to the conning tower. Lots of features are easily discernible on the wreck. The sub's upright with her attack periscope rising above the conning tower like a gravestone. The mount for the 20 millimeter gun is still in place on the wintergarten aft of the conning tower. Looking into the open hatches of the conning tower, galley, and torpedo-loading hatches, I can see a lot of debris and equipment inside the sub. There are two large holes in the pressure hull from the US depth charges. One is forward of the conning tower at the radio room and captain's quarters. The other is in the starboard side of the electric motor room.

As I look at the torn and jagged pressure hull, I can't help thinking about the crew's last minutes. Since Wolfgang Petersen's film *Das Boot* came out in 1981, I have watched the film a number of times.

Now peering into *853* it's as if I can see the scene in *Das Boot* when destroyers are pounding the U-boat with depth charges. Light bulbs are popping. Pipes are bursting. Water's spraying. In the strobe effects of the failing lights, I can see the sweat glistening on the captain's forehead and cheeks. The whites of men's eyes. Teeth biting lips. Some of the men are on their knees, praying. The captain's calling damage control and maneuvering orders to the crew. The sound of the destroyer hunting above grows louder. Yet another depth charge attack is coming.

For the next several years, Lori, the *Grey Eagle*, and I carry charters out to *853*. The boat's packed with clients on each trip. This is what we come to call "Sub Week." Eventually we not only dive *853*, but two others American subs sunk nearby, USS *Bass* and USS *L-8*.

The *Grey Eagle*'s Sub Weeks become popular with our wreck-diving clientele. The star of the show by far is *853*. A real German U-boat right in everyone's backyard with a compelling story. The diving's great when the weather cooperates, and Lori and I enjoy the camaraderie with our crew and clients, many of whom have become friends. Two of our close friends, Charlie and Suzette Walpole, have a dive shop in Narragansett Pier, a short distance from where we tie up the *Grey Eagle* in Point Judith. After dive trips we all go to the dive shop for air fills and showers. A large gang of us, led by Charlie and Suzette, head to one of the many local restaurants for dinner. The weeklong affairs become as much social events as diving trips.

Starting in June 1990 with the sixtieth anniversary of the sinking of the tanker *Pinthis* off Scituate, we begin doing commemorative dives on significant anniversaries. We have plaques made up for each diver with the diver's name engraved on it as a keepsake from the event. Before the dive we hold a brief memorial service and then do the dive, presenting the plaques to each diver afterward.

As the fiftieth anniversary of the Battle of Point Judith approaches, we plan to do the same thing. The date for the trip is May 5, 1995. Demand is high, and we have no problem filling the boat for two days of dives on *853* and the *Black Point*. We have black walnut plaques made up with laser engravings of the lost ships with a brief inscription and the individual divers' names. In addition to the plaques, we have two large floral wreaths prepared, one for *853* and one for the *Black Point*. Each has a ribbon with the ship's name and date printed on it.

On Friday, May 5, 1995, the *Grey Eagle* loads divers early at Point Judith. We have twelve passengers plus myself, Lori, and our friend Mark Blackwell, who's crewing for us. We get underway at about eight in the morning and head out to *U-853*. It takes slightly more than an hour to steam to the wreck. The plan's to make one dive on *853* and one on the *Black Point*. At each wreck we will hold a short ceremony, place the wreath on the wreck, and do the dive. After arriving back in Point Judith we'll present each diver with a plaque.

We arrive at the sub at 9:30 a.m. and make fast to the mooring line at the conning tower. The charter boat *Thunderfish* is already there and has divers in the water. Captain Bill Palmer's tied into the wreck with his own grappling hook. We hold a brief memorial, and the divers start suiting up. The plan's for me to go last and lay the wreath on the conning tower of *853*. But sometimes things don't go as planned. Sometimes a memorial service and a wreath for the dead hit way too close to home.

After about an hour or so at the wreck site, one of the divers from the *Thunderfish* surfaces with a problem. The *Thunderfish* is lying on its anchor line, parallel to us off our starboard beam about seventy-five feet away. Although I don't know it at the time, the diver in trouble is my friend Paul Gacek. He's hanging on the anchor line at the bow of the *Thunderfish* and clearly struggling. One of the guys from the *Thunderfish* jumps in and swims up to the bow to help him. They pull him back to the stern and help him out of the water. We hear Captain Bill on the *Thunderfish* radio asking the USCG for help on channel 16 as his crew helps Paul

Author preparing to dive on *853* with wreath, Kathy Murray and Hank Lynch in foreground
LORI TAKAKJIAN

out of his gear and administers oxygen. They are quite close to us, so we can see plainly what is going on. He has not been able to access his deco gas due to an equipment issue and he's bent. If he doesn't get medical attention, he could die.

On the *Grey Eagle* we listen on the VHF as Palmer talks with the USCG. We feel some sense of relief when we hear the USCG radio operator say a helo's being dispatched to evacuate the diver to the Navy recompression chamber in New London. But sometimes the rescue helos and boats can't get to a bent diver in time. We all know wreck diving means laying your life on the line every time you suit up. If you do this sport long enough, sooner or later death will try to snatch you or the guy next to you. Death can come when you least expect it.

You face constant dangers on a dive. Many threats like getting bent relate to the depth. If something goes wrong when you are 130 feet underwater, you cannot just shoot to the surface. Every 33 feet deeper you descend underwater, the pressure on your body increases incrementally. These increments of 33 feet are called "atmospheres of pressure." If you are on the surface, your body is functioning in one atmosphere of pressure. Thirty-three feet down, you are experiencing two atmospheres of pressure.

At "sand level," the wreck of *853* is 130 feet deep. Here you feel five atmospheres of pressure. But you don't feel this like weight pressing on your body. It's in your lungs, capillaries, and tissues where your body feels the difference. The gas that you are breathing from you tanks is four times more compressed than the air that you were breathing up in the boat. At the sand level of *853*, you use four times more air for each breath than you would on the surface. If you are anxious or panicked, you use much more. Running short of breathing gas before completing a dive is every diver's number one fear . . . followed closely by getting bent. Decompression sickness. DCS. The bends.

It's a shitty way to die. You can't dive to *853* at a depth of 130 feet for more than about ten minutes without making decompression stops before returning to the surface. The deeper and longer you dive, the more your blood absorbs nitrogen from the air you breathe from your tanks. If you ascend too quickly to the surface, nitrogen comes out of solution and bubbles build up in tissue outside the blood. These nitrogen bubbles can start with muscle pain, but if you don't get to a recompression chamber fast enough, you can die. A "chamber ride" can simulate taking you back down to depth, let your blood reabsorb the nitrogen in your tissue, and then slowly decompress you safely over hours.

When things go wrong with decompression, you can have a catastrophe like what happened to the father-and-son deep-wreck dive team of Chris and Chrissy Rouse in the fall of 1992. They died after diving the wreck of the WWII German submarine *U-869* off New Jersey. Chrissy Rouse was trapped in the wreck to the point where he was short of air when he got free. He panicked and bolted for the surface without fully decompressing. His father gave chase, and both men died agonizing deaths from the bends. My friends Tom Packer and Steve Gatto were aboard the *Seeker* when the Rouses burst to the surface. They were part of a team giving CPR to the Rouses until a USCG medevac helo could arrive. The memory of Chis Rouse saying, "Tell Sue I love her" still brings Tom and Steve to tears.

It takes me a while to shake thoughts of the Rouses and the deafening beating of the rescue helo's rotor blades from my mind, but by noon my head's back in the diving game. I'm really looking forward to this dive. It will be my thirty-fifth dive on the wreck of *853*, and I feel honored to be laying a wreath for the dead at the conning tower on this significant anniversary.

My plan is to make a short dive, just long enough to lay the wreath and come up. I go down the anchor line with the wreath over my right arm. I'm alone on the wreck. There's nobody else in the water. Visibility's pretty good, maybe fifteen to eighteen feet. When I get to the bottom, I attach the wreath to some piping on the side of the conning tower, with nylon twine. After attaching the wreath, I say a short prayer for the crew of *853* who lost their lives fifty years ago this morning. God bless you guys. You were doing your duty for your country and your shipmates. The war is over. You will not be forgotten.

After twelve minutes I'm on my way back up. My maximum depth has been 114 feet. I'm within the "no deco limits" for the dive. My ascent time is five minutes, and I make a three-minute safety stop (for decompression) at 10 feet before surfacing. It's pretty much a standard-profile dive at the time.

About five minutes after surfacing, I'm out of my gear. My gloves are off, but I'm still wearing my dry suit. I step into the cabin to see what's going on. Lori's messing with the holding tank, which has backed up because the damn sewage macerator pump has quit again. I put my right hand on the door jam and feel my two middle fingers go numb. Then the numbness spreads to the rest of my hand.

"I think something's wrong," I say.

"Really?" asks Lori. She's a very grounded, understated person, and at first she thinks maybe I'm exaggerating or fretting over something of little consequence.

I sit down on the starboard battery box, which is next to the doorway to the cabin. Almost immediately numbness and paralysis spread up my right arm and down my right side to my leg. I'm bent. No one has to tell me that if I don't get to a recompression chamber soon, I could be paralyzed for life. Or worse.

Lori sees what she calls an "oh crap" look on my face, and she whips into action. Her Coast Guard training to keep calm in an emergency kicks in. She helps me out of my suit. Then she, Mark Blackwell, Kathy Murray, and Tom Malloy roll me onto the top of the engine box. Kathy's one of the divers aboard, and she's a nurse. Tom's a firefighter and EMT. Mark and Lori have been trained in diving accident management and oxygen administration, too. Mark grabs one of the oxygen whips with a regulator on it from the surface deco setup and starts me breathing pure O2. It's the best short-term antidote for flushing the nitrogen from my tissues.

"What do you want me to do?" asks Lori. "Call a helo?"

"Yeah," I hear my voice say. It doesn't sound exactly scared. It sounds pissed. This is going to be a drill.

Lori fires up the engine in the *Grey Eagle*, drops the mooring, and starts for Point Judith. She's not waiting for the USCG to come to us. Meanwhile weird stuff is running through my mind. Not just my frustration that this fiftieth anniversary trip has to end this way for our clients, but other stuff, too. It's like I'm in *U-853* in her final moments, and everything is going to hell with the pounding of the destroyers' depth charges. The lights are flickering, pipes bursting. I'm sweating torrents.

A little after noon a USCG inflatable boat with a nurse and EMT come alongside and do a quick evaluation on me. A few minutes later a forty-one-foot utility boat shows up. Both boats were underway at the time Lori called the USCG and were returning to Point Judith, from the *Thunderfish*, so they were able to get back to us quickly.

An Air National Guard helo arrives at 12:45 and drops a Stokes litter and two rescue swimmers on the forty-one. The crews pass the litter to the *Grey Eagle* and strap me in. USCG and National Guard helos do not carry O2, so I take our portable unit with me for the ride. They transferred the litter back over to the forty-one, and the helo makes the lift from the stern of the USCG utility boat. As Lori watches the helo lifting me and the litter into the air, she thinks, with a touch of sarcasm, *Eric must really be loving this ride.*

I have done helo ops in the USCG many times over the years from both ships and small boats, and it's all a pretty routine operation for me. I have even commuted to work by chopper when I worked for SONAT offshore drilling. But lying on my back in the Stokes litter looking up at the bottom of the chopper as I'm being hoisted into thin air is a different experience. This time I'm the victim, the survivor, who needs the hoist. Hearing the beating of the rotor blades of the hovering helo, and the swaying back and forth in the air like a fish dangling on the line, it's almost like I'm one of those submariners trapped down there fifty years ago in *U-853* with the destroyers pounding away . . . with their depth charges and the rank scent of fear clotting in my nostrils.

Suddenly the hoist operator pulls me in the door, and I slide across the floor of the chopper in the litter. The helo picks up its two rescue swimmers. Then we peel off toward New London. One of the rescue swimmers does a vitals check on me as soon as he's aboard.

"You're going to be OK, buddy," he shouts.

I shoot him a thumbs up. You can't really talk much in a military helo. You're sitting just a couple of feet from a jet turbine engine that's running maxed out, and the rotors are thumping away.

Author in Stokes litter ready to be lifted off Coast Guard boat
LORI TAKAKJIAN

The flight to New London is quick. It seems like maybe ten minutes, fifteen tops, before we're landing on the pad outside the US Navy's recompression chamber facility at the submarine base. A couple of chamber techs in blue jumpsuits come out with a wheeled litter. They lift me onto it and wheel me into the room where the chamber is.

The chamber's a large double-lock recompression chamber. It looks like a long steel tube, sort of like the pressure hull of a submarine. It's actually constructed in a similar manner. It's about seven feet in diameter and about twenty or twenty-five feet long, painted white. There's a round steel hatch about three feet in diameter in the outer end of the outer lock and a similar hatch between the inner and outer locks. Acrylic viewports about six inches in diameter are fitted on one side of the chamber adjacent to the operator's station. Stainless steel tubing and valves, which supply oxygen, are attached to the outside of the chamber, along with sensors for pressure and gas content. The double lock allows personnel and patients to lock in and out via the outer lock, while pressure is maintained during treatments taking place in the inner lock.

Before entering the chamber I take everything out of my pockets. Fire hazards are a serious thing with chambers, due to the elevated oxygen levels inside, so anything metallic or any static accumulators must be removed before entering. I'm dressed in my thermal underwear that I wear under my dry suit undergarment. At this point I can walk, and a chamber tech and I lock through together. We enter the outer lock and sit on the steel benches.

"Can you clear your ears fast?" he asks. "We're going to be pressurizing down to sixty feet fairly quickly."

"Yeah," I say. My voice seems distant. Not my own. It's like I'm watching myself from outside the chamber.

"Good," he says, "because if you can't I'll have to puncture your eardrums."

Ugh.

We pressurize down to sixty feet in short order. The tech looks at me as we are equalizing, giving me the OK sign, which I give back. Then the tech frees the dogs on the airtight door and we enter the inner lock. When we get into the inner lock, I see Paul Gacek sitting there in an extra-large Depends adult diaper breathing pure O2. He has a chamber tech with him.

"Hi, Paul," I say. I'm still watching myself from a distance and catch myself flashing an embarrassed grin.

Hi . . . Eric?" He looks confused. "Hey. What are you doing here?"

"I'm bent just like you."

Quick as a flash one of the techs asks, "You see him like this often?"

"Only when we're diving." I give another one of those embarrassed grins. This is in the days before divers had "pee valves" in dry suits. Everybody wore diapers.

For the next six hours I sit in the chamber doing what the Navy calls a "Treatment Table Six," which is six hours at sixty feet breathing pure oxygen.

In the meantime Lori has her hands full. After I'm lifted off the USCG utility boat, she continues with the *Grey Eagle* back to Point

Judith and Point View Marina. Personnel from the Rhode Island Environmental Police are waiting at the dock. They spend hours taking witness statements from everyone on board. All the while Lori's got a killer migraine, and she's more than a little eager to get to New London to check on me. What was supposed to be an exciting dive adventure and anniversary celebration has turned somber and subdued. Nobody talks much as the divers on the *Grey Eagle* pack up their gear, collect their commemorative plaques, and head home. Finally, with the environmental police gone at last, the boat secured and unloaded, Lori and Kathy Murray drive to the chamber in New London.

By now I'm feeling much better. The chamber operator comes on the "comms" and says I have a visitor. I look up at the port, and Lori's looking in at me and waving. It's great to see her face. Toward the end of the treatment, the pressure gradually decreases so that after six hours the pressure in the chamber is that of sea level again. When I exit the chamber, I feel fine other than being tired and hungry.

I'm curious as to why I got bent in the first place. It was a serious Type II hit in my spinal cord. The master diver in charge of the chamber looks over my dive profile and asks me if I made any previous dives that day. I hadn't. It was my first dive of the season. He says we can rule out residual nitrogen as a factor, and I did not exceed my "no-decompression limit." He attributes my being bent to a combination of stress and dehydration.

I didn't have much to eat this morning, and all I had to drink was coffee, so I have no doubt that I'm dehydrated. He says to monitor my urine color, that darker urine indicates dehydration and clear urine indicates hydration. Today most of the world knows this, in 1995 not so much.

Was I stressed beyond the usual intensity that surrounds the first dive of the season, an offshore boat trip, and the management of twelve dive clients? I really don't know. Getting to the dive site to discover a bent diver and helo medevac was not exactly calming. Remembering the deaths of Chris and Chrissy Rouse put a knot in my stomach. And maybe subconscious thoughts about the memorial and death of sixty-six men in the U-boat and the *Black Point* stirred things up for me emotionally. There are a lot of ghosts down there. Some things you just can't know for sure.

Getting bent is both a learning experience and a turning point for me, particularly in my approach to decompression and hydration for diving. Going forward, I make changes in my diving protocols, paying close attention to hydration levels and drinking lots of water. Another major change I make is in my approach to decompression and safety stops. Prior to this on my air/no deco dives, I did safety stops on air. After this I switch to using oxygen for safety stops. On deep air dives I also switch to pure oxygen at twenty feet and ten feet, instead of just at ten feet. I have no doubt that this has made a difference going forward.

As for the *853*? It remains one of my favorite dives. I go back down to the wreck just a couple of months after getting bent. In the years to come I log well over fifty dives on the sub. But *U-853* has taught me you can never be too careful. No wreck dive is ever routine. In recent years two divers have been lost on this submarine.

CHAPTER FIVE

Ship Slayer

U-53 Wrecks

1996

FOR YEARS THE GREAT SOUTH CHANNEL HAS BEEN LOOMING LARGE IN my imagination as a nearly unexplored territory for shipwrecks. It's the deep-water passage between Nantucket Island and Georges Bank about sixty-five miles southeast of Cape Cod. The channel is a nutrient-rich marine environment that attracts large schools of cod and haddock, among many other species of fish. For this reason fleets of fishing vessels have been visiting this area for at least four hundred years. With its nexus at the Nantucket lightship, the Great South Channel is also a highly trafficked shipping lane between the Northeast Coast of the United States and Europe.

Hundreds of fishing boats and ships have been lost in this area to dynamic weather, rough waves, and unpredictable currents. Others like the *Andrea Doria*, *Republic*, and *Regal Sword* have been lost after collisions. Then during WWI and again in WWII, ships began disappearing in the Great South Channel for a new reason: The channel was a prime hunting ground for German U-boats.

One German submarine, *U-53*, changes the course of history here on October 8, 1916. In a single day it attacks and sinks five ships in the vicinity of the Nantucket lightship. It's the first time a submarine of any kind has crossed the Atlantic on a combat mission. These five ships are the first to be sunk by a submarine off the American coast since the CSS *Hunley* sank the USS *Housatonic* during the Civil War. The *U-53* attacks play a powerful role in leading the United States into WWI.

During the spring and summer of 1996 my wreck hunting with Tim is very successful. On just one day in Massachusetts Bay, Tim, our friend Rob Morris, and I use side-scan sonar east of Boston to find six wrecks, including USS *Eagle Boat 42* and an iron-hulled beam trawler called *Ocean*. We also find the WWI wooden steamer *Southland*. But these searches are just sideshows for my first big offshore expedition to find the wrecks of the five ships that *U-53* sank in 1916. To help with the search, I obtain a copy of the *U-53*'s logbook written in German from the National Archives in Washington, DC, and have it translated. The narrative that unfolds in the log, as well as in newspaper stories and magazine articles that I gather, tells a strange story of both audacity and compassion.

Commissioned in April 1916, *U-53* is one of about 350 submarines in the Imperial German Navy in WWI. She's a Type U-51 sub, 212 feet in length, built by Germaniawerft, Kiel. Powered by two 1,200-horsepower diesels, she can speed at 17 knots on the surface. Electric motors propel her at more than 9 knots when submerged. For armament she carries seven torpedoes that she can launch from two torpedo tubes in the bow and two in the stern. She also carries a pair of three-and-a-half-inch deck guns. Her ultra–low frequency radio is capable of receiving transmissions from central command at a distance of up to two thousand miles. Three officers and thirty-three crewmen man *U-53*. Over the course of thirteen patrols she sinks eighty-seven merchant ships and one warship.

The men who sail in her think of *U-53* as a lucky boat. Half of all U-boats in WWI (almost 180) are lost in combat. Accidents destroy another thirty-nine submarines. Five thousand of the seventeen thousand men who serve in WWI U-boats die at sea. But, as in WWII, the U-boats of WWI prove to be devastating weapons of war, sinking nearly five thousand merchant ships, with a loss of about fifteen thousand Allied sailors.

German naval engineers test the concept of an unterseeboot in the harbor at Kiel as early as 1851 with a prototype from engineer Wilhelm

Bauer. In the 1880s the Germans grow intrigued with designs of steam rams like the CSS *Stonewall Jackson*, employed during the American Civil War, and the British *Polyphemus*, as well as designs from engineers and inventors in Sweden and Spain. In 1904 Admiral Alfred von Tirpitz, head of the German Imperial Navy, becomes intrigued with a forty-foot experimental *unterseeboot* called the *Forelle*, built on speculation at the Krupp Germania shipyard. Using an electric motor and batteries for propulsion, the new submarine can run totally submerged without needing to intake air to supply a steam or internal combustion engine. Subsequent prototypes add gasoline engines so that the boats can move at high speeds for long distances while surfaced.

In the decade leading up to the start of WWI in 1914, von Tirpitz and other German military leaders anticipate a coming military conflict with England and its superior surface navy if and when Germany invades France and Belgium. To counter England's superior surface navy, German engineers rapidly move the design, technology, and construction of submarines forward. U-boat development makes a dramatic leap during these years with the development of reliable, lightweight diesel power plants, which avoid the use of explosive gasoline. Torpedo development moves forward quickly, too.

By the start of WWI's hostilities in 1914, the Imperial German Navy has twenty combat-ready U-boats, with at least fifteen more planned or under construction. War has hardly broken out when von Tirpitz realizes that the value in his U-boat fleet lies not, as originally conceived, as defenders of the homeland, but as commercial raiders ranging the high seas like Confederate Captain Raphael Semmes and his CSS *Alabama* during the American Civil War. England, an island nation, depends on merchant ships to keep it supplied with basic goods, food, and war materiel. Seeing that U-boats can stop that flow and neutralize England, the German navy shifts U-boat construction at Kiel into high gear . . . and *U-53* is born.

Thirty-one-year-old *Kapitänleutnant* Hans Rose takes command of *U-53* in April 1916. Born on April 15, 1885, in Berlin-Charlottenburg, Rose takes to the sea early as a cadet at the German Naval Academy at Kiel in 1903 and becomes a commissioned officer in 1906. Handsome and poised, Rose stands out among his colleagues with his dark, clipped mustache and goatee. It does not take him many years of service in the German surface navy to gain a reputation for courage, resourcefulness, and grace under pressure. Yearning for combat and finding it unavailable as a destroyer captain in the surface navy, he applies for a U-boat command in 1915. A year later he's in *U-53* . . . on his way to becoming the fifth-ranking U-boat ace of WWI and one of the most respected, highly decorated, and successful U-boat commanders of all time.

During the summer of 1916, WWI has been raging in Europe for two years with Germany, Austria-Hungary, and the Ottoman Empire battling Great Britain, France, Russia, and Italy. The United States still remains neutral and continues trading with both Axis and Allied nations, but as the war surges onward, US factories begin producing and shipping more and more military equipment to England and her allies.

Germany's Kaiser Wilhelm recognizes that it's essential to his plans of European domination to keep America neutral and thwart the shipment of materials to the Allies. He believes that a well-executed U-boat mission designed to intimidate the US government and its citizens can prove a deterrent to American thoughts of joining the Allies and entering the war.

Hans Rose will later write that he receives his orders in August 1916, "to attack and seek to destroy" British warships off the American coast, "then make an unannounced dash into Newport, Rhode Island, naval port to hand over for internment any British prisoners" he might have before returning to Germany. On the homeward voyage, he "could engage commercial vessels carrying contraband, under the normal prize rules." Rose's commander tells him that in the wake of *U-53*'s mission to America, the Kaiser plans to lift his ban on unrestricted submarine warfare, which has been in place since *U-20* sunk the British liner *Lusitania* in May 1915. In other words, *U-53*'s patrol to America will mark a change in German strategy and a turning point in the war.

No submarine has ever crossed the North Atlantic before, and Rose thinks his U-boat is "totally unsuitable" to the task. But orders are orders, so Rose and his crew prepare their boat for its mission. After converting some of the submarine's buoyancy tanks for carrying extra fuel and drinking water for a fifty-day voyage of between eight thousand and eleven thousand miles, and stuffing all available space in the U-boat with extra provisions, Rose judges *U-53* as barely habitable.

To add to the misery of the crew, the submarine must run on the surface most of the time to save time and fuel. *U-53* suffers constant battering from the waves. Soaked crewmen on deck watch in the conning tower resort to drilling holes in the bottoms of their sea boots to drain the water. Little by little, dampness seeps belowdeck until everybody's clothing and bedding is wet. The crew develops saltwater boils. The boat reeks of sweat and filth. Seven men come down with a mysterious flu off Newfoundland. Meanwhile the crew fights daily to repair broken radio antennas, oil leaks, and a cracked diving plane axle.

Finally, on October 7, Rose closes with the south coast of Martha's Vineyard island and anchors. Then he brings his entire crew on deck to refresh them, let their eyes feast on America, and prepare for the mission ahead. He orders everyone to shave and dress in his cleanest uniform. The next morning he submerges *U-53* to periscope depth and begins searching off the US naval port of New London, Connecticut, for British warships he hopes will be there to interdict German merchant ships, including the freighter submarine *Bremen*. But monitoring American radio stations, Rose hears that *Bremen* has been sunk before crossing the Atlantic, and he spots no English ships waiting in ambush.

"By late afternoon, it was obvious that we were going to be unable to carry out the most attractive part of our assignment," Rose remembers. "There was nothing left to do but bluff." So he heads his U-boat for Newport, where he encounters an American submarine, which greets him cordially and leads him into an anchorage that includes thirty-seven US warships.

Once anchored, Rose brought his crew on deck in full-dress uniform complete with medals. He made courtesy calls to both Rear Admiral Gleaves and Rear Admiral Austin M. Knight, commander of the Newport Naval Base and president of the Naval War College. He was told that because of United States neutrality, he could remain but a few hours in Newport or risk internment. Unfazed, he invited high-ranking naval

U-53 anchored in Newport with USS *Birmingham* in background
US NAVAL SUBMARINE FORCE LIBRARY AND MUSEUM

officials and their wives aboard the submarine for a tour and drinks, also inviting members of the press.

At one point Rose takes Admiral Gleaves's daughter into the conning tower and shows her how *U-53*'s periscope works by aiming it at the bridge of her father's ship. Before departing the city, the German skipper mails a letter and peruses local newspapers, possibly searching the shipping news for potential targets. Then, concerned that the harbormaster or the US Navy might forcibly intern his boat and his crew, Rose secures his vessel, weighs anchor, and heads for the Nantucket lightship . . . just two and a half hours after his spectacular entrance into Newport.

As for the letter that he sends, Rose has asked a journalist to post it for him. The letter is addressed to the German ambassador in Washington, DC. Inevitably the posting of the mysterious letter causes all kinds of speculation in the tabloids. Does it contain news of Rose's secret military and espionage intentions in stopping at Newport? Does it speak of Germany's future or clandestine military plans? Is it forewarning that Kaiser Wilhelm is about to declare war on the United States of America? None of the above. Rose has simply sent a friendly letter to the ambassador, like a postcard fired off while on vacation. Sort of. "I was surprised to find myself in your neighborhood. Wishing you well."

When the sun rises on the morning of October 8, 1916, *U-53* is drifting with the Nantucket lightship lying two miles off to port. The sea's calm, the sky's cloudless.

Rose writes in his log as his day of infamy unfolds:

0535 hours—Stopped American steamer Kansas *by a shot across the bow . . . Initiated Morse telegraphy with steamer . . . After initial difficulties the steamer sends a boat. Papers show Genoa as destination, with intermediate stop in Boston, cargo mainly soda—no controlled goods. Steamer released.*

0615 hours—Successfully jammed wireless telegraphy traffic from steamer after release. Headed south to the general shipping lane. Abandoned attack on a large passenger ship because of difficulties associated with rescuing the passengers. Stopped British steamer Strathdene, *from Glasgow, 4381 G.R.T . . . only after six shots had been fired did the steamer stop.*

0709 hours—Signal: "Leave the ship," because the steamer was clearly recognized as British. Approached two boats set out. Captain did not bring papers. Crew consisted of few white men, the rest were mainly Chinese and blacks. Gave the boats heading and distance to Nantucket lightship. They are sailing in that direction . . . Torpedo, set at depth of three meters, hit the aft cargo hold. The steamer's stern drops but does not sink.

0803 hours—Stopped the Norwegian steamer Christian Knudson, *3878 G.R.T . . . The captain brings papers but the steamer is seized because she carries diesel fuel for London. The captain is given orders to follow me to the steamer* Strathdene, *to abandon ship nearby there and to wait there for my return so that he can be towed to the lightship. The captain is pleasantly surprised by this news.*

0953 hours—Steamer Strathdene *sunk by firing grenades.* Christian Knudson *followed to approximately four nautical miles. The crew abandoned ship. Torpedo set at four meters depth, hit aft. The steamer does not sink. Opened artillery fire . . .*

1054 hours—Sank Christian Knudson *by hitting her with a second torpedo, since a second steamer is approaching from the east.*

1130 hours—Stopped steamer West Point, *3847 G.R.T., by firing shots across the bow and flag signal "Abandon ship." Steamer continuously transmits wireless telegraph signals, which are effectively jammed.*

1140 hours—Silenced wireless traffic through two shots to the stern. Crew leaves the ship in two boats . . . Sank the steamer with blasting cartridges. Test dive. Informed the crew that we would be returning home after the steamer crews were handed over to the Nantucket lightship. Towed the boats from the West Point *to the Nantucket lightship.*

1615 hours—Search for boats from steamer Knudson. *They are sighted near the lightship. Chided him that I had to search for him for a long time because he had sailed off. Boats sail to lightship.*

West Point port beam view
ERIC TAKAKJIAN

1655 hours—During the course of the day, a tremendously busy wireless telegraph traffic developed and the successful transmission of wireless messages by the steamer Kansas *could not be prevented.*

1715 hours—Stopped the Dutch steamer Blommersdyjk, *4850 G.R.T . . . signaled "Bring your papers." Before she can follow these orders a destroyer is sighted. Dived. The destroyer is part of the United States Navy, headed for the Nantucket lightship.*

1730—Surfaced. A sizable number of destroyers approaches from Newport in irregular intervals. The destroyer arriving first in the vicinity of Nantucket lightship appears to transfer the crews from the steamers, which were sunk during the morning.

1740—Ordered the steamer Blommersdyjk *again to bring papers. She lowers a boat. But before the boat comes alongside a steamer approached from the east. In order to prevent her coming closer, she was stopped . . . by firing several shots across the bow . . .*

1745—Meanwhile sixteen American destroyers, besides the two steamers and U-53 have assembled in a very small area requiring great caution in maneuvering . . . Now I sailed to the passenger ship to inspect her papers, but also to let her continue on her voyage in consideration of the passengers . . . I had already given the order to signal "you can proceed" when I became aware that everybody had already left the steamer and had been picked up by the American destroyers. The destroyers searched the ship from time to time with

Bloomersdyjk
ERIC TAKAKJIAN

75

searchlights and hereby allowed me to recognize the British flag at her stern and the name Stephano, *Liverpool, 3449 G.R.T.*

At about 7:50 p.m. (1950 hours), Rose sinks the Blommersdyjk *with two torpedoes. Then he sends a prize crew aboard the liner* Stephano. *When the prize crew is certain that all the liner's passengers and crew are off the vessel and safely aboard the American destroyers, they fire blasting cartridges in the ship.* U-53 *delivers the coup de grâce with her last torpedo. The time is about 10:30 at night when Hans Rose slips into the Gulf Stream current and heads east for Deutschland. US Navy destroyers carry 220 survivors, including 32 women and 10 children to Newport. There's no loss of life.*

A day later news of the attacks flashes across the front pages of major American and European newspapers. German papers herald the voyage of *U-53* as an exceptional example of the German Imperial Navy's initiative and reach. Allied newspapers voice British criticism of the American destroyers that stood by and did not stop the terror or destruction.

U-Boat 53 off Nantucket lightship, met by US destroyer *Benham*
WILLY STOWER IN THE PRIVATE COLLECTION OF ERIC TAKAKJIAN

American newspapers report their nation's shock that its neutral shores are so vulnerable to German sea wolves. In the White House and the halls of Congress, American leaders tell each other that *U-53*'s brazen entrance into Newport and her subsequent attacks are a clear message from Kaiser Wilhelm that America's sovereignty is in jeopardy and that the time is coming when Americans will have to shed their neutrality and help their friends in Europe stop the imperial ambitions of Germany and its bellicose partners.

By the summer of 1996, Tim and I think we know exactly where the *U-53* wrecks lie. We have spent a lot of time discussing hangs southeast of the Nantucket lightship and piecing together these hangs with the narrative and geometry of the events that took place on October 8, 1916. Having Hans Rose's log really puts into perspective the sequence of attacks as the five sinkings took place. Even though the log does not give positions in latitude and longitude, it describes the ships in relation to each other and to what the Coast Guard calls the "NLV 117" (*Nantucket Light Vessel*), where many of the survivors ended up. By comparing Rose's descriptions of his attacks to the hangs that Tim and I have collected from fishermen, I'm able to put tentative names on the hangs. The *West Point* is to the southeast. The *Strathdene* lies to the southwest, the *Knudsen* is more or less in the middle of the collection of hangs. The *Blommersdyjk* and *Stephano* should be close to the NLV, with the *Stephano* probably more to the east than the *Blommersdyjk*.

For several years I have been thinking about a lot of different issues associated with this project, not the least of which is expediency. There are some other people starting to do deep-wreck exploration off the East Coast. Much is happening these days in the technical diving evolution. Mixed-gas diving has opened the doors to a lot of wrecks that were previously either not practical to dive on air or just too deep.

Death or debilitating injuries from diving below ninety-nine feet (three atmospheres of pressure) on air have been known for more than a century, but in 1939 US Navy divers like "Swede" Momsen pioneer ways to avoid nitrogen narcosis, which impairs judgment and perception, while trying to save the crew of the submarine USS *Squalus*. They are trapped on the ocean floor in more than two hundred feet of water off Portsmouth,

New Hampshire, after a test-diving accident. While rescuing the crew and salvaging the *Squalus*, divers demonstrate that they can avoid getting narcosis by breathing a gas mixture of helium and oxygen called heliox. It's a blend that the US Navy has been experimenting with since shortly after the end of WWI.

Because of helium's atomic structure, it can pass out of human tissue faster than nitrogen can. And unlike nitrogen, helium has no known narcotic effect regardless of depth. By mixing helium into a diver's breathing gas, the diver can maintain situational awareness, coordination, motor skills, and peripheral vision in ways not possible when breathing normal air below ninety feet. In addition, reducing the percentage of oxygen in a diver's breathing gas inhibits oxygen toxicity below two hundred feet. The ideal gas mixture for a specific deep dive will have an oxygen percentage low enough to prevent toxicity at depth and enough helium to prevent narcosis.

But in the years following the *Squalus* rescue, US Navy divers discover that helium has its own problems. It conducts heat at six times the rate of air, so divers using breathing gases with high helium mixtures have found themselves freezing after using the gas to inflate their dry suits to adjust for buoyancy. They need to inflate their dry suits with a different gas, such as argon, to keep from freezing. Argon has twice the thermal capacity (ability to retain heat) of air and about eight times the capacity of helium.

While the navy continues experimenting with mixed-gas diving from 1940 into the 1980s, mixed-gas diving is virtually impossible for recreational divers until the late 1980s, when Florida cave divers begin experimenting with mixes they learn from the US Navy. In 1995 off the Virginia coast, wreck divers Steve Gatto, Tom Packer, Brad Sheard, Gary Gentile, and Ken Clayton prove the value of mixed gas when they dive to the German battleship SMS *Ostfriesland* in 380 feet of water.

As the benefits and effects of mixed-gas diving become better understood by the US Navy and, then, pioneering wreck divers like Gatto, Packer, Sheard, Gentile, and Clayton, a trimix of oxygen, helium, and nitrogen emerges as an alternative to air or heliox for dives over 150 feet. Today the term "trimix" has become a catchall for a variety of breathing-gas blends. What all of these variations of breathing-gas mixtures have in common is that they substitute some of the nitrogen in air with helium.

We divers usually refer to trimix varieties by the oxygen percentage and helium percentage. A blend of "trimix 20/40" has 20 percent oxygen, 40 percent helium, 40 percent nitrogen. When diving deeper than two hundred feet for any length of time, divers use a "bottom mix" with much less oxygen than air to avoid oxygen toxicity. But gas with a low percentage of oxygen will not support life on Earth's surface. Breathing a low-oxygen mix at the top of the water column, a diver will lose consciousness.

On dives with trimix with low oxygen percentages, divers use a separate "travel mix" with a higher oxygen percentage on the descent from the surface down to a depth of around thirty or forty feet. On the return to the surface, the divers breathe special decompression gases, so the travel mix is not needed for this phase of the dive.

I first start experimenting with mixed-gas diving in 1993 after meeting Billy Deans on my first trip to the *Doria* in 1992. Billy's one of the early pioneers in technical diving and at the time owns a dive shop in Key West where he teaches classes in mixed-gas diving. Having become nitrox certified in 1990, I jump at the chance when Billy invites me to come down to Key West to take a trimix class from him. Using mixed gas we dive on two deep wrecks off Key West, the salvage tug *Curb* in 180 feet and the light cruiser USS *Wilkes Barre* in 250 feet of water.

By the mid-1990s, using mixed gases, divers on boats out of New Jersey and Long Island are finding some of the so-called "Black Sunday wrecks" that were sunk by *U-151* in 1918, including the *Carolina*, *Texel*, *Winnecone*, *Jacob M. Haskel*, and *Isable B. Willey*. They also find the WWII U-boat *U-869*, as well as the WWI British Navy oiler *Sebastian* and the bow of the tanker *Pan Pennsylvania*, torpedoed seventy miles south of Nantucket by *U-550* in 1944, not far from the Great South Channel.

As the summer diving season begins to unfold in 1996, I know that if I want to be the guy who discovers the *U-53* wrecks, I need to get going. Besides the Long Island–New Jersey mixed-gas guys like my friends Pat Rooney, Tom Packer, and Steve Gatto, who call their diving club Atlantic Wreck Divers, there are other groups of deep-wreck, technical recreational divers emerging. They mostly have been pursuing wrecks off the coast of Maryland, Virginia, and the Carolinas, but I can see that it will not be long before some of these other deep-wreck divers decide to go looking for the *U-53* wrecks.

I have been talking about the *U-53* wrecks with friends at the annual Sea Rovers divers' clinic in Boston, and some of them are as interested in diving these WWI wrecks as I am . . . if we can find them. My problem is that my dive boat the *Grey Eagle* is not up to the task of a long, safe, multiday offshore search mission. Still, I feel that I need to make a move quickly to "plant the flag" and stake out my territory South of Nantucket and Martha's Vineyard. I'm trying to make a name for myself in the deep-wreck research world, not just as a diver but as a capable researcher and someone who can locate lost ships.

This *U-53* project will be a whole different ball game than looking for inshore wrecks on day trips out of Scituate, Cape Cod, or Rhode Island. To make the search, I need to charter a boat that's capable, pick a seasoned crew of divers and mariners for crew, and get out there and put Tim's and my research theories to the test. It's time to go big or go home.

I have a boat in mind. When I was doing my USCG Reserve duty at Chatham, one of our forty-four-foot motor lifeboats tied up at the Chatham fishing pier. Also at the fishing pier was a small green dragger that I have always admired. It belongs to my friend Bill Amaru, who counseled me during my search for the *Regal Sword*. She has a slightly raised foredeck, pilothouse forward, and large stern deck. Bill keeps the boat in great shape, everything neat and well organized. The *Joanne A III*'s a forty-four-foot long fiberglass Stanley dragger built in Maine with a 400-horsepower Lugger diesel.

In April 1996 I ask Bill about chartering his boat for an exploration expedition in the vicinity of the Nantucket light buoy. (The USCG took the last Nantucket lightship out of service in 1983 and replaced it with a buoy.) Bill's agreeable, and we decide to do it over a weekend. We will load up on a Friday and leave that night to steam about eighty miles out to the search area. Then we will search and dive Saturday and Sunday, getting back to the dock in Chatham early Monday morning.

Captain Bill Amaru aboard the *Joanne A III*
ERIC TAKAKJIAN

The next thing is to pick a crew. I want to be able to maximize our time and the number of dives over the two-day period, so I'm thinking the mission needs two teams of two divers each, ideally making a morning dive at one site followed by an afternoon dive at another site. In addition to myself, I need three other divers who are capable of diving deep wrecks in possibly less-than-ideal or unknown conditions from a platform that's not a dive boat. These divers will have to be team oriented, and I will need to trust them fully. The "espionage factor" that I experienced with the discovery of the *Baleen* is still infecting the wreck-diving community.

My first pick is my close friend Brian Skerry. Brian's an extraordinary underwater photographer; he and Brad Sheard, who's also a close friend of Brian's, are probably the two best shipwreck photographers in the world at the time. Brian and I have done a lot of diving together. We have dived many of the Massachusetts Bay wrecks. One year we did ten or twelve dives on the Bone Wreck. Brian has also occasionally crewed for me on the *Grey Eagle* and helped Lori on a trip south of Block Island that I wasn't able to make. Today Brian's one of National Geographic's leading underwater photographers.

My next two picks to round out the crew are guys who I met aboard the *Wahoo* on *Doria* trips: Captain Hank Garvin and Paul Gacek. Hank's one of the longtime *Wahoo* crew. He's a tremendous diver, super strong in the water, and a great guy. He's always interested in finding new wrecks, and as a licensed captain, he's a really capable boat guy as well. Paul's one of the longtime *Wahoo* customers. I got to know Paul on *Doria* trips. He's a conductor with the New Haven Symphony Orchestra, and he has lots of experience diving deep wrecks like the Doria and some of the deeper wrecks off North Carolina's Outer Banks. I know he'll be up for an adventure.

The *Joanne A III* has an open stern that's low to the water, but the boat needs a dive ladder, so my brother Kyle and I weld up an aluminum ladder similar to the one I have on the *Grey Eagle*. Then the team picks

Exploration team, L to R, Paul Gacek, author, Hank Garvin, Brian Skerry
ERIC TAKAKJIAN

a weekend that looks like a good weather window and coincides with everyone's schedule. As it turns out the date is near a new moon or full moon, which means higher tides and stronger currents. I still have a lot of lessons to learn about diving on Nantucket Shoals and in the Great South Channel. Nobody has ever done any diving in the Great South Channel. We will be the first, and there will be a steep learning curve.

Our team meets at the Chatham fish pier on Friday, May 31. I get there in the late morning, with my gear, the ladder, and all the food and drinks. I also have a briefcase full of research material, a small three-ring folder with stats on all of the ships, a copy of the *U-53* log, my chart marked with hangs, a list of hangs, and plotting sheets I have made up for the different wrecks. Better to have more info than less. Lori has made a pie and an apple crisp.

Bill's there early too. We load most of the gear in the fish hold along with some ice to keep the food cold. The other guys trickle in over the course of the day. At one point Bill says, "By the time the 150th tank goes into the fish hold, I realize you guys are pretty serious."

No question, this is going to be an expedition. The weather becomes calm and clear, and we get underway around 7:00 in the evening. Bill steers us out of Chatham Harbor and over the treacherous, shifting sand shoals known as the Chatham Bars. After that, Bill, Hank, Brian, and I take turns standing watch at the wheel.

Our first search will be in the area of the *West Point* wreck, the hang farthest to the southeast. We get there on Hank's watch. It's around 4:30 in the morning, still dark. We cut the engine and drift until daylight. Shortly after dawn, everyone's up, eating breakfast. We're all keyed up and hyper alert. It's not long before we're making passes over a set of hang numbers that I think will be a good candidate for the *West Point*. It's a bad hang where a lot of draggers have lost gear.

We're steaming slowly back and forth in a search pattern we call "mowing the lawn," and it doesn't take long before what looks like a big wreck shows up like spikes on the *Joanne A III*'s depth sounder display screen. We make more passes over it to plot how the wreck's positioned on the seafloor measured by the LORAN navigation receiver. When we have a good idea of how the wreck is lying and what appears to be the center of the wreck, we maneuver and drop a weighted shot line with a small anchor and lead weight on the bottom and a tuna ball on the top.

Brian and I suit up while Bill positions the boat up current of the buoy. I'm wearing a pair of high-pressure tanks called "one hundreds" with an isolation manifold filled with 17/50 trimix, on my back. Under each arm I carry an aluminum "80" filled with deco gas. One has 36 percent nitrox in it and the other pure oxygen. My trusty Blue Water Technologies dive light is clipped to my chest harness. No question, this stuff adds up to at least two hundred pounds of gear.

Then we both jump in. I grab the shot line, but Brian misses it and starts drifting down current. Bill circles the boat around. Finally Brain's close enough to grab the wire to the paravane hanging from the outrigger, and Bill tows him up to the shot line. This current's no joke; I'm having a memory of the aborted dive to the *Regal Sword*.

Once we're together, Brian and I do a final gear check and head down the line. It's a long pull and kick to get to the bottom but nothing like the struggle I had trying to get down to the *Sword*, thank God. The water's very clear, and I can see the bottom long before we touch down in nice, clean white sand. There's a steel mast

Author and Brian getting ready to make the first dive on the *U 53* wrecks
ERIC TAKAKJIAN

lying in the sand next to us. Looking straight ahead, I can see the wreck. We're more or less amidships. Together we swim forward and up over the wreck. There are hull plates and steel beams everywhere. To our right the wreck goes up higher, probably twenty-five feet above the sand.

We start swimming slowly over the wreck, looking around to take it all in. The whole superstructure's gone, and the hull's broken down. But the wreck's upright, and I can see clearly it was once a big freighter. All the research that I have been gathering for the last four years about the *West Point*, her sister wrecks, and *U-53* comes flooding into my head.

Looking down I don't see the bones of a long lost shipwreck. I see the *West Point* as she was in her glory days and in the photograph I've received from the Peabody Essex Museum in Salem, Massachusetts.

She's 375 feet long with a sleek, dark hull, displacing 3,847 gross tons. With her low-slung, white bridge structure amidships, a single funnel, and her two tall masts—one far forward and the other far aft—she's a classic example of an English merchant ship built shortly after the outset of the twentieth century. The *West Point*'s still a young ship. Furness Withy, her owner, has spared no expense in her construction. Irvine Shipbuilding and Engineering Company at Strathclyde, Scotland, launched her in 1912, just a mere four years before U-53 sinks her.

Today she's sailing light, bound from London for Newport News, Virginia.

Her captain, Frederick Harnden, will declare that his ship's an unarmed vessel but "doing Admiralty business." In other words, she's voyaging on behalf of the English navy to carry war materiel from America to Great Britain.

Harnden will never forget this morning:

The first intimation that there was any trouble was when the submarine came upon our starboard bow and fired one shot. I put my helm hard at starboard, swung away from the submarine, and stopped. We had no passengers, had about 300 tons of miscellaneous freight. We were about forty-five miles southeast of Nantucket when the submarine appeared. The commanding officer of the submarine gave us plenty of time to abandon ship . . . No complaints to make about treatment received.

Aboard the Nantucket lightship, the crew has been following the events surrounding U-53's arrival in the area on the morning of October 8, by monitoring the radiotelegraph transmissions from the steamer Kansas, and later, the West Point. The radioman on the lightship has also heard anonymous distress calls, probably from the steamers Strathdene and Christian Knudson, which have already been stopped by Hans Rose. The lightship crew has also "heard a hundred or more shots fired, the reports being very clear, apparently not many miles over the horizon."

At about 10:30 in the morning, the lightship crew spots lifeboats sailing its way. This is the crew of the Strathdene. *They're welcomed aboard the lightship, which already has seventeen shipwrecked fishermen from a schooner sunk the night before.*

Things really start getting crowded aboard the lightship at about 2:00 in the afternoon when the crew from the West Point *starts arriving. The master of the lightship will say,*

The submarine, after sinking the West Point, *had taken their boats in tow and towed them within sight of the lightship. Although the line parted several times while being towed, the submarine returned and picked them up again. All passengers arriving on board assert that they were treated with the utmost courtesy by the submarine captain. The captain of the Strathdene stated that after being sunk the German captain slapped him on the back and said, "Well, old man, I wish you luck" and also gave him his bearing to the lightship.*

I'm still marveling over Hans Rose's old-school gallantry toward his victims when I spot a couple of cargo winches and some machinery below me. Brian and I are over what used to be the engine room. I realize we have been here before and our exploration has taken us back to where we started. A quick check of my dive timer shows we have been on the bottom for about twenty minutes. Time to start back up.

Coming up from 260 feet, we have about ninety minutes of decompression stops at 10-foot intervals, starting at 120 feet, before we can surface safely. We're using the Key West Consortium tables to plan our decompression stops. These have been calculated by our close friend Dr. Bill Hamilton, a diving physiologist who does a lot of consulting work for the offshore oil industry. Dr. Bill's a great friend to tech divers like us during the first years of using mixed gases to dive deep wrecks, and he's definitely instrumental in the technical diving revolution. He created all of the original early deco tables for mixed-gas diving by developing algorithms for different gas combinations. His work makes it possible for us to do these dives. These are in the days before software programs and arm-mounted dive computers give us real-time deco stop solutions. Eventually tech divers can make their deco calculations with an app on a smartphone. But not in 1995.

When Brian and I surface and hang on the shot line buoy, Bill circles the boat around and picks us up. After we get out of the water, I'm buzzing with adrenalin. Like, "Holy shit, guys. It was right in front of us. A large steel freighter, sitting upright on the bottom." Everything's checking out. This wreck has to be the *West Point*.

After lunch we head several miles west of our current location in search of the freighter *Strathdene*. After about twenty minutes of circling around at the next search sight, sure enough, we come across a really large target on the sounder. This one has a lot of relief, much more so than the *West Point*. Water depth is 230 feet, and the wreck comes up to nearly 180 feet. Wow. Next up on the dive schedule are Hank and Paul. Excited to see what's down there, they suit up right away. Bill maneuvers the boat into position, and we drop the shot line as we did this morning.

Once Hank and Paul are ready, we swing around up current of the buoy. They jump overboard and swim to the line. Now we sit and wait. Hank and Paul are planning about twenty minutes of bottom time, which will put them back on the surface in just under two hours. If it turns out that this hang is just a pile of rocks, they will come right back up after a short deco.

The guys don't surface for an hour and forty-five minutes. Even before they come back aboard the dragger, I know we can chalk up another discovery.

When Hank and Paul finally get back aboard, they're clearly excited. They say they found a big steel ship that was either turned turtle or lying on its side. The way the line is positioned over the wreck they ended up on the smooth side of the hull. They say that they swam quite some distance down the wreck and then back to the anchor line. But other than the wreck being steel and very large with a lot of relief (off the bottom), there isn't much else they can say about it. Just as with the wreck we found this morning, this one bears more exploring.

It's only midafternoon . . . so where to next? There are three wrecks left from the *U-53*. The *Christian Knudsen*, a Norwegian tanker; *Blommersdyjk*, a Dutch collier; and the real prize, the British passenger ship *Stephano*.

Bill turns his dragger in the direction I think the *Stephano* and *Blommersdyjk* could be. This is an area where Tim and I have collected a lot of hang numbers. When we get to the next search area, the sun is getting close to the horizon, making it tough to see the sounder and LORAN digital displays because of the sun's glare each time we turn to the west. So we decide to stop and have dinner, a short break, and some coffee before resuming looking around at hangs.

After the sun dips below the horizon, it's much easier to view the electronics in the wheelhouse without the glare. We start making passes on a group of hangs north of the light buoy, and it's only a few minutes before we see some debris on the sounding machine. A few more passes reveal a large wreck coming fifteen to twenty feet off the bottom. By now it's probably close to 10:00 p.m., so we decide to call it a night, get some rest, and dive this new target in the morning. Bill lowers a trawl "door" as an anchor, and we lay to for the night.

The next morning dawn's bright and calm. We eat breakfast and start prepping our dive gear. Bill winches in the door, while we get the shot line ready and deploy it. Brian and I suit up, and Bill drops us at the surface buoy. It's a long pull down the shot line. Once again the bottom is white, clean sand. There's wreckage everywhere, rising fifteen to twenty feet off the bottom. The wreck's pretty badly broken up, but the unique whaleback hull design of the *Blommersdjk* is clearly evident. The US Navy heavily depth charged the wreck during WWII thinking it was the wreck of Nantucket lightship *LV-117*, which they did not want U-boats to hide next to. The way this wreck is broken in pieces is consistent with depth charge attacks.

We've found three of the five *U-53* wrecks. Only two more to go.

But we're out of time and good weather. The prize among the wrecks, the *Stephano*, with all the artifacts and valuables that you can find on a passenger ship, will have to wait. We're going to have to save her for another expedition. I'll say it again: Hope drives deep-wreck divers.

CHAPTER SIX

Ghosts on Devil's Bridge

The SS *City of Columbus*

City of Columbus at Boston
PEM

2000

AFTER DISCOVERING THREE OF THE FIVE WRECKS FROM *U-53*'S ATTACK, I'm hot to find more of New England's legendary virgin wrecks. One, of course, is the *Stephano*. But another that really seizes my imagination is the *City of Columbus I,* a passenger liner like *Stephano* . . . but with a much darker story. The sinking of the *City of Columbus* off Martha's Vineyard in 1884 causes the loss of over a hundred souls and fuels a media frenzy.

But before committing time and resources to search for the *City of Columbus* or *Stephano*, we need a bigger and tougher boat. So in September 1996, Lori and I sell the *Grey Eagle*. Eventually our search for the perfect research vessel leads to Nova Scotia and the forty-two-foot fishing vessel *Darren & Treena*. She becomes the *Quest*, a superb exploration and diving platform for both inshore and offshore work and the flagship of our new company, Quest Marine Services.

Once we have the new boat, the Quest Marine team begins polishing its exploration techniques by searching for wrecks in Massachusetts Bay. Using new technology like side-scan sonar, we hope to uncover the wrecks of dozens of ships scuttled during the Great Depression in an area just to the east of the site of the Boston lightship station (now a light buoy). It's one of the largest artificial reef areas in the United States, if not the world.

During the Great Depression of the 1930s the US government began a program to help provide employment for the masses of people left unemployed after the stock market crash of October 1929. President Franklin Roosevelt began this program, known as the Works Progress Administration, or simply WPA. WPA projects varied from road, dam, and bridge building to academic projects such as cataloging various types of prevalent architecture throughout the country. Under the WPA the Federal Writers Project paid authors to write and publish the American Guide Series of history and travel guides to each state. The WPA also sponsored artistic projects like mural painting in public buildings and commissioned original dramatic and dance compositions.

While researching the massive number of hangs that Tim Coleman and I have collected in Massachusetts Bay, I discover that one of the WPA projects involved disposing of all the derelict ships that have accumulated in the various backwaters of Boston Harbor over the preceding thirty to forty years. Between 1930 and 1942, WPA workers removed a total of sixty-four ships from the harbor and scuttled them in what became known as the Dumping Ground about ten miles east of Boston.

After the project ends, an amazing array of ships lies at the bottom of the ocean. The vessels scuttled in the Dumping Ground represent most of the various types of ships in existence during the late 1800s and early 1900s. Included in the various types are wooden coal schooners, wooden cargo and passenger steamships, wooden tugs, various types of barges, a Great Lakes freighter, an iron-hulled cargo ship, four iron-hulled steam trawlers, five lighters, two dredges, and a steel-hulled US Navy Eagle Boat, which is a WWI version of a destroyer escort.

The Boston Dumping Ground Exploration Project becomes Quest Marine's longest-running shipwreck research effort. Our initial research begins in the spring of 1988, and by the late 1990s we are deep into it. Our objective is to locate as many of the scuttled ships as possible, record their correct locations, and document their existing condition. In the end we hope to have an accurate inventory of the vessels that the WPA has scuttled.

Working in collaboration with Captains Heather Knowles and Dave Caldwell of Northern Atlantic Dive Expeditions of Salem, Massachusetts, we begin putting names on the wrecks that lie in an area approximately six miles wide by ten miles long. Mixed in with the scuttled ships in the same general area are an equal if not greater number of ships lost by various casualties. It's a wreck diver's paradise. Among the many wrecks we find, dive, and identify are the intact 230-foot schooner *Snetind*, originally a lumber schooner built on the West Coast, and the WWI-era freighter SS *Southland*.

But Lori and I haven't gone to all the expense of buying and fitting out the *Quest* to document the Dumping Ground wrecks or salvage artifacts to decorate our home. The old addiction constantly nags, and it's not really the dream of finding a treasure down there … although a payday might be nice. It's like a siren's song calling me to go in search of the stories of tragedy and heroism that only a few wrecks like the *City of Columbus* and *Stephano* can tell.

So it is on a Sunday in June 2000 that I find myself diving in search of phantoms . . . and suddenly having second thoughts about the whole adventure. I'm drifting with the light current down tide along the crest of an underwater ledge called Devil's Bridge. And for the first time in more than seventeen years of imagining and planning for this dive, I'm contemplating failure.

My mind keeps whispering, What the hell? Really?

Maybe the rumors that I've heard along the waterfronts of Cape Cod are true. Maybe the divers who have more experience in these waters are right. Maybe I'm on a fool's errand. Maybe there's no shipwreck to be found down here. Maybe one of the two most deadly maritime disasters in New England history is never going to surrender its secrets no matter how many clues I have gathered, no matter how much I hate the idea of ever giving up on anything.

No one has ever accused me of being short of initiative or persistence. But I may be hitting a wall. Maybe the wreck of the *City of Columbus* has become nothing more than a phantom, just a flickering like the brief flash of a striped bass's tail fin, like the 103 souls who perished when the liner sank somewhere near here on a clear, cold winter night in 1884.

My teeth grit with frustration into the mouthpiece lugs of my respirator. The water is surprisingly warm here for early June, over sixty degrees, and inside my dry suit I'm suddenly perspiring. I can feel sweat breaking out over my shoulders and starting to slide in drops down my spine. This sucks.

I'm about fifteen feet below the surface of Vineyard Sound, ten or fifteen feet above the white sand bottom. For the last ten or twelve minutes I have been swimming west. I'm tethered to the anchor with the 1/8-inch white nylon line connected to the wreck reel in my left hand. But now I've come to the end of the 250-foot line. The visibility is just about as good as it ever gets in New England waters. I can see more than 30 feet in every direction. The problem is that I see nothing but the sandy crest of this ledge and its sloping sides sliding down into the dark gray haze of Vineyard Sound.

From my early youth growing up in Piermont, New York, along the banks of the Hudson River, I have always been fascinated with steamships, particularly the steamships built shortly after the American Civil War. Ships with iron hulls. Ships that are both steamers and sailing vessels, odd hybrids as the maritime industry transitioned from sail power to steam. Ships like the *City of Columbus*.

Before I ever thought about searching for the wreck of the *Columbus*, I could tell you the ship's history and that of its owners. Forming in 1872, the Ocean Steamship Company of Savannah, Georgia, takes over the operation of the Empire line of steamships, owned by the Georgia Central Railroad. Rail travel following the Civil War is still relatively basic, slow, and costly. If you want to travel distances up and down the Atlantic Coast of America, steamships are the way to go. You can travel twice as fast by steamer (about three days) as by train from Boston to Savannah at half the cost. Steamers like the *Columbus* have good food, grand main salons, and well-appointed private cabins. If you're coming from ports like Boston and others farther east, your route inevitably takes you around the eastern edge of Cape Cod. Then to avoid Nantucket Shoals, your steamer sails through the protected waters of Nantucket Sound and Vineyard Sound, past Devil's Bridge, and back out into the open Atlantic.

A lot of freight (as well as human cargo) travels this route, too. The Ocean Steamship Company provides transport between the cotton export wharves of Savannah, Georgia, and the northern manufacturers of New York and Boston. Cotton travels north to textile mills in Massachusetts towns like Lawrence, Lowell, and New Bedford. New England–made garments, shoes, furniture, and rum head south. Rail connections at both ends of the line provide freight and passenger service to the interior of the country and the West.

As the popularity of the line increases, the Ocean Steamship Company, commonly called the Savannah Line, begins building new ships. In the fall of 1877, John Roach & Son shipyard in Chester, Pennsylvania, launches the sister ships *City of Macon* and *City of Savannah*. Both ships prove to be major improvements in comparison to the older vessels in the fleet. So pleased are the managers of the Savannah Line with the two new steamships, a few months after their delivery the line orders two more ships from the same yard. During June and July 1878, the somewhat larger sister ships *City of Columbus* and *Gate City* slide down the ways into the Delaware River.

The *City of Columbus* sails on her maiden voyage from New York on August 28, 1878. She arrives in Savannah to a tumultuous welcome on September 2. The elegantly appointed ship is 275 feet long and displaces 2,200 gross tons. A two-cylinder compound engine developing 1,500 horsepower drives the ship at a speed of 15 knots. Four circular tube–type boilers provide steam. The hull's built of wrought iron plates riveted together. The superstructure is pine trimmed with mahogany, bird's-eye maple, rosewood, and walnut. The ship has two masts rigged with sails, as is common on steamships of the era, in case of boiler failure.

The *Columbus* serves faithfully on the Savannah to New York route until 1882. Then the Nickerson Company of Boston purchases her along with her sister ship, the *Gate City*, to be the flagships of what is called the Boston and Savannah Steamship Company. Weekly sailings between the two ports is the norm.

The City of Columbus *leaves Boston on the afternoon of January 17, 1884, heading unknowingly for Devils Bridge and oblivion with a mixed cargo of furniture, shoes, butter, and rum . . . along with eighty-seven passengers and forty-five crew. Although the sky's clear on the day of departure, a stiff northwest wind's blowing, making it seem much colder than the thirty degrees registered on the thermometer when the passengers board the* City of Columbus *on the afternoon of January 17. As the ship eases away from Nickerson's Wharf in Boston bound for Savannah, many on board are anticipating the pleasant climate of the South as an escape from the bitter winter cold of New England.*

Under the command of Captain Schuyler E. Wright of Dartmouth, Massachusetts, the City of Columbus *settles into its normal routine for a southbound voyage. While the ship skirts the outside of Cape Cod, passengers enjoy a leisurely dinner in the main saloon. Many stayed up to socialize, drink tea, or quaff distilled spirits. Some play cards in the main saloon or the smoking room after finishing their evening meal.*

Later that night after traversing Nantucket Sound westbound, the ship turns southwest into Vineyard Sound, the last leg of confined waters before venturing into the open ocean for the remainder of the journey to Savannah.

Approaching Tarpaulin Light on Naushon Island, Captain Wright gives the order to Second Officer Augustus Harding, "When Tarpaulin Light bears north, go west southwest." Harding came on watch at 2:00 a.m. Wright steps into his cabin, which is directly aft of the pilothouse. Resting in his cabin, which opens into the pilothouse, Wright has every reason to believe his ship's bound safely down Vineyard Sound.

At approximately 3:15 a.m., the lookout spots a buoy on the starboard bow in a position where one should not be. Harding issues an order to steer the ship to starboard. Captain Wright, alerted by the actions in the pilothouse, comes on the bridge and orders "hard aport," bringing the ship still farther to starboard and, hopefully, out of danger. Wright immediately recognizes that the ship's perilously close to the rocks on Devil's Bridge. The Gay Head lighthouse is plainly visible on the top of the cliffs of Martha's Vineyard to the southeast. A moment later the ship strikes bottom on Devil's Bridge. Believing the ship only slightly damaged if at all, Wright orders the engines reversed in an attempt to back the ship off the ledge. This is a fatal mistake. With her bottom badly punctured by rocks in several places, the City of Columbus *begins to sink. Quickly.*

There's little time to send a distress message, fire flares, or get the sleeping passengers and crew out of their cabins and into lifeboats. When the majority of the passengers and crew reach the upper decks of the ship, they do the only thing possible to save themselves. They try to climb into the rigging. But in the wicked wind and freezing spray, the effort to climb proves challenging to many women, children, and elderly. One by one the sea washes these unfortunate souls overboard. Only seventeen crew members and twelve passengers survive.

I have spent my entire working life as a professional mariner. Thoughts of the disaster and death on Devil's Bridge can sometimes bring a tightening deep in my gut. The tragedy seems entirely too close to home, too much like, "There but for the grace of God go I." So now, searching for the wreck underwater, I try to steer my mind away from dark thoughts and focus on what's here, right now in front of me.

I look down and spot what look like little black buttons. Maybe these are something. But then the buttons shift and the sand around them quivers. I'm chasing ghosts down here. These buttons are not part of a

City of Columbus wreck on Devil's Bridge
THE MARINERS MUSEUM AND PARK

coat sleeve of a long-lost shipwreck victim. The buttons are the eyes of a fluke, a summer flounder, hiding beneath a layer of sand.

There's no sign of a wreck. No remnants of the *City of Columbus*. No clue that over a hundred people perished here. Once their deaths were front-page headlines in a host of local and national newspapers. Once the wreck of the *Columbus* was the most deadly shipwreck on the New England coast—and that's saying something. Since the arrival of the Pilgrims in 1620, at least two thousand ships have been lost on the shoals to the east and south of Cape Cod. Once, the story of the *City of Columbus* accidentally steaming onto Devil's Bridge was an oft-told New England legend. Both the tellers and listeners of the tale would shiver when they thought about steep waves washing overboard mothers and children traveling aboard the liner. They shivered to think of that forty-degree water. Shivered to imagine being one of the twenty-nine survivors, most of whom climbed into the rigging and hung there drenched with spray, blasted by wind, coated in ice for hours before rescue belatedly arrived.

But today's world—except for a few historians and wreck divers like me—has all but forgotten the horror that happened here over a hundred years ago.

Still, how can the monument to such human tragedy have vanished without a trace? How can a 275-foot steamer with a hull of thick wrought iron just disappear? Could it be that after all my research and calculations, I'm wrong about the location? Could I have anchored the *Quest* in the wrong place on Devil's Bridge? Did salvagers strip the wreck clean a century ago then leave the remains of the huge wreck to bury itself beneath the sand like the fluke? Or could the wreck not be on Devils Bridge at all?

There's nothing I can do at this moment but turn around and swim back to the *Quest*'s anchor and hope that my dive buddy Charlie Warzecha has had better luck searching the ledge east of the dive boat's anchor. As I reel in my wreck line, my mind starts to drift again, not a smart move for a diver. Being alert, keeping mindful of the details of your environment, your diving gear, and your body's use of the limited compressed air in your tanks, is all that stands between you and death underwater. Vigilance is my best assurance that I can finish my business down here and return to Lori waiting aboard the *Quest* for her turn to dive.

I'm not worried. I'm just damned frustrated. But to be sure there are multiple dangers here. If a diver ever needs a reality check on the dangers here on Devil's Bridge, he needs only to remember that right in these waters is where director Steven Spielberg filmed *Jaws* in 1974. Spielberg chose this setting not just for the quaint, summer resort ambiance of the island, but also because these waters around Martha's Vineyard are truly home to lots of sharks, including great whites. During the summer there are additional dangers. Small powerboats on sport-fishing outings crisscross Devils Bridge at high speeds with no concern for the "Divers Down" flags on dive boats anchored here, no awareness that there are divers in scuba gear swimming dangerously near whirling propellers.

If thoughts of racing speed boats or giant, finned predators hunting here are not enough to remind me that I'm an alien in a hostile environment when I dive here, then thoughts about Devil's Bridge will do it. The name of this ledge says it all. With its ridge dotted with spiky, giant

Author helping Charlie Warzecha suit up for a *City of Columbus* dive
ERIC TAKAKJIAN

boulders, Devil's Bridge stretches out underwater more than a mile from the southwest corner of Martha's Vineyard. The ledge is an evil place. Over the past four centuries, Devil's Bridge has more than earned its name. Watercraft of all shapes and sizes have been swept to their doom by the strong and capricious currents that meet here.

Devil's Bridge and the nearby cliffs and promontory at the western corner of the Vineyard—known to local Wampanoag Indians as Aquinnah and to English colonists as Gay Head—are the places where the currents of the tides in Vineyard Sound meet the currents of the North Atlantic. Even on a rare, windless day, the currents stir eddies and the water bubbles and boils. The waves can sweep inattentive mariners onto the rocks. Beware if you try to dive here. These currents can pull you beyond the reach of your dive boat or tangle you in the fishing gear caught in the boulders.

It's with this knowledge that I have waited until nearly slack water at the change of the tides to make this dive. But now, after more than twenty minutes of fruitless searching underwater, the window on this dive is starting to close. In another hour or so the current will start to rip over Devil's Bridge again. As I reach the *Quest*'s anchor, I know I don't have all the time in the world. I need to focus on this search for the elusive *Columbus* before this dive becomes a total bust or worse.

"Stop, breathe, think," I tell myself. This is the diver's mantra at moments of confusion. Looking around as I hover over the *Quest*'s anchor, I see my dive buddy's wreck reel line leading off to the east, but no sign of Charlie. Maybe he's found something. Follow the yellow brick road, Eric.

I haven't traveled more than twenty feet along the course of Charlie's wreck reel line when something large, dark, and metallic looms in the distance.

As I swim closer, I see two large iron bitts, the kind used for tying a mooring line to a vessel. These are attached to a hull plate from the bow of a ship.

Holy shit, this is it! This is the *Columbus*! Then my eyes spot a woman's shoe. As I reach for it, my mind seems to bark, Not so fast, guy. What are you going to do if you find bones?

Later, aboard the *Quest*, my mind slips back to the night of January 17, and the morning of January 18, 1884.

Mooring bitt on bow
ERIC TAKAKJIAN

Someone on the bridge of the City of Columbus *is shouting to his crew to sound the whistle. He wants continuous blasts, the international signal to alert anybody nearby that the vessel's in distress.*

But the seawater's pouring into the hold. It douses the fires in the boilers so quickly, cools the steam lines so fast, that the whistle will not hoot. As the ship sinks, she lists sharply over to port. Then she briefly rights herself before starting to settle. People are screaming. A woman is handing her child to a crewman. "Save my baby." Almost everyone who can is climbing the ratlines into the rigging to get above the breaking seas. Monstrous waves are sweeping women and children overboard.

The crew launches two lifeboats, but both swamp in the rough seas. The howling of the wind is so fierce that the cries for help and the shouts to God vanish even as they are spoken. The first boat escapes with only five people in it. The second drifts away empty. One passenger, a Nova Scotia sea captain named

Vance, swims to the unoccupied lifeboat and climbs aboard. He will be rescued later on the 18th by the US Navy tug Speedwell *steaming down Vineyard Sound.*

In his official testimony Horatio N. Pease, *keeper of the lighthouse and lifeboat station at Gay Head says,*

Leather shoes, possibly cargo or personal effects
ERIC TAKAKJIAN

At one o'clock Friday morning I left the light in charge of an assistant keeper, Frederick Pool. At five o'clock Mr. Pool saw a white light on the Bridge and noticed that it did not move. At six o'clock I was called, and an hour later, after talking over the matter, we called the neighbors. The light we saw on the wreck burned until five o'clock Friday afternoon. I took the watch and sent Pool to alarm the neighbors for the lifeboat. He started a few minutes before seven for the nearest house, which is 150 rods away. The neighborhood was aroused and at daybreak I took the sheet with which I cover the light and held it up as a signal. I wanted the sufferers to know we saw them, and I afterwards learned it put new courage in the men.

I then went down and assisted in launching the lifeboat . . . The crew were natives [members of the Wampanoag/Gay Head clan] without exception. The wind was blowing fresh from the southwest and there was a heavy swell. It was thirty minutes before the boat reached the wreck. It was inexpedient to go too near on account of the drift, and seven people were picked up to leeward. The crew had been pulling for two hours and were so fatigued on returning that they did not go out again.

At about 12:30 in the afternoon the revenue cutter *Samuel Dexter* comes to the rescue as it is steaming into Vineyard Sound on its way home to nearby Woods Hole from an offshore patrol. At about the same time a second volunteer crew of native men from the Gay Head Lifeboat Station launches a boat. They reach the wreck at the same time as the *Dexter* and rescue thirteen men, whom they transfer to the cutter. A third rescue boat swamps in the breakers and is smashed, but the crew reaches shore. It's wicked weather. Captain Gabrielson from the *Dexter* testifies,

The wind was blowing a gale from the westward, and a terrible sea was running. As we approached we saw the vessel was a steamer, and the waves were breaking over her. We discovered men clinging to the rigging, and finally anchored on her starboard quarter, 200 or 300 yards away. The cutter was at once lowered, manned by five men in charge of Lieutenant Rhodes, who brought off seven men. A return trip was made and one man was brought to the vessel.

First crew of Wampanoag Gay Head Indians manning a lifeboat
THE MARINERS MUSEUM AND PARK

Lieutenant Kennedy was then dispatched in the gig with four men and took off four or five men. Meanwhile the lifeboat transferred several men to the cutter and at length the rigging was clear. The vessel sank in about four fathoms of water and the railing at the bow was the only portion of the hull visible. We found the men in the fore and main top and rigging. It was impossible to row over the vessel, as the boats would have pounded in pieces. The men in the rigging were forced to jump into the sea, and we caught them as they arose to the surface and pulled them into the boats. Some of the men could not swim, but nearly everyone in the rigging was saved.

One man, Eugene McGarry, jumped from the rigging. Lieutenant Rhodes reached for him but the boat was lifted fifteen feet on a crest, and it was necessary to give way to starboard to avoid being swamped. The poor man was not seen afterwards. And the same instant, nearly, McGarry's brother was pulled into the boat. Captain Wright was among the last to leave the ship. Two men who were frozen so stiff that they were unable to relinquish their hold on the rigging, were at length the only persons remaining on the ill-fated vessel,

Captain Lori Takakjian on *RV Quest*
ERIC TAKAKJIAN

excepting the captain. Lieutenant Rhodes asked him to jump, but the captain shouted back, "Save those men first."

"They are frozen," was the lieutenant's answer. The captain then jumped, and, although he could not swim a stroke, he was rescued by Lieutenant Kennedy. I did not see any bodies floating, although the sea was strewn with wreckage.

A day later bodies start washing up on the shores of the Vineyard. In the weeks to follow, newspapers and magazines sensationalize the sinking of the City of Columbus *and the loss of 103 lives with lurid sketches of the catastrophe. It is, in fact, one of the worst shipping disasters of its era.*

Now, 116 years after the tragedy, we have found the last resting place of this ill-fated ship and far too many of its unlucky passengers. I feel a sense of closure. But discoveries like this, dives like this, can be hard on you. I think of that woman's shoe. What can you say except, "Rest in peace"?

CHAPTER SEVEN

Survivors' High

The SS *Stephano*

Stephano
STEAMSHIP HISTORICAL SOCIETY OF AMERICA ARCHIVE, WWW.SSHSA.ORG

2000

FINDING THE *CITY OF COLUMBUS* BRINGS A GREAT SENSE OF ACCOMPLISH-ment, and it puts to rest rumors that the ship had been salvaged to a greater or lesser extent or that the ship was no longer there at all. These rumors had persisted about the ship in various forms for years. But for me the real prize is not the *City of Columbus*. It's the one I have not stopped thinking about. It's the passenger liner SS *Stephano*, the last of the five ships to be sunk on the night of October 8, 1916, by Hans Rose in *U-53*.

Divers love exploring liners because, in their heyday, liners were virtual floating cities. When you dive on the wreck of a liner, especially a virgin wreck, it can feel like you are discovering the lost continent of Atlantis. There's so much to see, so much to explore, and—often—treasure in the form of personal valuables, rare cargo, and nautical artifacts that went down with the ship. In the wreck of a liner you can find a lot of items that collectors crave, not just crockery and cutlery, but fine art, ornate fixtures, and expensive nautical hardware including engine order telegraphs, compass binnacles, and helms.

Recently my New York and New Jersey dive buddies have found and dived on the liner SS *Carolina* about sixty-five miles off the coast of Atlantic City. By all accounts it's a great wreck, with a rich history and an excellent dive. Serving on the New York to San Juan, Puerto Rico, packet run, the *Carolina*'s last voyage came in early June 1918. Departing San Juan for New York, the *Carolina* had 217 passengers on board. On June 2, 1918, less than a day from reaching her destination, the German submarine *U-151* torpedoed the *Carolina* off the New Jersey coast in what has been called the Black Sunday Attacks. All 217 passengers and the ship's crew took to the lifeboats. One lifeboat capsized, killing sixteen occupants. Two lifeboats managed to reach the New Jersey coast some eighty miles away. The other survivors were rescued by passing ships.

Today the remains of the *Carolina* lie on a white sand bottom 240 feet below the surface of the Atlantic. The wreck is upright with the superstructure collapsed. Pieces of the ship's china with the steamship line logo are lying all over the midships area. Divers have found ornate sinks from the passenger cabins with the logo and a rope design among the wreckage. Portholes and brass ships fittings are everywhere. I think the SS *Stephano* should be just as great a wreck if not better . . . if I can find it.

Belonging to the Bowring family's Red Cross Line, whose maritime roots in Newfoundland stretch back to the early 1800s, the *Stephano* is the fleet's flagship at the time of her loss. The story of the Bowring group of companies begins in St. John's Newfoundland in 1811. By 1823 the company owns three sailing ships, trading to Europe and the United States. Bowring enters the lucrative sealing business in the 1830s, and by the 1850s the company owns a small fleet of tramp steamers. By the mid-1880s, the company has entered the passenger business with the purpose-built SS *Miranda* and SS *Portia*. These ships provide passenger and limited cargo service between St. John's, Newfoundland, and New York. With a stop in Halifax, Nova Scotia, the Bowring liners can make the trip in five days.

Constructed at the yard of Charles Connell and Son in Scotland, the *Stephano* slides down the ways on February 4, 1911. Her owners take delivery of her in June of the same year. She's what mariners call a "pretty ship," with the long sleek looks you associate with passenger liners. The *Stephano* has a plumb bow, the bridge on the forward third of the deck, a single funnel midships, and two tall masts, one over the forward cargo hold and one over the aft hold. Her hull's built of heavy steel for breaking ice and painted black. The superstructure's white. The funnel has a black stripe at the top and one at the bottom with a large white field in the middle. A huge red X, the Cross of St. Andrew, spans the white field, marking the *Stephano* as a liner of the Red Cross Line.

Her principal dimensions measure 323.4 feet in length overall, 46.5 feet in beam. She displaces 3,449 gross tons. Her triple expansion steam engine propels her at a service speed of 13 knots. Four coal-fired, water-tube boilers supply the steam. The *Stephano's* elegantly appointed for passenger service, with ornately carved interior woodwork in mahogany and Burmese teak, passenger cabins fitted with plush bunks and cabin fittings, and a magnificent main dining room. Scotland's known at the time for having some of the world's best shipyards and producing some of the world's finest ships. The *Stephano* is no exception.

The liner and her sister ship, the SS *Florizel*, have been built expressly for the Red Cross Line's St. John's to New York passenger service. But during the early spring the *Stephano* and *Florizel* participate in the annual Newfoundland seal hunt to gather tens of thousands of seal pelts for sale to the garment industry. The ships transport the seal hunters in the cargo

Red Cross Line route map
ERIC TAKAKJIAN

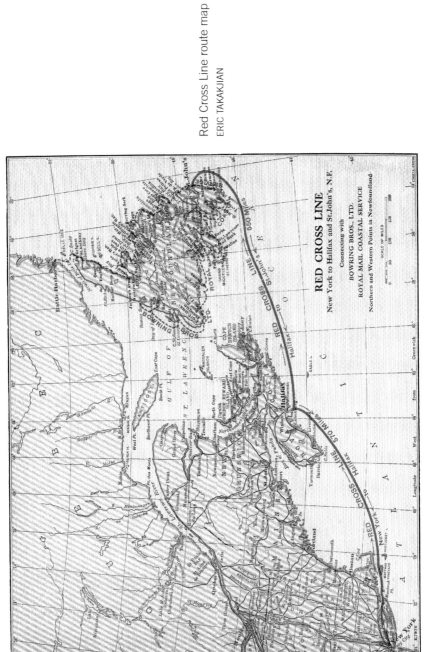

holds, not the passengers' quarters, to the ice floes where the seals congregate off Newfoundland's north coast. When sudden blizzards hit, these expansive frozen masses of floating seawater can trap the sealing ships in the ice and crush their hulls. Between 1906 and 1914 the ice claims five ships and reduces the country's sealing fleet to twenty vessels.

During the winter of 1914, both ships are on hand when the SS *Newfoundland*'s crew of 132 sealers becomes separated from the ship on the ice for fifty-three hours in a blizzard. The wooden-hulled *Newfoundland* can't push through the thick ice to reach her stranded crew. Eventually Abram Kean, captain of the steel-hulled *Stephano*, is able to break through the thick ice to rescue some of the *Newfoundland*'s crew members left stranded. Captain Abram Kean's son, Westbury Kean, is captain of the *Newfoundland* at the time of the incident. Of the 132 men trapped on the ice for over two days, seventy-eight perish in the catastrophe, known as the Great Newfoundland Sealing Disaster. Two years later the *Stephano* transports the *Newfoundland* and Labrador regiment of the British Army to Europe during the early stages of WWI.

But despite her luck, her heroics, and her colorful voyages, the SS *Stephano* dies nearly a new ship.

On October 8, 1916, she departs Halifax, Nova Scotia, and Captain Clifton Smith points her toward New York for the remaining leg of the voyage that began in St. John's. By evening, the SS *Stephano* becomes the last chapter of a significant event in maritime history that's unfolding off Nantucket.

Smith's narrative of events is short and to the point.

We sighted the German submarine at six p.m., October 8, 1916. She fired across our bows. We stopped immediately and commenced to lower our boats. Everything was done in a perfectly orderly manner. The commanding officer of the submarine gave us plenty of time to abandon ship. We were unarmed and carried ninety-four passengers . . . I left the Stephano *in a launch belonging to the US destroyer, which picked up the passengers and crew of the* Stephano. *There were fifty-four women and children on the* Stephano. *There were thirty-four shots fired in trying to sink her, and a torpedo was finally used. Have no complaints to make.*

Clifton Smith's official narrative given to the US Navy in Newport, Rhode Island, is definitely in the tradition of centuries of maritime incident reports in which the governing caveat is, "The less said, the better."

But quite a few of his passengers have a lot to say to the press. Articles in New York, Boston, Providence, Halifax, Long Island, and New-foundland papers about the sinking quote survivors extensively. Some passengers speak of their personal terror during the initial phase of the attack. Everyone remembers how German submarine U-20 *attacked and sunk the British liner RMS* Lusitania *on May 7, 1915 off the Old Head of Kinsale, Ireland. Rescue boats and ships picked up 764 passengers and crew from* Lusitania, *but of 1,959 passengers and crew, 1,195 were lost. Even though Germany's Kaiser Wilhelm has forbidden surprise U-boat attacks on liners following the loss of the* Lusitania, *the passengers and crew on the* Stephano *have no way of knowing if* U-53 *shots across the liner's bow are a warning or the start of a full-scale attack. At this moment a heroine emerges.*

Greg Kennedy, part of the ship's crew, tells the *New York Times,*

I wish I could tell you the name of a young American woman who, when the raider halted us and it began to look as though we were going any minute, began going around among the steerage women laughing and talking to them. I think that young woman did much to halt a panic. She told them the American warships were nearby and would save them. She put her arms around an old woman who began to weep and made the old woman smile. She refused to take a seat in the boats until all the women and children were taken care of. It is likely she will hide from publicity. She is that sort.

While the unknown heroine of the SS Stephano *is there to bring calm to the passengers and crew of the liner during the evacuation, a flotilla of US Navy destroyers has arrived on the scene from Newport to rescue evacuees as soon as they abandon their ship in the lifeboats. The sinking of this liner will not be like the* Lusitania *massacre. Hans Rose sends an officer and men aboard the liner to make sure everyone is safely off the ship. Like the heroine aboard the* Stephano, *he's "that sort." But then he does his duty as a German officer and sinks his enemy's pretty liner.*

The Stephano's *survivors travel by US Navy ships to Newport, then by train to their final destination, New York City, with quite a story to tell. One woman complains to the* New York Times, *"I lost everything I owned when the* Stephano *went down. All my wedding presents and all my household goods are now at the bottom of the sea."*

To varying degrees, she speaks for the entire ship's company. But no lives have been lost. Things can be replaced, and sometimes things lost on the bottom of the sea can be recovered.

On Friday, July 22, 2000, the summer sun is low, almost at my back, giving the sea ahead a misty, violet glow. It's about 8:30 at night. The *Quest* rises and falls in a long ground swell as she steams southeast at 9 knots. A half dozen gulls are following us, squawking away over the rumble of the engine. They think we are a fishing dragger or a lobster boat likely to toss some trash fish over the side for them. They're hoping for a bit of good luck. So am I.

After years of research and preparation, I'm finally outbound in search of the SS *Stephano*. Now, with a good offshore dive platform in the *Quest*, we can venture on long, multiday searches in the Nantucket lightship area without the expense of hiring a boat like Bill Amaru's dragger. We left D. N. Kelly's Shipyard in Fairhaven about ninety minutes ago. I've steered the *Quest* across Buzzards Bay, through Quicks Hole Passage between the Elizabeth Islands chain, and across Vineyard Sound. Ahead the reflection of the setting sun has begun to flare in the windows of the houses on the western shore of Martha's Vineyard. If the lighthouse at Aquinnah/Gay Head has begun to flash out its alternating white and red lights every fifteen seconds, I can't see it. The sun has turned the whole lighthouse into a pillar of gold.

As we pass near Devil's Bridge, I think again of the 103 lives lost aboard the *City of Columbus* and hear the shouts of women and children swept overboard by towering seas. I feel the bone-chilling wind freezing those men clinging to the rigging all night until they look like ice statues.

Then I think of that woman's shoe I found and how diving on the *Columbus* was one of the most haunting dives of my life. I'm really hoping this trip in search of the SS *Stephano* can land my emotions in a sunnier spot than that expedition to the *City of Columbus*.

So far so good. The weather forecast predicts clear skies with light winds and calm seas all weekend. Over the course of the afternoon, the crew arrive at the boat in ones and twos. Tom Packer and Steve Gatto drive up from New Jersey and arrive first. Steve Scheuer from Westport appears a little later. Dave "Mort" Morton comes straight from work in Lexington, Massachusetts, having packed his truck the night before. Lori shows up in late afternoon, having picked up some of our favorites takeouts including cubed marinated pork *caçoila* and *carne no espeto* from Antonio's Portuguese restaurant in New Bedford.

I could feel the energy of the team as we carried plastic totes full of diving gear, dozens of bottles of breathing gas, bags of ice, vegetables, Gatorade, bottled water, and coolers of steak aboard the *Quest*. We had a couple of six-packs of Sam Adams for the end of the day after the dives, but, in truth, we rarely do much drinking. I can still hear Tom Packer saying, "Hey, Eric. Let's get this show on the road. Let's go find a shipwreck." The guy's a constant source of optimism and can-do spirit.

Now, with the sun dropping below the western horizon, we pass between Noman's Land Island and the south side of Martha's Vineyard and set rotating watches, one and a half hours each, for the rest of the twelve-hour trip out to the search area. The guys and Lori settle into berths in the fo'c'sle. The sky seems to be raining stars. They start to fade, along with a sliver of a moon around 4:00 in the morning, and by 4:30 the eastern horizon has a milky glow. We arrive in the search area around 8:30. I have made up a plotting sheet of hangs where Tim and I figure the *Stephano* to be.

We located the Blommersdyjk four years ago on the trip out here with Bill Amaru. She was the next-to-last ship sunk by *U-53*. The *Stephano* was the last, and I know that Hans Rose stopped the two ships close to each other. The Blommersdyjk's a couple of miles east of the site of the former Nantucket lightship station. From Rose's log, the accounts of the American destroyers who came to the rescue after Rose started sinking merchant ships, and statements by Captain Smith of the *Stephano*, I believe the *Stephano* lies to the northeast of the *Blommersdyjk* along a line to Halifax, Nova Scotia, where she was coming from.

Tim and I have collected one particularly large group of hang numbers at the same spot in this area. The hangs look like a good candidate for the *Stephano*. We also have another group to the west of these hangs. We think the hangs to the west may be the fishing vessel *New England*. Years from now we will find out differently. It will turn out to be another ship entirely, and an amazing find. But that's a story for another time.

At the helm of the *Quest* I set up a search pattern on the Northstar GPS receiver, and we start "running lines," mowing the lawn over our target area. Everyone is awake, sipping coffee, eating bowls of cereal, and gathering around the Furuno video sounder in the wheelhouse. We're watching for telltale sign of a wreck to appear on the screen.

I'm getting a good feeling about today, and it isn't long before we start seeing little spikes popping up on the sounder. Then, just after I finish making a turn to port to head back south on the next search line, I get a big spike. We have something. It's big and most likely a large wreck. There are no large piles of rocks dropped by glaciers on Nantucket Shoals. The Laurentide glacial ice sheets that covered New England twenty thousand years ago never reached this far out to sea.

"Hot damn," says Steve Gatto. "Piece of cake."

"No kidding," says Tom. After thirty years of diving, Tom and Steve have been on more search missions for virgin wrecks than they care to count, and they know finding the prize is rarely this easy.

After a couple of more passes over the area with the *Quest*, I have a feel for where the center of mass is on this target. It lies in 170 feet of water. We get the shot line set up, and I maneuver the *Quest* into position for the drop. Out here eighty miles offshore on the edge of Nantucket Shoals and the Great South Channel in Bill Amaru's dragger four years ago, we learned to attach a small anchor to the end of the shot line along with the weight. It helps keep the weight from being dragged out of position if there's current running when divers go down the line to tie in.

I steer the *Quest* toward the target from the east, stemming the current until we make the drop. It's a bright, blue morning, flat calm and sunny, but not hot. Mort and I suit up quickly. We're both pumped to get in the water and go down and see what's on the other end of the line. At the helm Lori maneuvers us up to the buoy on the end of the shot line. I jump in with Mort right behind me. After a quick gear check we start down the line. The water's clear with visability a solid thirty feet, and I'm thinking that this trip could be epic. The only question is *how* epic.

As we come down the line, I can see the white sand bottom well before I get there. The ambient light from the surface is still pretty strong, and I don't think I need my dive light. Touching down on the sand before we get to the hook, we see we're off the wreck a little ways. I spot a shadow in the distance directly up current of us. I clip my wreck reel line off to the shot weight, then Mort and I swim toward the shadow. Soon I see the steel side of a ship materialize in front of us. We swim toward it, then up onto the edge, maybe five or seven feet off the bottom. The hull is broken down right above the turn of the bilge. Yellowtail flounder are all around in the sand next to the wreck.

Reaching the top of the wreck, I can see more than forty feet to the other side of the hull. I see four boilers below to our left. The engine room is more or less right in front of us with a huge triple-expansion steam engine leaning over to port, toward us. These discoveries are almost enough to make a positive identification of the wreck, because my research has shown that the *Stephano* is the only wreck in this vicinity with four boilers.

At this point Mort and I have a pantomime conversation about what to do next. We're about fifty feet away from the shot line weight. Mort suggests dragging the weight and line over to the wreck to tie in. I think about it for a second but decide it's too far of a hump in the current. We should go back up and make a better drop. Tom and Steve can come down next and tie us in.

Heading back up the line, Mort and I keep checking in with each other, especially at our deco stops. When I look into his face mask, I can see his eyes smiling like a kid who has just seen Santa for the first time.

We have found the *Stephano*, an Edwardian-age British passenger ship that has been lost from the view of humans for eighty-four years.

It doesn't get much better than this. I can't wait to go back down on the wreck. It's going to be really amazing to explore. And who knows what treasures lie amid the rubble?

After Mort and I surface, Tom and Steve Gatto suit up. I maneuver the *Quest* back to the spot roughly amidships. This time when we drop the weighted shot line, it seems like a better drop. I can see the trace of the line on the echo sounder display as it goes down, and the line seems to land right on the wreck. By now Tom and Steve Gatto are ready to go, so I circle around to drop them at the buoy.

About ten minutes later two white foam cups pop to the surface, indicating that they have us tied in on the wreck. Now it's time to wait. By my rough calculations they will make a twenty- to twenty-five-minute dive and be back on the surface in about an hour and a half after completing their deco stops.

Meanwhile, Mort and I start swapping our gear over to fresh sets of double tanks. And as we eat a lunch of cold-cut sandwiches and hydrate with bottle after bottle of water, we can see the tidal current is starting to run. We can't dive if it's running more than about half a knot, so we're hoping for another period of slack current later in the day.

We have learned some things about diving out here over the past few years. One is to avoid the more extreme phases of the moon, like new and full moon. At certain places on the shoals and in the Great South Channel, the tidal current runs stronger than others. It runs particularly hard close to the edges of drop-offs. Usually you only get two slacks in a twenty-four-hour period, and only one of those will be during daylight. But sometimes, during periods of a quarter moon, there can be four slacks.

To identify these times of slack current, sometimes called "slack tide," when we can dive, we have learned to hang a weighted line from the starboard stern cleat of the boat and watch the angle of the line in relation to the transom. The closer the line is to vertical, the more slack the current. We keep notes on the strength of the current during the day and at night when standing anchor watch. These data points are key in helping us plan for safe dives.

When Tom and Steve Gatto finally surface, the current's starting to run pretty hard and still increasing. After they climb back aboard, and spit out their regulators, you can hear the excitement in their voices. They say we're tied at the engine room on the starboard side, aft of amidships. They have spent most of their dive swimming aft from amidships on the wreck and have seen a lot of wreckage spread around both inside and outside the hull.

"It's loaded," says Steve Gatto. There's a huge grin on his face. This is the grin of a collector thinking about the kinds of valuables he can find by digging in the sand down there. He's imagining artifacts he can add to his collections of tea sets, jewelry, and nautical hardware from the *Andrea Doria* and other wrecks displayed in glass cases around his home. No question: Everybody's thinking there are treasures down there . . . if we can find them. If we can get another slack for diving.

But for now all we can do is wait, hydrate, try to kill time, and hope the tide will go slack again before it's too dark to dive. Some of the guys fiddle with their gear, making tweaks just for the sake of something to do. Lori catches some sun on the bow and thumbs through *This Old House* magazine. I keep rereading my binder full of research material and newspaper articles I have accumulated about the *Stephano* and looking over the set of plans of the ship I had brought along. There are clues in here about the valuables that sank with the ship and where they may be located.

But as the afternoon turns to evening and the tide is still running, it becomes clear that we're going to have to wait until tomorrow for our next chance to get in the water. We've all been in this bind before on dive trips. It's the moment when Neptune makes it clear he's not giving up anything more to a bunch of frogmen today.

It's time to fire up the gas grill on the aft deck and get ready to start putting dinner together. Food's always a big event for us on offshore trips. Whether we find a wreck or not, whether we score some artifacts or not, we always have the first night's feast at sea to look forward to. It's kind of like a camping trip thing, complete with sea stories as well as teasing and steady banter featuring Steve and Tom. These guys are legends in technical wreck-diving circles. Probably no one has more time diving on the *Andrea Doria* than Steve and Tom. They were part of the team that found the German *U-869*, featured in the best seller *Shadow Divers*. And they've recovered the bodies of the crew of the tug *Thomas Hebert* off the New Jersey coast. Robert Kurson, author of *Shadow Divers*, has called Steve and Tom the most formidable wreck-diving team in America. Tonight the camaraderie, the brotherhood, I feel with these guys and everyone else aboard the *Quest* comes with steaks, string beans, and portobello mushrooms from the grill, a big salad, and one of Lori's homemade strawberry rhubarb pies.

After dinner we settle into our rotating watch routine. Even at anchor we stand watches to keep an eye out for changes in the weather, and ship traffic. We are at least ten hours away from safe harbor, and we need to be aware if the seas pick up or a thick fog blankets Nantucket Shoals. We must keep a sharp lookout for ship and fishing vessel traffic. All of us remember the catastrophic collisions out here that sunk the *Andrea Doria*, *Republic*, and *Regal Sword*. Boats at anchor out here in the major traffic lanes for both East Coast and transatlantic shipping are exceedingly vulnerable. Just a few miles from this spot on May 15, 1934, the liner RMS *Olympic* rammed and sank the Nantucket lightship *LV-117*, killing seven of her crew.

Tonight our luck holds. When I stand my watch from 10:30 until midnight, I try to read. It's one of my favorite pleasures, but tonight I can't. Tonight my watch slips by as I stare up at the sky and look for stars of the first magnitude. The "Dog Star" Sirius, Alpha Centauri, Arcturus, Betelgeuse, Polaris, Vega. These are some of the road signs in the night sky that guided European explorers like Bartholomew Gosnold and Henry Hudson through these waters four hundred years ago. They are the same stars that steered Hans Rose in *U-53* and Captain Smith in the *Stephano* to their fateful meeting on October 8, 1916. The same stars that shone on a little girl in a lifeboat later that night.

While researching the sinking of the SS *Stephano*, I have discovered that one of the survivors lives near me on Cape Cod. After I make contact with ninety-year-old Wilma McLean Tucciarone, she welcomes me to her home in North Truro and shares with me her memories of the sinking and a large collection of newspaper articles and memorabilia that she has collected over the previous eight decades.

In October 1916, Wilma's a "wide-eyed seven-year-old" when U-53 attacks the SS Stephano. She's with her mother, grandmother, and two younger siblings on their way home to Hempstead, New York, after a Nova Scotian vacation to visit relatives. She has traveled in small boats before, but a trip aboard a liner is something new and exciting. On the night of the attack, she has just finishing playing in the ship's parlor with some young friends she met aboard and is heading toward the first-class dining area with her grandmother when she hears a commotion. "Everyone's running on deck. I'm one of those curious children and want to know everything that's going on."

When Wilma gets topside, she sees people pointing at a low dark shadow on the waves. They say it's a submarine and that it has fired on the liner. Meanwhile her mother is with her younger brother and sister on their way to dinner when a crewman stops them and says to get into lifejackets and report to their abandon ship stations. "My mother's frantic until she finds me on deck, hands me a life jacket, and tells me we're going on a little trip. The life jacket comes down to my knees."

Adult passengers like her mother and grandmother descend a rope ladder into a lifeboat, but crewmen hand down Wilma and her siblings.

She will always remember "search lights shining on us and sailors calling to us to pull our lifeboat to this huge destroyer." Still fascinated, she watches from the deck of USS Ericsson as the U-53's guns hammer away at the thick, ice-breaker hull of the liner before the U-boat torpedoes the ship. "There are lights still on in Stephano. They flicker as the ship goes down. It seems to take a long time." It's an image you don't forget even after eighty-four years.

I'm curled up in my berth still picturing the *Stephano*'s sinking lights through Wilma McLean Tucciarone's eyes when I smell the morning coffee brewing in the galley. Those of us off watch start rising, brushing teeth, and getting into our diver's long underwear for the day. The weather's calm and sunny. Small birds called Wilson's storm petrels dart over the surface of the water searching for baitfish. Sometimes they land on the *Quest* to catch a breather. We like seeing them. Some of the crew offer them pieces of bread. They are hunters like us, a long way from home.

It's common for us to have more and more "visitors" after we have been anchored up for a day or so over a wreck. The birds and sea creatures

Stephano survivors on steps of Newport Naval Hospital, Wilma McLean in center bottom row
US NAVAL WAR COLLEGE MUSEUM

seem to get used to the boat being here and approach us more closely. Not just birds, but often dolphins, whales, sharks, and big schools of tuna. In the later part of the summer, we often see tropical fish that have been spun off from eddies on the edge of the Gulf Stream.

All we need now is a slack tide. And at about 9:00 in the morning the current looks to be easing. Mort and I suit up and hit the water. Tom and Steve follow with Steve Scheuer right behind them. Soon the five of us are pulling ourselves down the anchor line like ants on a long, arching blade of grass. Once on the bottom, Mort and I swim slowly around in the engine room before starting forward. At 323.4 feet in length, the *Stephano*'s a big wreck. There's a lot to see. Artifacts like portholes, cabin fittings, and machinery lie everywhere.

Moving forward from the engine room, we spend time looking around the four large boilers, which are roughly amidships on the wreck. This is a good place to search for artifacts like brass steam gauges. But before we find anything, a check of my dive computer indicates that our

Steve Scheuer with a porthole recovered from the *Stephano*
ERIC TAKAKJIAN

window for discovery is closing. It's already time to head back to the anchor line. Our planned twenty-five minutes of bottom time will soon be up. So it goes.

On my way back to the surface, hanging at my deco stops at ten-foot intervals from seventy feet up to twenty feet, I can't stop thinking about what an amazing wreck this is. I wonder if and when any of us will snag a major artifact like the ship's bell.

By now it's midday Sunday. We have planned to head back to Fairhaven tonight, so at best we will only get one more chance to dive. I wish we could stay another day, but we just can't. Work commitments call us, and we only brought enough grub and tanks for a two-day expedition. Aboard the *Quest* you can feel a subtle urgency in the way the crew polishes off their sandwiches and gulps water. We are men caught between two worlds. It's the world of October 1916 that calls loudly to us, but we can't go back there unless we catch a break from the tide.

Late in the afternoon the current finally starts going slack again. Mort and I jump back in followed by Steve Scheuer. When we get to the bottom, we head forward on the wreck. I wanted to get to the bow if possible and see what it looks like to confirm it has the distinctive shape I have seen in photos of the *Stephano*.

Moving forward from the boilers, we cross an open patch of sand where the plates on the side of the hull have fallen away. Perhaps this is just a weak point in the hull, but more likely the sides of the ship broke here from the force of *U-53*'s torpedo. Beyond the sand patch we find the nearly intact wreckage of the bow section. The tip of the bow lies upright but leaning to port. This is the bow I have seen in the photos of the *Stephano*. No doubt in my mind now about this wreck . . . but it sure would be great to find an artifact that nails down the ship's identity.

I'm looking around in the sand just aft of the bow section for a clue, an artifact, a little bit of treasure that might identify the wreck for certain, when I see something sticking out of the sand. Swimming closer I realize it's a partially buried brass engine order telegraph pedestal for relaying speed and direction changes from the bridge to the engine room. The distinctive round shape of the base is protruding from the sand, with the bolt holes visible. It's heavily tarnished with the dark greenish-brown color of bronze that has been in the ocean a long time. Without a doubt it is a British Chadburn-style engine telegraph from the Edwardian era. The distinctive shape of the base gives away its origins. This telegraph, the four boilers, the size of the wreck, and the shape of the bow clearly mark this wreck as the SS *Stephano*.

And here comes the payday. It's not someone's lost wedding gifts, but, still, a major score. I swim up to the telegraph and start digging. The base section comes out of the sand easily, but the head with the face and handles is buried deeper. Mort comes to help. We are down on our knees scooping up sand like dogs, stirring up a cloud of silt, when we come across the helm, the ship's wheel.

But, damn, a check of our dive computers shows that we are running out of bottom time, and we have a long swim to get back to the anchor line before starting up.

I decide to bring the telegraph base with me and come back for the rest on a later dive. My options are to either send the base up on an inflated lift bag from where we are, or get it back to the anchor line and send it up from the bottom of the line. Preferring to have the bag come up closer to the boat than farther away, I decide to try to drag the telegraph back to the anchor line, then send it up. But the base is too heavy, and I can't swim with it. For a moment I think maybe I'm going to have to abandon the telegraph. But then Mort comes to my aid. We put a short line on it, and the two of us drag the telegraph back to the anchor line.

We're running really short of bottom time so once we reach the anchor line, we hustle to get a lift bag attached to the telegraph with a plan to inflate it with air from my doubles and send it up attached to the end of the line on the wreck reel attached to my waist. Free floating lift bags are always at risk of being lost. But with the telegraph attached to my reel line, if there's a problem with the bag, we will still have a line on the telegraph, which will make recovery a lot easier.

This method of using the reel line proved its worth several years back when I sent up the steam whistle from the tug *Mars*. The bag sank shortly after reaching the surface. When I saw the lift bag failing, I had to cut short my deco stop to surface for a second and pass my reel up to the

Returning from *Stephano*, L to R, Steve Scheuer, Tom Packer, Dave Morton
ERIC TAKAKJIAN

guys on the boat with instructions to put a buoy on it. After completing my deco, and surfacing safely, I explained what was going on. Mort, who was on that trip, jumped back in with a bigger lift bag, dove down, and sent the whistle up a second time. This time we snagged the lift bag with a boat hook and hauled the steam whistle aboard.

Today there's no drama. The bag surfaces next to the boat and stays afloat. The team hauls it and the telegraph aboard. On the way up the line doing our deco, we pass Tom and Steve Gatto on the way down for their dive. They shoot Mort and me thumbs up.

It feels like a salute.

Maybe they have already seen the *Stephano*'s bridge telegraph attached to the lift bag. They know the buzz of adrenalin I'm feeling right now. It's not just from finding the telegraph. It's from knowing we've pulled off a long, difficult, and dangerous expedition. Like the passengers and crew of the SS *Stephano*, like Wilma McLean Tucciarone, we will have a story to tell about the day we bore witness to the wreck of an ocean liner and felt momentarily blessed by the gods of the sea. It just doesn't get better than this for a deep-wreck diver.

CHAPTER EIGHT

Way Out There

Ghost Ship on Georges Bank

2005

HERE'S THE TRUTH. DURING THE FIVE YEARS FOLLOWING MY DISCOVERY of the SS *Stephano* in 2000, good fortune and I become strangers. But these difficult years prepare me for a ghost liner called the *North American* and the most challenging searches and most demanding dives of my life.

In 2001 the *Quest* team heads back to the wreck of the *Stephano* with hopes of recovering the top of the telegraph, the helm, some of the fine dining room china, and silverware that once graced the table of Wilma McLean Tucciarone and other first-class passengers. But just a couple of miles shy of the wreck site, the propeller shaft coupling on the *Quest* lets go, bending the shaft and destroying the bolts holding it together. Not only can we not get to the wreck or dive, but we have to spend hours making a jury-rigged repair then hope it will hold for the eighteen hours that it takes us to limp back home to Fairhaven. Fishermen call voyages like this "busted trips."

As if the cost and disappointment of our failed expedition and the expense of repairs to the *Quest* aren't enough, I follow it by spending time and money I don't have taking long shots and chasing phantom wrecks. One of these phantoms is the largest ship to ever sink off the New England coast. On New Year's Eve 1976, on a passage from England to Somerset, Massachusetts, the 642-foot oil tanker SS *Grand Zenith* disappeared with her crew of thirty-eight somewhere east of Cape Cod.

I never come close to finding the *Grand Zenith*, but time and money slip away as I hunt for her and other phantoms. During these years I do find some virgin wrecks, like the tug *David Winslow* fifty miles south of Martha's Vineyard. But I find few valuable artifacts. And having some marketable artifacts to sell through a broker or through the developing online markets could make a huge difference in my life at this point.

People will collect anything, particularly when the material objects stir strong emotions. We all know the guy who has a "football room" full of memorabilia from his favorite college or pro team. Well some people are drawn to the golden age of ocean liners and steamships the way others are drawn to Lladro china figurines. A quick Internet search will turn up many websites advertising maritime collectibles for sale or available through auctions. The last time I looked, eBay had over fifty pages of *Andrea Doria* collectibles for sale.

Serious collectors love china with names, designs, and logos of a shipping line on them, and the china's worth a lot more if it comes from a wreck. Some sellers on eBay claim their china has been salvaged from the *Doria*. You can also buy money like Italian lira or US one dollar silver certificates allegedly salvaged from the wreck. A dinner plate with a paper trail and photos to prove that it came from the wreck will cost a collector over five hundred dollars. A single one dollar silver certificate can cost you four hundred to twelve hundred dollars depending on its condition and preservation. Hundreds, if not thousands, of plates have been recovered by divers from the *Doria*, so a plate from the ship is not very rare compared to a compass binnacle, an engine telegraph, a whistle, a bell, or a porthole. These things can command many thousands—sometimes tens of thousands—of dollars from collectors.

Don Leavitt has been running his business, nautiques.com, for nearly twenty years. He says money is no object to serious collectors. He has seen collectors pay tens of thousands of dollars for pieces to flesh out their collection of china from a particular shipping line like Cunard or P&O. A longtime enthusiast of luxury liners and steamships, he started his business as a hobby, but for more than the last decade he has been selling his maritime collectibles and antiques full-time. "I make more money than I did at my old job, and this is just fun," he says.

Don has thousands of customers from all over the world. But he says many of his most avid customers come from Australia and the United States. Not all items, even similar pieces of china, draw the same amount of attention from collectors. Collectibles from the transatlantic liners like the British "*Queens*," SS *France*, and the SS *United States* are big sellers. But their prices do not compare to items off a famous shipwreck like the *Andrea Doria*. A certain segment of serious collectors are connoisseurs of tragedy. These folks prize anything off liners like the *Lusitania*, *Mauritania*, *Normandie*, and, of course, *Titanic*.

Many famous and tragic wrecks are protected by governments and/or private owners who have gone to court to "attach" the wreck, making them legal owners of its contents. Today recovered items from these ships sell on the black market. I've heard rumors of two small bowls from the RMS *Titanic* selling for twenty-five thousand dollars. The taboo on buying and selling artifacts from some of the most famous wrecks adds new value to both existing artifacts from those wrecks and artifacts from second-tier steamship companies like the Red Cross Line and its *Stephano*.

Recovered artifacts from well-remembered New England wrecks like the SS *City of Columbus* and RMS *Republic* can draw high prices as well. The greater the tragedy, the bigger mystery surrounding the loss. Prices rise. Ten years ago a second-class passenger list from the *Titanic* sold at auction for more than thirty thousand dollars. A bronze porthole from the wreck of the *Lusitania* went for five thousand dollars. An ice bucket from the *Normandie* commanded eight thousand dollars.

Don says that 95 percent of his customers are male. Many of them have a "ship room" in their house where they display their collections the way we divers have our artifact rooms. But while collecting may be fun and trading collectibles can be a thrill and lucrative, there are a lot of counterfeits out there. Don knows of one dealer who bought up a trove of engraved silverware from a retired liner. When the dealer ran out of the real knives, forks, and spoons, he started making and selling counterfeits. A similar situation occurred around the selling of deck chairs and other furniture from a famous liner after she made her last voyage. When the dealer ran out of stock, he had fakes made.

It's during these years when Lori and I are just scraping by with the *Quest* that my mind starts obsessing on the wreck of a much-loved lost liner that most definitely holds a huge cache of china and other collectibles. The SS *North American* is a 280-foot Great Lakes passenger steamer lost off Cape Cod in 1967. Built in 1913 by the Great Lakes Engineering Works in Michigan with a hull of high-grade steel and a wooden superstructure, the *North American* and her sister the *South American* are the first purpose-built cruise ships in the United States.

With a beam of 47 feet, a draft of over 18 feet, a displacement of 2,317 gross tons, a 2,200-horsepower quadruple-expansion steam engine, and three boilers, the *North American* is big, as Great Lakes passenger steamers go, for her day. For forty-nine years she carries over four hundred passengers at a time on luxury vacation cruises of the Great Lakes for the fabled Georgian Bay Line. Her route is generally Chicago, Mackinac, Detroit, Cleveland, Buffalo, and return. Generations of

SS *North American* getting under weigh from dock in Detroit River.
JOHN LOCHEAD COLLECTION, STEAMSHIP HISTORICAL SOCIETY OF AMERICA ARCHIVE, WWW.
SSHSA.ORG

passengers, particularly from the Midwest, remember family cruises and honeymoons aboard the Georgian Bay Line's "Americans."

The cruise ship's slim white hull, tall topsides, forward wheelhouse, and twin stacks give the *North American* the look of an immense yacht from the Roaring Twenties. The ship has a yacht-like interior as well, complete with a ballroom, multiple dining rooms, and a ladies' card room. There are vaulted ceilings in the saloons. Silver oak raised paneling adds opulence to the bars and other public rooms. Corinthian columns support the dining rooms' ceilings. Clerestories bring in natural sunlight and moonlight. Cherry trim highlights the staterooms. Passengers flock to a verandah cafe and the "Egyptian lounge" to see and be seen after their daily rounds of the promenade deck.

But in 1963, after nearly fifty years of steaming back and forth from Chicago to Buffalo, the *North American* is tired and losing money. The Georgian Bay Line decides to sell the ship and continue operating her younger sister, the *South American*, on still-profitable summer cruises to Lake Superior. After a brief stint with a new company on Lake Erie, the *North American* is laid up because of financial problems. Then new USCG regulations ban large passenger ships with wooden superstructures, following the burning of the liner *Yarmouth Castle* on her way from Miami to Nassau in 1965. The *North American*'s cruise ship career's over. She sells at auction for thirty-two thousand dollars to the Seamen's International Union, which plans to use the ship as a dormitory for trainees in its merchant mariners school at Piney Point, Maryland.

In early September 1967, the tug Michael McAllister *takes the old ship under tow in Erie, Pennsylvania, and heads through the eastern Great Lakes and St. Lawrence Seaway bound for Piney Point, Maryland, on Chesapeake Bay. But the tow proves to be too much. Later some of* North American's *old crew will say their "girl" is heartbroken to leave the lakes and "just gives up." Others will say she succumbs to flooding through an open valve that the* McAllister *crew did not notice before taking her under tow for weeks and hundreds upon hundreds of miles.*

With no riding crew aboard the old liner, nobody knows for sure what sinks her. At 4:00 in the morning on September 14, 1967, the wind and seas on the western edge of Georges Bank, 140 miles southeast of Boston, are moderate. It's a dark night with no moon when a deckhand aboard the tug bursts into to the wheelhouse of the Michael McCallister *shouting, "Captain the ship is gone!"*

He had been watching the North American's *running lights glowing from the ship at the end of a twelve hundred–foot hawser when the lights just disappeared. Captain Charles Shaw on the tug immediately stops his vessel before the sinking ship tied to his stern can take down the tug too. As soon as Shaw verifies that the* North American *has vanished beneath the sea, he records his position. He tells his crew to take a fire ax and sever the eight-inch hawser tethering him to the wreck. Then the tug proceeds to her base in Norfolk, Virginia. Insurance pays the Seamen's International Union for the loss.*

Maybe the *North American* would have moldered away down there, undisturbed, full of her china servings for over five hundred passengers and crew, loaded with nautical artifacts, if I were not obsessing over her. At this point in time, no one in New England has ever tried to find and dive a wreck as far offshore as Georges Bank. It's a place known for its wicked weather, brutal currents, and confused seas that can look more like haystacks than waves. But over the years something keeps drawing me to the wreck and what fishermen call "Georges."

Located in the Gulf of Maine, Georges Bank gets its named from English explorers and colonists in 1605 who called the rich fishing ground St. Georges Bank. The English were hardly the first to discover the bank or fish here. Basque fishermen found the bank about a thousand years ago. In the centuries that followed, fishermen from Europe crossed the Atlantic to this place that virtually boils with fish. Georges Bank is a major feeding and breeding ground for cod, haddock, herring, and sea scallops as well as many other aquatic species.

Oval shaped and about the size of the state of Massachusetts, Georges is an elevated part of the continental shelf stretching beneath the North Atlantic from Cape Cod to Nova Scotia. At approximately 150 miles long and 75 miles wide, it was once part of the North American mainland. But as the climate warmed following the end of the last ice age about eleven thousand years ago, the sea level rose and turned Georges into an island.

As the sea level continued to rise, Georges flooded about six thousand years ago. Today, at its nearest point, it lies about sixty miles east of Cape Cod. Its depth ranges from a dozen or so feet to over two hundred feet, but the bank is over three hundred feet shallower than the Gulf of Maine to its north. It lies to the west of other prolific fishing grounds like the Grand Banks off Newfoundland. Over the years Georges has claimed more than its share of shipwrecks, including the SS *North American*.

I learn about the *North American* and her sister ship the *South American* in a roundabout way. In 1987 I'm working for Zapata Gulf Marine running a tug from Miami to Puerto Rico with container barges, but I leave Zapata in the early winter of 1987 to take a job with McAllister Towing in Philadelphia as captain aboard the tug *Theresa McAllister*. It turns out that McAllister's yard's in Camden, New Jersey, across the Delaware River from Philly on the site of the old New York Shipbuilding yard. Many of the covered slipways where New York Shipbuilding built vessels are still in existence in 1987, along with a lot of the equipment used in the yard.

"Mac" occupies the northernmost covered slipway and an adjacent open finger pier where they tie up their tugs and a floating office/workshop fashioned from an old coffee barge. Inside the covered slip at this time, on the side opposite the tugs, lies the SS *South American* in a derelict state, waiting for a ship breaker to dismantle her. Seeing the *South American* there really piques my interest in the ship and the story behind how she got here. Asking the guys in the yard, I hear the story that she was towed from the Great Lakes with the intention of being used as a training ship for the Seafarers International Seaman's Union based in Maryland. The guys in the yard tell me she's actually a replacement for another ship that was also towed around from the lakes but had sunk en route off Cape Cod. After the first ship sank, the *South American* was towed as far as this slip in Camden. But the old liner never got any farther. The Seafarers International Seaman's Union decided against using the ship.

After doing some digging in the Boston Public Library archives and asking more questions of the guys in the yard on my next tour at work, I find out that the ship that had sunk is the *North American*. The tug *Michael McAllister*, which towed the liner to her doom near Georges Bank, is currently assigned to the fleet in Philly where I'm working. The fates, it seems, are binding me to the lost liner.

Over the years I begin collecting information about the *North American*. When I become a member of the Steamship Historical Society of America (SSHSA), I purchase a number of back issues of the society's journal *Steamboat Bill*. Some of these issues have articles on both the *North American* and *South American*. Many members of the SSHSA were passengers aboard both of these ships when they were in service, and some were actually crew members. Later I become friends with Sue and Bill Ewen, who spent their honeymoon aboard the *North American*, and Donald Nevins, a chief engineer for the United States Lines who sailed on the *South American* as an oiler early in his career. Each of these connections draws me closer to the liner. At some point I begin having dreams of piles of china stamped with the Georgian Bay Line logo lying mounded in its hull. I imagine excavating the remains of an Edwardian pilothouse to find valuable nautical collectibles like the big brass compass binnacle.

By 2004 Tim Coleman and I are discussing at length the possibilities of where the wreck of the *North American* might be. Based on the newspaper reports and statements made by the crew of the tug *Michael McAllister*, and after extrapolating the probable course and route the tow would have taken, we come to the conclusion that the wreck is somewhere between Western Georges Bank and the lower end of the Great South Channel. There are a number of large wrecks and bad hangs in this area, so the question we have is this: Which one is the *North American*?

A number of contemporary fishing boats have sunk in this area, and we have a pretty good idea as to their locations based on USCG reports that more or less coincided with hang numbers that we have. Some of the hang data support our conclusions with notations as to the origin of the hang, which in many cases originated with sinkings that were witnessed by other fishermen or a sinking site that has circulated among the fleet. In the process of sorting through the known wrecks in the area, we develop a list of unknowns. Then we narrow down that list of unknowns to targets within the area we believe to be the SS *North American*'s location.

"There's only one way to find out what those things are, and that's to swim down there and knock on the sides of the wrecks and see," says Tim.

We decide that the summer of 2005 is the time to go and do just that. My plan is to point the bow of the *Quest* east and steam farther than we have ever gone. On August 11 we load the boat up at Kelly's Shipyard in Fairhaven for the 150-mile trip to Georges Bank. Kelly's has been our base of operations for many years. It's an ideal place to stage dive and research operations, a shipyard that caters primarily to fishing vessels and other large commercial vessels. The yard has all the equipment one might need, including forklifts and cranes. It also gives us the ability to tie the boat up in a location where we can back a truck up to the boat and lift gear aboard. One thing is for certain, we can never make more noise or more of a mess than the yard does on a daily basis, so the *Quest* team can do whatever we need to prepare for a long and challenging diving expedition. Loading dozens of tanks, huge plastic totes full of diving gear, personal sea bags, sleeping bags, and hundreds of pounds of provisions aboard would probably get us evicted from a fancy marina with people sipping cocktails in nice clothes.

As the date for our expedition approaches, we're watching the weather closely. I can see that we have a weather window, but there's a chance that the weather could close in on us near the tail end of the expedition sooner than the forecasters are predicting. We better get going.

After loading my gear aboard the boat, I drive over to Crystal Ice in New Bedford and load up on block ice. This is my usual routine prior to an offshore trip. I then go grub shopping for everything else except the meats, which I purchased earlier in the week and have frozen at home. The crew starts to trickle in by early afternoon. Pat Rooney's first to arrive, followed by Tom Packer and Steve Gatto, who have come up together in Tom's truck from Jersey. Then Dave and Pat Morton come down from New Hampshire. It's going to be a long eighteen- or twenty-hour steam to the east on the *Quest* so once we're all loaded up and the gear's stowed, including the all-important Portuguese takeout from Antonio's, we shove off. With some luck we can arrive at the search area by sunrise.

It's suppertime as we head out across Buzzards Bay, and we start chowing down on pork alentejana and paella, while catching up with each other on how our individual dive seasons have been going. After dinner we set our watch schedule before the crew heads off to their racks to catch some sleep. I'm too keyed up for this trip to nod off for long. I find myself analyzing every beat of the engine, every roll of the boat, every creak and groan to make sure all is well. The last thing I want is a breakdown like the prop shaft issue we had on the second trip to the *Stephano*. As the fishermen say, we are heading out where "the buses don't run." Help will be a long, long way off if something goes wrong. This is not like a trip to *U-853* or even the *Andrea Doria*. A USCG or Air National Guard rescue chopper will need more than an hour of flying to get to Georges Bank. And problems at sea can turn into catastrophes in an hour.

Over the course of the night, fog starts to set in, and by morning it's thick. It really hasn't been much of an issue for most of the night, but by the following morning, we're crossing the Great South Channel a little after daybreak and there are a lot of scallop dredgers working the west edge of the channel. We have to thread our way through the fleet using the radar. Even for seasoned mariners like our team, this is tedious work, keeping track of all the scallopers on the radar display as they stop, start, and change course. There are moments for all of us this morning when we think about how fog just like this set up the collisions that sunk the *Doria* and *Regal Sword*. We keep two sets of eyes on the radar scope at all times and two guys on watch for shadows of fishing boats and ships in the fog.

"Well, hell, that was a lot of fun," says Tom to kind of cut the tension once we reach the other side of the channel from where the scallop fleet's working.

The fog sticks with us, but there's virtually no traffic the rest of the way to the target area. By late morning we reach the spot where there's a collection of hang numbers Tim Coleman and I have identified as a good candidate for the SS *North American*. From the standpoint of location it make sense to us. We know it to be a bad hang where several boats have lost gear. Gradually slowing down about a mile or so away from the location, I gather my notes and take the wheel.

As usual the echo sounder's running while we're steaming along in case we run over something. As we approach the GPS coordinates of the hang, I shift the sounder from 200 kHz to 50 kHz. Doing so gives us a wider cone of detection while searching around the hang numbers for a target. Once we locate something, we can shift back to 200 kHz to pinpoint the location under the boat. I have purposely set up the *Quest*'s GPS antenna directly over the echo sounder transducer for pinpoint accuracy.

Once we reach the area of the hangs, we don't have to look around very long. After a few passes over the possible wreck site, we start picking something up on the sounder. Then right after making a turn, we run over something big on the bottom. I shift to 200 kHz and make another pass. The mass on the bottom appears again probably 20 to 25 feet high in about 230 feet of water.

Out here we like to grapple into a wreck and then tie the hook in (as opposed to using a shot line) due to the current. Shot lines even with a small anchor tend to get pulled off a wreck. So now we rig the grappling hook and ready it to drop from the bow. I make another pass, and the wreck shows up high again on the sounder's display. Up on the bow Tom and Steve drop the hook and pay out about 250 feet of line. The grapple has 20 feet of 3/8-inch chain on it as well.

The hook grabs almost right away. Tom and Steve make the line fast on the bow bitt. Now the waiting begins. We're all anxious to get in the water and go down to see what's on the bottom, but we have to wait for the current to go slack as measured by the weighted line we dangle over the stern. In addition to the current, we have another variable that will be tough to predict: fog. It has really set in thick, to the point that the visibility by 10:00 a.m. is down to one hundred yards or less. Georges Bank is a major fishing ground. It is also along the great circle route between the United States and Western Europe, so we keep a constant watch on the radar display for ships and fishing boats. If we have to buoy the line off and get out of the way of another vessel bearing down on us in the fog, any divers still in the water could be lost. If a diver has to make a free ascent and come up off the anchor line, we will likely never see him from the boat. He will not be able to see the boat either.

A number of years ago my friend Bill Campbell surfaced from a dive to the *Andrea Doria* in thick fog. While swimming back to the stern of the dive boat, he lost his grip on the line running aft and was swept behind the boat in the current. No one heard him yell, and before he knew it he was well down current of the boat. The boat crew realized what happened a short time later but had to wait until the other divers were out of the water before they could start searching. The boat captain set up a search pattern and started working down current from the wreck location in visibility of one hundred yards or less. Bill ended up drifting all night and was pushing blue sharks away with his camera housing by the next morning when the boat found him.

No one wants to go through what Bill did, so we wait. And wait. Over the course of the day everyone slows down and gets into that relaxed mode that we morph into on offshore trips away from the daily distractions of cell phones, e-mails, and schedules. We tinker with dive gear, chomp sandwiches and chips for lunch, speculate about the wreck, read, and nap to kill the time.

The fog hangs around thick all day, and the current never seems to let up much. The good news is that no other vessels come into range and force us to scramble out of the way. But as the day wears on, it's becoming evident that we will have to wait until tomorrow to have a chance to get in the water.

By evening when we're firing up the grill for dinner, we still have thick fog. The current continues running at more than a knot. It's going to be a long, dark night. The waiting has taken down the crew's energy on the boat, but probably not anybody's anxiety. Guys turn into their berths early, but all night long I can hear them parading back and forth to the toilet or wandering aft onto the work deck to see if the current or the fog has cut us a break. As usual we are all taking turns standing anchor watch and keeping an eye on the radar for other vessels.

Meanwhile I'm thinking about the weather and listening on the VHF and single sideband radios to the updated forecasts for Georges Bank and the waters south of Nantucket and Martha's Vineyard out to the edge of the continental shelf. Sometime close to midnight the sky begins to clear. This portends two things. The end of the fog. Good. The approach of the next frontal system and stiff breezes. Not so good.

Dawn comes bright and clear. As everyone gets up, has coffee, and eats breakfast, we're encouraged by the conditions. Sitting around the galley table with our coffee, we discuss the dive plan for the day. Pat Rooney and I will go down first and tie in. Then the crew in the boat will shorten up on the scope of the anchor line to make the descents better. The second dive team will be Tom and Steve, followed by Dave and Pat Morton after Pat Rooney and I come up. We have a feeling there will be a slack tide this morning.

About 8:30 the current's slacking off, so Pat and I suit up quickly and jump in. The water's really clear, typical for this area. With the light current it doesn't take us long to get down the anchor line. At a depth of maybe 130 to 140 feet, we can make out a large dark shadow below us. Once we reach 160 to 170 feet, we see the side of a ship and a row of windows. The ship's lying well over on its port side. We touch down on the wreck at a depth of around 210 feet near the row of windows where the hull meets the deck above. We tie in the grappling hook at lightning speed, shake hands like a couple of guys who are about to summit a peak like El Capitan, and start swimming forward.

Almost immediately I realize something's wrong. As we're swimming forward along the upper deck, I look down and see a steel pipe about five inches in diameter that has rotted away in places. Inside the pipe I can see a long worm screw. I know right away what this pipe and screw are. They are not something that you would find on any passenger ship. It's an ice screw for moving crushed ice from an icemaker to a fish hold. This wreck can't be the *North American*.

But what is it?

As Pat and I swim forward, we reach the front end of a large deck-house and then the ship's pilothouse. The superstructure is covered with a thick beard of sea anemones and draped with torn trawl nets. Forward of the pilothouse the deck drops to a long, wide area with hatches in it and a very large double drum winch mounted directly in front of the deckhouse superstructure. Looking forward, I spot a raised foredeck in the distance, the crew's fo'c'sle. This wreck's an immense fishing trawler. The visibility's excellent, probably at least fifty feet, and I can see large schools of cod flashing in and out of the beam of my dive light. The bottom's clean white sand. Faint shafts of sunlight cut through the blue. Everything looks so peaceful. The North Atlantic this morning is in one of its calm moods.

But the weather can change in a hurry out here, and there's no place to hide. If I have to guess, I'd say this trawler got caught by one of the storms we call a "nor'easter," rolled, down flooded, and sank. Everyone who fishes out here knows how wicked things can get. And since the book and the film *The Perfect Storm* came out a few years ago, the general public now has a sense of how overwhelming the North Atlantic can be, especially when a low-pressure system spins up southeast of Nova Scotia and the wind shifts out of the east or northeast. So after twenty minutes on the bottom, I'm ready to stop picturing the crew of this trawler with the panicked, hopeless looks on their faces like the men of the sword fisher *Andrea Gail* when a wave rolled them over in *The Perfect Storm*.

Heading back up the anchor line, I'm feeling disappointed that this wreck is not the *North American*. But at the same time I'm really curious as to what we just found. Judging by its nearly intact condition, it hasn't been on the bottom any longer than about thirty or forty years. And it's huge, way larger than any of the typical New England fishing boats that frequent Georges Bank.

Could this be the wreck of one of the foreign trawlers that crossed the North Atlantic from the Soviet Union, East Germany, Poland, Bulgaria, Portugal, and Spain to fish Georges Bank in the 1960s or 1970s? Until the 1960s relatively small boats like wooden schooners, family-owned trawlers, and "longline" fishing boats the size of the *Quest* ventured from the United States and Canada to Georges Bank to fish. But in the 1960s large, steel fishing ships came to Georges Bank from all over the world to catch what then seemed an endless abundance of cod and other ground fish. These new arrivals were what are known in the fishing industry as "factory trawlers." They had the ability to stay at sea for up to a year, fish nonstop, make their own ice, and freeze their catch into huge blocks. Some factory trawlers could clean, cook, and can their catch onboard. Some worked in pairs to tow immense nets between them. In the process they nearly wiped out Georges Bank's stocks of haddock, cod, yellow-tail flounder, and herring while decimating the New England fishing industry. The increasing scarcity drove the price of fresh fish higher than the cost of sirloin steak.

How often I've heard my commercial fishing friends like Dave Dutra and Bill Amaru talk about the early 1970s, when the seas east of Cape Cod seemed filled with Soviet Block ships. They wonder whether overfishing could turn the waters into a dead sea. A USCG air patrol in the 1970s logged over two hundred foreign fishing vessels operating in the Northwest Atlantic, including about ninety Russian ships. One Russian ship was over five hundred feet long and carried a crew of about six hundred.

In an attempt to halt the devastation, the International Commission for Northwest Atlantic Fisheries placed some of Georges Bank off-limits and introduced a catch quota. But this wasn't enough. In 1975, with the New England fishing fleet in economic shambles, the Massachusetts congressman from Cape Cod, Gerry Studds, introduced legislation called HR 200 into Congress to protect American fishing stocks and the fishing industry. In 1976 President Gerald Ford signed into law what would become known as the Magnuson–Stevens Fishery Conservation and Management Act. Among other things the law divided Georges Bank between Canadian and US fishing grounds and excluded foreign trawlers from fishing within two hundred miles of the US coast. But the damage was already done. The New England cod, haddock, and yellowtail fleet has never recovered.

I feel like we have just discovered the bones of a monster and a watery grave. The wreck reminds me of the Soviet factory trawler I visited once in West Africa when I was working there aboard a research ship. In the years to come, I will search the Internet and USCG records for clues to the mammoth ghost trawler's name, home port, and news of its loss. But I will always come up empty-handed.

Why didn't the crew of this sinking ship call the USCG for help? Did they not want the Americans to know that they were here? Perhaps the ship was fishing Georges Bank after the establishment of the two hundred–mile limit, and she was sneaking into US territorial waters to poach fish. But there's another possibility. This ship probably sank at the height of the Cold War. Possibly the wreck was more than a foreign trawler poaching fish in American territorial waters.

During the Cold War, Soviet and Eastern Block spy ships often disguised themselves as trawlers to get close to the US coast and snoop on military operations and communications. The US Navy called them AGIs, Auxiliary General Intelligence ships. They were known to hide among legitimate trawlers working off North America. And they often tried to monitor activities at the major US submarine base at Groton, Connecticut.

Is this wreck an actual spy ship? Probably not. But who knows? It's a mystery. One thing I know for sure: If I were on a Soviet spy ship in trouble off the US coast, I would not be calling the USCG or anybody

Soviet trawler and freezer ship off Cape Cod 1962
US NAVAL HISTORY AND HERITAGE COMMAND

else for help. I would destroy all the sensitive material on my ship. Then I would hope for rescue from a friendly Russian or Eastern Block ship . . . or go down with my vessel.

Here lies a ghost ship of the first magnitude. It's sad to think that somewhere in the world there are families of fishermen who are still wondering where, when, and why their loved ones vanished. Maybe it would be some comfort to them to learn of the final resting place. Maybe it would give them some sense of peace if they knew that the *Quest* had found the remains of the lost trawler and that the wreck lives again as habitat for the cod.

When Pat and I come to our twenty-foot deco stop, we meet Tom and Steve coming down the line. I write on a slate that the wreck's a fishing trawler and for them to untie the hook. As Pat and I get back in the boat, Dave and Pat Morton are suiting up and getting ready to dive. We tell them what we saw and to wait on getting suited up, that Tom and Steve will be rigging the hook to pull out. I have another target a short distance away, and if we can steam over to the next location quickly enough, there might be enough time before the tide turns for the Mortons to make a recon dive and see what the next target is. It's a long shot, but worth a try.

After Tom and Steve surface, we break out the hook, and soon we're at the next target area. After a few passes a large target shows up on the echo sounder, with over 30 feet of relief in about 250 feet of water. I stop the boat above what looks to be the highest point on the wreck. But it's not long before the *Quest* drifts over the flat expanse of sand off to the side of the wreck. The tide has turned. We have missed our window for diving for the day. The next slack water for going deep will not be until tomorrow morning.

Realizing this, I make more passes over the wreck to get dialed in on how it's lying on the bottom and the height of the wreck in different locations. It seems that one end is considerably higher than the other. This site has been a bad hang as well. From my conversations with fishermen, I know that numerous boats have lost gear on this wreck. Maybe this is the *North American*. It's big enough. Maybe all that china and those valuable artifacts are just 250 feet directly beneath us.

But after listening to the weather forecast again on the VHF radio, I see that we can't stay out here another night. There's a system about to build in from the east with increasing winds and seas. Forget it. We're 150 miles offshore and looking at eighteen to twenty hours of steaming back to Fairhaven. None of us wants to be like the crew of that trawler we found, reported overdue and presumed lost somewhere in the vicinity of Georges Bank. At this point all we can say about this expedition is that it has been a mixed bag. We have found a ghost ship. We eliminated one possible site of the *North American*. And we have pinned down a very promising-looking target. But we are heading home empty-handed.

Before noon we turn our bow back toward the west and head for land . . . hoping we can stay ahead of the coming storm. I set a waypoint into the GPS chart plotter for the *Stephano*. If the weather is still good enough when we reach the wreck, we might be able to get a dive in. I might be able to recover the rest of the telegraph and the helm.

No way. By the time we reach the *Stephano*, the wind is already blowing about 20 knots out of the east. The boat's riding well, but we know we should keep going. We don't need *The Perfect Storm* to remind us that nor'easters are no joke, and we have a long way to go to safe harbor.

A few hours later the wind has increased to 25 knots with gusts to 30. The seas going by us have crests as high as the pilothouse roof. It's still a downwind run. The boat is loaded with gear, so we're riding well and pretty comfortable. But we're glad we're not taking these seas on the beam or on the bow. Ten- to 12-foot seas are never the kind of things you take lightly. When the *Quest* arrives back at Kelly's Shipyard around 8:00 in the morning, the boat's crusted in salt. So are we. But we're thankful that the *Quest* has done her job flawlessly and pretty damn relieved we do not end up like those poor buggers in the ghost trawler or the men of the *Andrea Gail*.

CHAPTER NINE

Fate Is the Hunter

The SS *North American*/MV *Oregon*

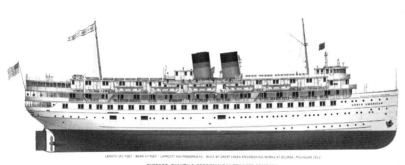

CHICAGO, DULUTH & GEORGIAN BAY TRANSIT COMPANY
S.S. NORTH AMERICAN

JOHN BELLIVEAU

2006

THE HUMAN MIND IS A FUNNY THING. ONCE I'M BACK ASHORE, I KIND of forget what a sketchy place Georges Bank is. I forget about how risky it is voyaging so far offshore to a place known as a ship killer. I forget about how dangerous it is diving with brutal, unpredictable currents and diving in such deep water. I even forget about that mystery trawler, the Cold War spy ships, and death in *The Perfect Storm*.

By the winter of 2006, I'm again leafing through my file on the SS *North American*, lingering over photos of her in her glory days on the

Great Lakes and picturing how she might look lying down there in the white sand at Georges Bank. In my mind she doesn't look like the ghost trawler we found out there draped in a web of fishnets. She looks shiny, golden, like the wreck of the RMS *Titanic* as it blooms again from the depths of the North Atlantic in brilliant color near the beginning of James Cameron's epic film.

But there's another virgin wreck, too, that keeps tugging at me, and I don't quite know why. The name of this ship is the MV *Oregon*. What a haunting story she could tell. Built in 1941 by the US Maritime Commission in Tacoma, Washington, the *Oregon* measures 397 feet on deck, 60 feet abeam, 24 feet in draft, 6,759 gross tons displacement. Powered by twin diesel engines, she's an all-steel, high-speed merchant ship of the most modern design capable of traveling at more than 15 knots. She's built to excel at her job for decades, but she disappears off Cape Cod a mere four months after her launching . . . taking more than fifteen of her forty-two-man crew with her.

Oregon on builders trials in Puget Sound
STEAMSHIP HISTORICAL SOCIETY OF AMERICA ARCHIVE, WWW.SSHSA.ORG

Three days after the Japanese attack on Pearl Harbor on December 10, 1941, and with the United States entering into WWII against Japan and Germany, the *Oregon* is on the final leg of a voyage from South Africa to New Bedford, Massachusetts, with a cargo of five million dollars' worth of wool for New England textile mills. All's going well until about 4:30 in the morning. South of the Nantucket lightship, she comes afoul of a flotilla consisting of the battleship USS *New Mexico* with her three escort destroyers.

Over the years I have heard waterfront wags talk about the wreck of the *Oregon*. Wreck hunters have made two attempts to salvage her. One of the salvagers thought the contents of the wreck to be so valuable that after announcing his attempt to find and buoy the wreck, he located a decoy wreck buoy far from the actual suspected wreck site to mislead anyone trying to jump his claim. These stories peak my interest. Why would anyone go to the trouble to try to salvage a ship full of salt water–soaked wool? Digging deeper, I find rumors that in addition to the cargo of wool, the *Oregon* carried a large load of Thompson submachine guns and possibly other military cargo of enduring value.

But before I can get too fired up about searching for the *Oregon*, the March Sea Rovers clinic in Boston rolls around. At the clinic I hear a craving in the voices of my *Quest* teammates when they mention the *North American*. Everybody has forgotten the scary stuff about that trip. We all want to get back out there and continue the hunt. It's like we can smell treasure. As I have said before, deep-wreck diving is not a totally rational enterprise.

Priority number one is to get back to the big target we pinpointed last summer to see if it's the *North American*. So on Friday, July 14, 2006, we load the *Quest* at Kelly's for a trip back out to Georges Bank. By midafternoon everyone's in the boat with all gear stowed and ready to go. Lori sees us off and takes a photo of us pulling out of the shipyard with our Zodiac inflatable on the stern under the A-frame and huge load of scuba tanks on deck—something like twenty-three sets of doubles and forty-six stage bottles. On board are Heather Knowles, Dave Caldwell, Pat Rooney, Tom Packer, Steve Gatto, and me.

North American first trip July '06 crew, L to R, Dave Caldwell, Heather Knowles, Tom Packer, Eric Takakjian, Pat Rooney, Steve Gatto

LORI TAKAKJIAN

The trip out to Georges Bank is perfect. We have a typical midsummer night as we cross Nantucket Shoals. The sea is close to flat calm with a long, low swell. The sky's partially clear with lots of stars and a waning moon. It's a night when it's hard to keep your mind from wandering. But tonight my mind isn't chewing over details of the *North American*. It skips to the declassified "action report" I scored through correspondence with the US National Archives in Washington, DC, about the loss of the MV *Oregon*.

At 4:30 in the morning on December 10, 1941, the battleship USS New Mexico *is passing to the west of Georges Bank and transiting through the Great South Channel en route to Hampton Roads, Virginia, with destroyers* Sims, Hughes, *and* Russell *providing an antisubmarine screen. The night's partly overcast with a half moon. Visibility's about two miles. The battleship and her destroyers are traveling at 14 knots on a base course of 236 degrees true. The wind's blowing about 20 knots out of the southwest.*

The bridge crew aboard the New Mexico *is on edge because of the events of the last three days. On December 7 the battleship was on a "neutrality patrol," trying to deter German U-boat attacks on merchant ships east of Newfoundland when the ship got word of the Japanese raid on Pearl Harbor. Over the ship's PA system, the crew heard a radio broadcast of President Franklin Roosevelt's famous "a day that will live in infamy" speech and his declaration of war against the Japanese. Until as recently as May the* New Mexico's *homeport has been Pearl Harbor, and now the loss of her sister battleships the* Arizona, Nevada, *and* Oklahoma *has everybody stunned.*

As if these events are not enough to rattle the crew of the New Mexico, *the ship has received new orders to proceed to Hampton Roads with all haste for reassignment to the Pacific Fleet to replace the lost battleships. Wartime combat conditions are now in effect. The battleship and her escorts are traveling with all lights extinguished. Rumors on the ship prophesy that at any moment Adolph Hitler will declare war on the United States and his U-boats are at this very moment hoping to get a shot at the* New Mexico. *The rumors are not wrong. Hitler will declare war against the United States on December 11, and at least one U-boat has already been detected in these waters.*

At 4:32 a.m. the officer-on-deck, Lieutenant (Junior Grade) H. L. Waliszewski is in charge of the bridge on the New Mexico. *He spots a ship broad on the port bow showing no lights at a distance of perhaps five thousand yards. For a few seconds he wonders if he's seeing one of the escorts, but he quickly accounts for the three destroyers. Immediately, he calls the ship's commanding officer, Captain Walter E. Brown, to the bridge, saying that there's an unknown ship off the port bow crossing from port to starboard. It looks to Waliszewski like a cruiser class warship. Actually, it's the MV* Oregon, *and its bridge crew does not yet see any of the American warships. Heads up!*

That's what I'm thinking as the *Quest* approaches the east side of Nantucket Shoals and the Great South Channel. My thoughts are swerving in two directions. On one hand they are still drawn to the events unfolding for the *Oregon* and *New Mexico* in these waters sixty-five years ago. On the other, they veer abruptly toward the large fleet of scallopers that I'm picking up on the radar display. Heads up. We don't want to get boxed in between a bunch of boats moving in different directions with different individual agendas. We don't want to become another statistic on the list of vessels lost on Georges Bank.

Everybody's talking just a little too fast and a little too loud after we thread our way between the scallopers and slow down a mile or so away from the wreck site. It's now a bright, sunny morning. Maybe this is going to be a good day. Soon the probable wreck we found last summer appears on the sounding machine as a high peak coming off the bottom. I make a couple of passes over it with all of us looking at the sounder. We have learned to distinguish wrecks from large rocks on the sounder by the presence of "scour," a sort of shadow, around the bottom contours we see on the sounder display. Wrecks tend to have scour close to the edges of their contours, particularly with sand and mud bottoms. Large glacially deposited rocks do not have scour. This target's showing significant scour. It's a big wreck for sure.

Once the anchor line's set on the wreck, we deploy the "granny line," a rope leading thirty feet straight down from the starboard stern corner of the boat to a twenty-pound weight. At the weight another sixty feet of line runs to a weighted sliding hook that is riding on the anchor line.

This setup allows divers to grab a line as soon as they jump in at the stern and pull themselves below the surface away from the boat, which may be rolling or pitching.

The granny line also guides them to the anchor line without having to transit on the surface. This setup enables divers to make deco stops near the surface while being somewhat isolated from the pitching and surge of the anchor line in rough weather. We deploy the surface-supplied oxygen setup for the final deco station as well, with two eight-foot whips of oxygen hose coming off a Y valve clipped on at the twenty-foot level.

After setting up the granny line and deco station, we set our current meter and wait for slack tide. Finally, in late afternoon, the current goes slack, and it's time to get wet. Pat and I suit up and hit the water carrying over two hundred pounds of gear each. We have great visibility on the surface, and it remains clear as we head down below 150 feet. But little by little the water begins filtering out the sunlight from the surface, and the color of the water changes from almost clear to indigo.

At about 180 feet it's dark enough to switch on dive lights. With my light I can see something dark starting to come into view below. Moments later I spot the outline of a ship below. We touch down on the top of the bow at around 220 feet and lash the hook into a steel deck beam. At this moment Pat and I are the first two people on the planet to see the wreck of the SS *North American*.

There's no doubt in either of our minds what we are looking at. The bow's intact and leaning well over to port. Rows of window openings and portholes line the sides of the hull. Inside, the wooden bulkheads separating the staterooms have rotted away leaving sinks attached to the steel plating. Both anchors are still housed in their respective hawse pipes. The windlass is still in place under the foredeck. A large nylon hawser, an artifact of the last voyage, hangs down from the bow and extends out into the sand off the starboard side. Pat finds the remains of the crew's shower up in the bow. The floor's lined with octagon-shaped black-and-white tiles.

On our way back up to the *Quest*, we are at one of our deco stops when Tom and Steve pass us going down to the wreck. But I barely notice them. My mind is drifting back to the *Oregon* and *New Mexico* again.

Heather, Steve, and Dave suiting up
ERIC TAKAKJIAN

At 4:40 on the morning of December 10, 1941, the officers aboard the Oregon *are as uneasy as those on the* New Mexico. *They, too, have been distressed by news of the attack on Pearl Harbor and the declaration of war. They, too, have been told that as a US-flagged ship they must travel blacked out to deter submarine attacks. Now as they close with the US coast and the shipping lanes leading to the major US Navy bases at Boston, Newport, New London, and New York, they fear they might be a target of opportunity for a U-boat. They know their best chance for safety is running like this at night, blacked out, toward the safety of New Bedford . . . as fast as they can.*

The Oregon's *diesels are clattering away at nearly full speed. The ship's making nearly 14 knots. Both Captain Elton P. Gillette and his second mate are on watch aboard the freighter. They're out on the starboard wing of the bridge when they spot a shape four points off the starboard bow at a distance of a mile or less. Captain Gillette orders his running lights turned on . . .*

Steve just up from a late afternoon dive
ERIC TAKAKJIAN

Dave Caldwell suited up and ready to dive
ERIC TAKAKJIAN

Sunday dawns flat calm with patchy fog. Everyone's up early and eager to dive, but we have to wait as usual. The ever-present current is rolling along like a river during spring runoff. It's lifting the dive ladder out of the water and holding our current meter line well aft. It doesn't let up until late afternoon. As soon as it does, we hit the water in the same order as the day before, making twenty-minute bottom times so we don't end up with huge deco obligations and we can get the first team out of the water in enough time for the last team to have a semblance of slack.

Pat and I explore the bow section and start working aft. The farther aft we go on the wreck, the more the hull appears to be broken down. The entire wooden superstructure of the ship is gone, rotted away in the salt water and swept off by the currents. We don't spot any china or artifacts. In particular we would like to find the bridge equipment like the telegraph pedestal that I scored off the *Stephano*. But no luck. The currents and storms on Georges Bank seem to move the sand around a lot on the bottom, burying wrecks and artifacts.

Monday morning the current slacks off early, and we get in the water by 10:00. On the bottom we notice a big difference in the amount of ambient light. The previous dives have all been late afternoon, and it was dark on the bottom. Today it's clear and bright on the wreck. Pat and I take advantage of the bright light along with the good visibility to look for the bridge equipment out in the sand off the port side. Still no luck. Tom, Steve, Heather, and Dave recover several portholes. By 2:00 we're all out of the water and steaming home.

As we start back, I'm feeling a bit reflective. Maybe I'm just tired now that my adrenalin high of the last three days has worn off. The rest of the crew must be feeling it, too, because when they aren't on watch they head off to their bunks. Yes, we have found another major virgin wreck, and we all have had safe and thrilling dives. I'm thrilled that we have found the *North American* and really look forward to further exploring the wreck. But going so deep in these currents comes with a physical and emotional price. The cold water and the struggle to swim with two hundred pounds of gear wear you out.

And then there's the fear factor. Here at Georges Bank you just never know when the currents are going to start ripping again and you will have

Tom, Heather, Dave, Pat, and Steve enjoying dinner
ERIC TAKAKJIAN

a fight for your life to get back up to the boat. There's another thing, too. If we're honest with ourselves, we all might wish we were coming home with some beautiful brass bridge artifacts and china stamped with Georgian Bay Line logos, not just a couple of portholes. It's in this mood that my thoughts turn back to the *Oregon* and *New Mexico*. The story of their impending catastrophe tugs at me like a half-remembered nightmare.

When Captain Brown on the New Mexico *reaches the bridge of his battleship, he sees the running lights of another vessel about to cross his bow port to starboard. The crossing ship is only about a half mile ahead. This isn't good. Brown orders the battleship's running lights turned on and goes out on the port bridge wing. He recognizes the silhouette of the crossing ship as a merchantman not a cruiser, as his young lieutenant imagined, and waits to see what action the freighter will take now that it must surely see the* New Mexico's *lights.*

According to Rule Fifteen of the International Rules of the Road, "When two power-driven vessels are crossing so as to involve risk of collision, the vessel which has the other on her own starboard side shall keep out of the way and shall, if the circumstances of the case admit, avoid crossing ahead of the other vessel." This rule applies to the Oregon, *and Brown fully expects that the freighter will reduce speed and or change her course to avoid a collision.*

Lieutenant (Junior Grade) Waliszewski asks the captain if he should turn the New Mexico *to the right. Brown considers and then says that the battle-ship's "obliged to hold course and speed." He's following Rule Seventeen of the Rules of the Road. "Where, by any of these rules, one of two vessels is to keep out of the way the other shall keep her course and speed."*

Meanwhile one of the screening destroyers is urgently sending a Morse code signal to the freighter with its signal lamp to keep clear. But the crew on the Oregon *does not see the destroyer's light signal nor does it change course and speed.*

Seeing that the freighter is not changing course and that he must do what-ever he can to avoid a collision, Brown orders, "Hard right rudder, full speed astern." The ships are now only about seven hundred yards apart, and the New Mexico *sounds her sirens to alert her crew and the other ship of imminent danger.*

Aboard the Oregon *Captain Gillette orders the helm put hard left and the engines full astern. Finally, both ships are turning to avoid a crash. But at 4:42 a.m. the bow of the 32,000-ton battleship slams the starboard side of the 6,700-ton freighter forward of the bridge, adjacent to the forward cargo mast. It's the beginning of the end for the* Oregon.

After the ships back away from each other, stop, and identify themselves, the searchlights from the New Mexico *survey the* Oregon. *There's a triangu-lar-shaped hole in the topside from the edge of the deck to a few feet above the waterline. Water appears to be lapping in.*

At this point the destroyer Sims *comes alongside the wounded merchant ship and receives orders from Battleship Division Three Command to standby the* Oregon *to "ascertain if the ship could proceed unescorted."*

After being notified by a wireless telegraph message from the Oregon *that she's safe and aims to head for Boston, the Commander Battleship Group Three orders the* New Mexico *to proceed on course at full speed and reminds Captain Brown that a U-boat "has been reported in the vicinity."*

The Sims *remains in company with the* Oregon *and directs her to the* *Nantucket lightship and the Boston inbound traffic lane. Around 11:00 a.m.* *the freighter's radio officer sends a message saying his ship has six feet of water* *in her number two hold and two feet of water in her number four hold. Pumps* *are controlling the flooding, and she's proceeding toward Boston at 13 knots.* *The* Oregon *has no injuries aboard. The* Sim's *need not escort the freighter* *further. Everything's under control.*

But this is the North Atlantic. Anything can happen, particularly in *regard to weather. Sometime after the* Sims *leaves the* Oregon, *a cold front* *blows offshore from Cape Cod. The wind shifts around abruptly out of the* *northwest and begins to honk. As seas build, the* Oregon *starts shipping water* *through the hole in her starboard side and starts flooding. At twenty minutes* *before noon, she sends out an SOS message to the USCG radio station at Cha-* *tham. She's sinking and in immediate need of assistance.*

The Sims *turns back north to help, and the USCG dispatches an observer* *aircraft as well as vessels. Shortly after the SOS, the tanker SS* Tydol Gas *radios that she's in sight of the* Oregon *and standing by to render assistance.* *The* Sims *receives orders to turn around again and gives chase to her battleship.* *The USCG observation airplane circles the sinking merchant ship and takes* *photos of her with her bow awash. By 2:00 in the afternoon the crew of the* Oregon *has abandoned ship and the freighter is heading for the bottom about* *eighty miles northwest of the site of her collision with the* New Mexico. *But* *while some of the crew make it to Boston aboard the tanker, and the USCG* *brings eight survivors to New Bedford, only about twenty-five of the crew,* *including Captain Gillette, survive. The rest of the forty-two men perish.*

I'm beginning to see why I've been thinking about this collision so much over the last few months, thinking about the *Oregon*. It's not about arti-facts or collectibles. Not about a cargo of wet wool or even Thompson submachine guns and war materiel. I haven't even been thinking about the bragging rights that come with finding another virgin wreck.

I've been thinking about those lost men. In my research I read a story in the *New York Times* filed the day of the collision from New Bedford. I can still remember the names of some of the dead cited in the story. Robert Tanner, Alexander Landreau, Byron Applegate, Whitney Morris

... it's almost as if I can hear their voices calling me, asking me to find their ship and the rest of their lost shipmates.

Is it possible that my near obsession with the *North American* has just been an excuse to get out here on another mission far more important than harvesting china from the bones of a cruise ship?

"We're going to take a little detour over to a place fishermen call the Cove of the Rip," I say to no one in particular on the *Quest*. There are two collections of hangs at the cove. One I believe may be the SS *Oregon*.

When we arrive at the Cove of the Rip, we find a wreck in about 210 feet of water. On the sounder display it looks solid but not really large. It's definitely too small to be the *Oregon*, so it's probably a scalloper or trawler. But there's another hang not far away, and soon we're seeing something huge on the sounder. It's resting on a slope in about 140 feet of water, with a lot of relief. This is clearly a large wreck covering a large

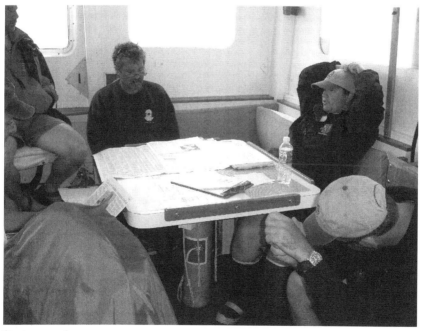

Strategy conference
ERIC TAKAKJIAN

area. A blast of adrenalin rocks my body. There's a really good possibility this is the *Oregon*.

The current rips through here. Chances are we will add to the fatalities that already haunt this place if we try to go down for a look. But, really, there's no need. Something feels sacred about this place. Sacred like the wreck of the ghost ship we found on Georges Bank during our first trip out here. Sacred like the bones of the *City of Columbus*. Sacred like do not disturb. So as we stop over the wreck of what is surely the *Oregon* and drift above the graves of a bunch of all-but-forgotten merchant mariners, I tell the crew the story of this lost ship, her men, and their bad luck.

This is how we remember them. We tell their stories. They're men sailing in a ship with a mortal wound, but they believe they can bring her and her cargo home to America safely. They know that New England's textile mills need all that wool in their holds to make uniforms for the men and women who will have to fight this new and awful war. They're among the first of thousands of American merchant seamen to make the ultimate sacrifice for their country in WWII. Sailors at the wrong place at the wrong time, trying to outrun the fickle finger of fate.

CHAPTER TEN

We're Rich???

The SS *Newcastle City*

SS *Newcastle City* at anchor
UK NATIONAL MARITIME MUSEUM

2008

IT'S ALWAYS STRANGE, THE WAYS YOU FIRST LEARN ABOUT SHIPWRECKS.
The thing that draws me to one of the most memorable wreck discoveries
of my diving career is a single, rather long sentence in a book Lori gives

me for Christmas one year, *Life on the South Shoal Lightship* by Gustav Kobbe.

The sentence reads, in part,

> *A few winters ago, the* Newcastle City *went ashore on one of the shoals near the lightship and strained herself so badly that although she floated off she soon filled . . .*

I first read these words in the very early days of my research into wrecks south and east of Nantucket and Martha's Vineyard, when finding such a ship seems like a fantasy. It's the late 1980s, and it will take me years of collecting hang numbers and learning how to conduct effective library and archive searches for lost ships before I can actually find a ship like the *Newcastle City*.

Finding wrecks is a guessing game, a riddle in the shoals. Which of these hangs matches up with which ship? At first I haven't a clue. But as I get better at matching library and archival research with hang numbers, the *Quest* team starts finding long-lost ships like the *North American* and *Oregon*. So it is in 2008 that I feel like I have gathered enough archival information that I can correlate to hangs to lead the Quest to the bones of the *Newcastle City*.

Over my years of research, I have been growing more fascinated with the *Newcastle City*. She's a "rare bird" so to speak. The ship's from that narrow period in time when steam was replacing sail for propulsion and iron was replacing wood for ship construction. She was one of the original five freighters of the Furness Line, which is known for building first-class ships during the Victorian era. It would be amazing to find a vessel like this and see how it has held up over time. And, no doubt, it contains some historically significant artifacts.

Then there's also a big question in my mind about the *Newcastle City*. What does it mean on the shipping reports when they say she's carrying "general cargo"? Sometimes that phrase is used to mask a high-value shipment: treasure. Could wealthy shipowner Christopher Furness have been sending some of his riches from England to New York for safekeeping aboard the *Newcastle City* in case of catastrophe or political/economic upheaval in the United Kingdom?

In 1882 Furness creates the Furness Line. Later it becomes Furness Withy, after a partnership in 1883 with shipbuilder Edward Withy. Today Furness Withy is one of the world's largest shipping companies, operating hundreds of cargo and passenger ships in several different divisions all over the globe.

But the Furness Line begins on a much smaller scale when Christopher Furness contracts for five ships to be built in 1882 for the cargo trade between Europe and North America. The SS *Newcastle City* is one of those ships built for Furness at Edward Withy's shipyard. Constructed with a raised fo'c'sle, poop, and bridge deck, the ship has a hull of iron plates with web-type frames and four bulkheads. Web frames are an innovation that Withy develops to increase hull strength while allowing for hold spaces unobstructed by vertical supports. The *Newcastle City* has two boilers and a compound steam engine of 220 horsepower.

The ship is also rigged for sail. The sailing rig is that of a brigantine, consisting of a foremast rigged for square sails and a mainmast rigged for fore-and-aft canvas. With an overall length of 285 feet, a 36-foot beam, and a depth of hold of 24 feet, the ship displaces 1,384 deadweight tons. Four hatches provide access to the cargo holds, with two forward of the amidships house and two aft.

The River Tyne, where the *Newcastle City*'s built, has long been a center of shipbuilding in North East England. Great technological changes are afoot here as the nineteenth century comes to a close. Iron hulls and steam propulsion are rapidly replacing wood and sail as a means of construction and power for oceangoing ships. The last wooden ship slides down the ways here in 1880, and the last sailing ship in 1893.

As the technology evolves from paddle wheels to screw propellers, and from simple, direct-acting steam engines to compound engines, steamships become both more powerful and reliable. With this reliability comes efficiency in the use of coal. The major breakthroughs in this area are the principals of compounding and condensing. Compounding allows steam exhausted from a high-pressure cylinder to be redirected into a low-pressure cylinder of a larger diameter, instead of being exhausted to the atmosphere. This is a much more efficient use of the steam generated by a ship's boilers.

Eventually engineers expand upon this principal to create triple and quadruple expansion engines. An additional efficiency is a condenser that traps the exhausted steam coming from the low-pressure cylinder and turns it back into water that returns to the ship's boiler. This saves the ship from having to carry massive amounts of fresh water. These changes in technology give birth to cargo ships capable of longer voyages between coaling ports and vessels able to adhere much more closely to scheduled arrivals and departures. As steam becomes a more reliable and efficient means of propulsion, sailing rigs begin disappearing on steamships. Still, some steamers in the 1880s like the SS *Newcastle City* carry sails.

During August 2008 a team from the *Quest* is back out at the edge of Georges Bank searching the wreck of the *North American* for the mother lode of collectible artifacts we know sank with the wreck. But Michael Dudas, Steve Gatto, Joe Mazraani, Tom Packer, Pat Rooney, and I come up empty-handed once more after two days of hard, difficult, and danger-ous diving. We're feeling frustrated by the way currents and storms have drifted deep ridges of sand over the wreck and thwarted our search for artifacts and collectibles. The guys aboard the *Quest* are in a somber mood as we depart the *North American* and head for home.

But wreck divers are naturally an optimistic bunch, and there's almost nothing better than finding a virgin wreck—except recovering sunken treasures—for pumping up my shipmates. So as we steam west toward Nantucket Shoals, I'm thinking tonight could be the perfect time to go hunting for the *Newcastle City*. She's a virgin wreck . . . and there's a chance she's got a high-value cargo aboard. The guys are game. They already know the ship's story.

Departing Newcastle, England, on November 29, 1887, bound for New York, the SS Newcastle City *is carrying twenty-five hundred tons of general cargo. This cargo consists of dry cement in casks, steel billets, coils of steel wire, and mysterious, unnamed "general cargo." The weather during the course of the voy-age is poor from the outset. The ship encounters continual heavy seas and thick rain all the way across the Atlantic. Very few celestial navigation observations can be made during the voyage due to the poor visibility. But on December 21*

Tom and Steve navigating
ERIC TAKAKJIAN

the ship's officers are able to determine their position by use of the lead line to measure depth while approaching Nantucket Shoals.

On the evening of December 22, the skies clear. Captain Robert Thornton spots the Nantucket lightship in the distance on the ship's starboard bow. He takes out his sextant and obtains his latitude by observing Polaris, the North Star. With a compass bearing on the lightship and an observation of Polaris, Thornton is able to accurately fix his ship's position. He orders his helmsman to steer a westerly course to carry his ship south of the lightship and clear of any dangers marked on his chart.

With the ship's position known and a safe course set for New York, Thornton leaves the navigation watch in charge of the ship's second officer and retires to the chart room directly below the bridge. As the ship passes south of the lightship, the weather continues to clear. But with the clearing weather, as is so often the case, the wind begins to increase in strength from the northwest. Soon it's blowing a gale. And as the wind builds, so do the seas. Before long the Newcastle City *is laboring heavily against the westerly gale.*

Conditions deteriorate to the point where the lookout posted on the fore deck has to retreat to the bridge for safety. The men on the bridge stare into the dark with hollow eyes. They grit their teeth and try to ward off the dizziness that comes after days of nothing but bread, water, and dry heaves. They have no idea how much more miserable their lives will get in the coming hours.

At approximately 1:30 on the morning of December 23, 1887, the Newcastle City *slips into the trough of a wave. The ship shudders. Then a hard jolt rocks the ship. Men on the bridge crash against the spokes of the large wooden helm and stumble against the engine telegraph pedestal. Flames flare from the open fireboxes beneath the boilers in the engine room. Stokers drop to their knees. Coal tumbles from the bunkers, and seawater starts spraying through seams in the iron hull plates as rivets stretch.*

Thornton can feel it. The after part of his ship has grounded on a shoal or possibly a wreck. The Newcastle City *remains stuck fast for about a half hour. But the bow continues to rise and fall in ten- to fifteen-foot seas. Back aft waves rake the deck. Upon inspection of the cargo holds, Thornton and his officers see that their ship's taking on water aft. Fast.*

Men curse their gods. After weeks of miserable weather crossing the North Atlantic, now this?

With the stern stuck fast and the bow still afloat, the westerly gale forces the ship around until the Newcastle City *is facing east. Thornton spots a chance here. Maybe the gale is driving his ship off the shoal or obstruction. He grabs the lever on the engine telegraph and rings the engine room. He's telling them to stop trying to back the vessel and give him full speed ahead.*

Down in the engine room, the chief engineer is shouting an endless stream of invectives at his stokers. "Heave the blasted coal, you buggers! Heave for your lives, boys!"

The stokers and coal passers are already calf-deep in icy water and getting soaked in spray. The coal explodes like little firecrackers as it hits the boilers and evaporates. The crew can feel the ship grinding over the bottom like a sled skidding over gravel. It's a horrible sound when you're more than fifteen feet below the waterline of a ship being beaten to death by a Christmas gale.

But then the rumbling and the shaking stop. All that the "black gang" in the engine room can hear is the churning of the massive prop shaft, the hissing of their fires in the furnaces, and the popping as spray continues to hit hot metal. A cheer erupts as the stokers feel the ship rise and fall and begin to rock rhythmically in the waves. But the water is already reaching their knees. Two assistant engineers are scrambling to get every pump on the ship sucking out the water.

With the ship free of the shoal, Thornton tries to point the Newcastle City *toward the lightship. But it's a struggle. The lightship lies almost directly to windward, and the gale is increasing. As daylight approaches, water overwhelms the furnaces in the engine room. The engine loses power. Then it stops altogether. The pumps cannot keep up with the flooding. Thornton knows this is the beginning of the end. He orders the black gang out of the engine room and has his deck crew fire signal flares in the direction of the lightship, hoping there is some way the crew of the lightship can render assistance.*

It's around midnight when we anchor the *Quest* over a hang and a sonar target that could be the *Newcastle City*. As soon as dawn breaks, we grapple into the target below. As usual here on Nantucket Shoals, a strong current's running. When it finally goes slack, Pat Rooney and I head down the anchor line to make the tie-in and see if this wreck could be the *Newcastle City*. As we near the bottom in 130 feet of water, I see iron hull plates and a loose bronze porthole lying in the white sand. Riveted iron hull plates spread out in front of us like a path. To my left is a large shadow. Swimming in the direction of the shadow with Pat, we spot two large iron boilers ahead.

Beyond the boilers we find an immense compound steam engine listing sharply to starboard. Cargo in the form of barrels and coils of wire are scattered around inside of what used to be the ship's hull. A pile of steel billets lies outboard of the engine to port. Aft of the engine, the propeller shaft stretches through short tunnels used to cover the shaft below the hatch openings. The ship's hull has flattened out, for the most part, on the seafloor, but some portions of the hull plates protrude a few feet from the bottom.

We're drifting about ten feet off the bottom, following the propeller shaft toward the stern when, at the very after end of the ship's cargo hold, we spot a huge pile of metal ingots. It's like a scene from the movie *Fool's Gold* with Matthew McConaughey when he discovers treasure at the

Newcastle City engine and boilers
STEVE GATTO

bottom of the sea. Like one of those *National Geographic* pictures of gold stacked in Fort Knox. Right there in front of me and Pat is a somewhat jumbled stack of ingots twenty-feet long, eight feet wide, and five or six feet high.

The metal bars are covered with a film of sand and sea growth. But on top of the pile is one ingot that had been broken and polished by the abrasive sand in the currents. The ingot shines bright silver in the clear water. I can feel myself breathing faster and my heart surging against my ribs as Pat and I swim up to the ingot. We pick it up for closer inspection and pass it back and forth. It's about ten inches square and two inches thick, and it weighs about thirty pounds. If this is silver . . . and silver is selling for about $225 a pound . . . and there are thousands of these ingots? We have just nailed a treasure worth millions.

I can hear Pat yelling into his mouthpiece as we kneel on this huge pile of ingots. And I can hear myself trying to shout back, "We're rich.

We're freaking rich." Our voices sound like garbled versions of Alvin and the Chipmunks or Mickey Mouse.

It takes us a couple of minutes to settle down, but eventually we hatch a plan. We stuff two of the ingots in my mesh goody bag along with the porthole I spotted earlier. Then we drop the bag at the *Quest's* anchor and head out across the sand to find the forward sections of the ship, trailing a reel line so we don't get lost.

The hull sections forward of the boiler are much lower to the sea-floor and are partially covered with fine white sand. 'Tween deck hatch coamings protrude above the sand forward of the boilers. Deadeyes along with other evidence of the foremast and standing rigging are vis-

Grapple hook, porthole, and ingots in bag at bottom of anchor line
TOM PACKER

ible forward of the boilers. Just aft of the ship's bow, a rare Porter anchor lies flat in the sand. Forward of this anchor is the ship's anchor windlass. To starboard of the windlass, we spot a large Trotman anchor protruding from the sand.

Both of these anchors are clues to the wreck's identity. This is an English-built ship from the late nineteenth century for sure. While most of the hull is flattened out and buried in this area, the forward most section of the ship's bow rises above the sand, partially intact and listing to starboard. It has the blunt look of the SS *Newcastle City* that I have seen in photos gathered through my research.

By sunset each member of our dive team has completed two dives on the wreck. Pat and I have retrieved our ingots using lift bags. While grilling steaks for dinner on the after deck of the *Quest*, we try not to think about those ingots. We will not know what they are until we can

Wreck site drawing
ERIC TAKAKJIAN

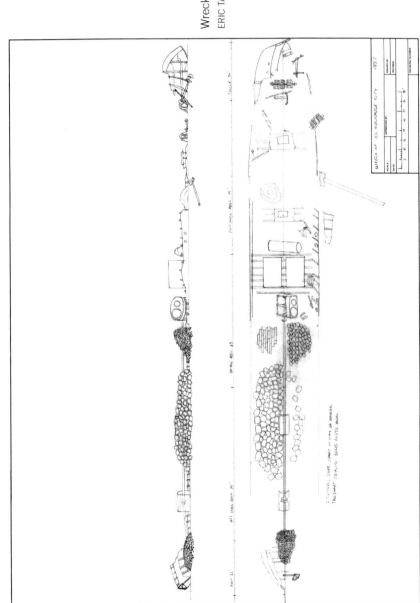

send out samples to labs for testing. Meanwhile we take stock of all that we have seen on the wreck and feel all but certain we have found the *Newcastle City*. Everything is adding up. The blunt bow, the construction of the hull, the types of machinery we have seen, the rigging deadeyes that we found lying in the sand along with part of a mast indicating a sailing rig, the mixed cargo in the ship's hold. The wreck's location relative to the position of the Nantucket lightship also supports our theory. But however compelling the supporting evidence is, we do not yet have conclusive proof this wreck is the *Newcastle City*.

In the fall of 2008, the *Quest* team returns to the wreck over a two-day weekend equipped to further explore, document, and record the site. Machinery specifications listed in *Lloyd's Register of Ships* for *Newcastle City* list the two cylinders' bores of the compound steam engine at thirty-eight inches and seventy inches with a thirty-six-inch stroke. Armed with a tape measure and a couple of steel scrapers, Pat and I head down

Pat and Eric with ingot at sunset
STEVE GATTO

to check it out. We're tied in just forward of the boilers, and it's a short swim to the engine. First we scrape off the mussels covering the larger cylinder and measure it. Seventy inches exactly. Then we clean the growth off the smaller one, thirty-eight inches on the money. The dimensions of both the high-pressure and low-pressure cylinders on the wreck's engine match the specifications in *Lloyd's Register of Ships* exactly. We try to measure the stroke of the pistons, but collapsed hull plating prevents access to the crankshaft.

Back aboard the *Quest* we let the rest of the guys know what we found.

Dave Morton says, "All you need now is something with a name on it."

"The day's not over yet," I tell him.

Meanwhile Tom Packer and Steve Gatto take photographs and video footage of the wreck site, while Dave Morton and Tom Mulloy examine the remains of the cargo. In the videos I can see the same barrels of concrete, coils of wire, and stacks of ingots that I have pictured sinking beneath black water as the holds of the freighter flood in my dreams.

By 8:00 a.m. on December 23, 1887, Thornton realizes that the Newcastle City *is running out of time. With the ship drifting to leeward before the gale away from the lightship, he orders the crew into their warmest clothes, sea boots, and foul weather gear. Then he calls for the lifeboats to be swung out on their davits in preparation for lowering. The first boat lowers shortly after 8:00 a.m. with fourteen people on board. As soon as the boat hits the water, the crew starts rowing toward the lightship, which is barely visible in the distance. It's a miserable go against the howling wind and breaking seas. But if you're one of the men with an oar, you are pulling with your back to the worst of the weather, and the effort is keeping you warm.*

An hour later the second boat lowers with Thornton, the chief mate, the chief engineer, and the remainder of the crew. The decks are awash as the captain climbs into the lifeboat. The Newcastle City *is now listing hard to port. Fifteen minutes after the second boat departs, she slips beneath the waves, stern-first. It's late afternoon when the lifeboats reach the red-hulled Nantucket lightship, which is only three and a half miles away.*

The ten men aboard the lightship Nantucket New South Shoal No. 1 *haul the survivors aboard and try to make them as comfortable as possible in the rough conditions. The surf breaking over Nantucket Shoals to the north, west, and south of the lightship fills the air with freezing spray and a deafening thunder. The lightship itself is tethered to a stockless mushroom anchor, weighing several tons, by over 150 fathoms of two-inch chain. The ship pitches and rolls with odd, irregular jerks unlike anything the deep-ocean mariners of the* Newcastle City *have ever felt before. Standing up for them after their long row, and with the lightship bucking and tossing about, is not possible. Seas are sweeping the deck of the 103-foot vessel. The huge bell on the foredeck clangs with the pitch of the church bells on Christmas Eve back in Newcastle.*

"Let's hope the anchor holds," says one of the lightship crew, "or ya may be going to Bermuda."

He's not kidding. At twenty-four miles off the coast of Nantucket, this is the most remote and exposed lightship in America and perhaps the world. Over the course of her service between 1855 and 1892, this ship has parted her anchor and been blown off station twenty-five times. During an October gale in 1878, she snapped her anchor chain and drifted nearly eight hundred miles to Bermuda . . . before she could raise her small sails and work her way back to the United States.

By sunset on December 23, the wind has moderated just a bit. The sky's clear. Crewmen light the oil lamps on the 75-foot masts. The 228-ton, double-hulled wooden ship rolls a bit more easily. But the bell has not stopped its clanging. Seas are still running over 10 feet. Nantucket Shoals are white with foam.

"Sankaty," shouts the lookout. The crew of the lightship all run to the deck. The shipwreck sailors follow, but they have no clue what the urgency is.

The watch officer is pointing with his arm almost directly off the bow, which is cocked to the northwest. The men can see a light winking faintly just above the horizon every seven and a half seconds. It's Sankaty Head Light in Siasconset at the northeast tip of Nantucket.

"Right where she should be," says the skipper of the lightship. This is a ritual during every gale.

When there are clear skies, the crew searches for Sankaty Head Light to get a bearing and assure themselves their lightship is not drifting for Bermuda again or that they have not been blown into oblivion. Lightship duty is beyond harsh. As one former New England lightship captain tells a reporter from Century *magazine in 1891, "If it were not for the disgrace it would bring on my family, I'd rather go to state prison."*

It's not uncommon for the lightship to provide shelter for shipwrecked survivors. But in most instances these survivors are a few fishermen whose craft has foundered during bad weather on the shoals. But twenty-seven members of a steamship's crew present a problem of space and provisions for the men of the lightship. Still, nobody's complaining. Thornton has lost none of his men. Surprisingly nobody's in rough shape after the long row.

The next day, Christmas Eve, the lightship hails a passing schooner, the Agnes I. Grace, *bound for Baltimore. But Captain Thornton elects to remain on the lightship instead of taking a chance trying to board the schooner in the ugly seas. Instead he asks Captain Seavey on the schooner to report the wreck and the plight of the survivors aboard the lightship when the schooner arrives in Baltimore.*

On Christmas Day there's a strong northeasterly wind howling. The lightship's pitching and rolling heavily again, but belowdecks the men are in a jolly mood. The crew of the lightship has decided to throw a Christmas party of sorts for their guests. They've decorated a small blue spruce brought out to them a couple of weeks ago by the lightship tender Verbena. *Now they're showing the Brits how to weave the famous wicker Nantucket lightship baskets and presenting the guests with little gifts of dry clothes and soap.*

The men of the Newcastle City, *for their part, are teaching the Americans traditional English Christmas carols. The cook serves up a feast of turkey and cranberry sauce along with a traditional Yankee pot roast, complete with boiled potatoes, carrots, cabbage, and onions. There's a keg of apple cider for drinking. It has been aging for more than a month and has a bit of fizz to it now. The cider is getting "hard," to the delight of the Englishmen who have been missing their daily ration of rum. As the cider makes the rounds, thirty-six voices sing in a rough but hearty harmony. The main saloon of* Nantucket New South Shoal No. 1 *echoes with chorus after chorus of "God Rest Ye Merry Gentlemen." Men smile with the knowledge that their lives right now could be much worse . . . or not at all.*

Almost two weeks later the weather abates. On January 6 the tender Verbena *reaches the lightship. It delivers much-needed provisions to the lightship's crew and carries the* Newcastle City's *survivors ashore to Hyannis on Cape Cod. After landing, the shipwrecked sailors travel by train to New York, where they board the Furness Line ship* Durham City *for the voyage back to England.*

In England a British Board of Trade inquiry convenes to examine the circumstances of the disaster and to decide if any action should be taken against Captain Thornton or any members of the crew. Over the course of two days, the board reviews the navigation practices aboard the Newcastle City, *specific charts used, details of the ship's compasses, courses steered after sighting the lightship, and actions taken after the ship struck bottom. In the end the Board of Trade determines that the ship struck an uncharted shoal. Since this shoal was not indicated on the current edition of the British Admiralty chart of Nantucket Shoals, the board judges that Captain Thornton and his officers navigated the ship "in a safe and prudent manner taking all necessary and prudent precautions as would be deemed reasonable under the circumstances." In other words, like the SS Oregon, the SS Newcastle City was simply a ship in the wrong place at the wrong time. The North Atlantic and Nantucket Shoals did what they do best. They played havoc. But in the aftermath a group of new friends found their voices and sang.*

On the second day of our fall trip to the wreck, I make a dive to the engine room. While swimming forward past the boilers on the starboard side, and following along the edge of the exposed hull plating, an object begins to come into view in the distance. At first it appears to be a small cargo winch. But upon closer inspection the thing appears to be the carriage for a manual helm. It's lying on its side in the sand. Swimming up to the object, I see this is, in fact, the ship's helm with the hub of the wheel still in place. All of the spokes of the wheel along with its outer rim are missing, long since rotted away.

Pat Rooney's shooting video footage nearby, so I signal him to come over and video the helm. Knowing that the face of older ship helms are occasionally inscribed with the ships' names, I begin to carefully scrape away the marine growth from the face of the helm's hub. Slowly letters begin to appear. The first is a W, then an E and an N. As I slowly scrape away the growth with my gloved hands, I see the words NEWCASTLE CITY, WEST HARTLEPOOL engraved in two-inch-high block letters around the face of the helm.

It's like that moment finding the ingots for the first time. Some things are even better than ice cream or fireworks. The SS *Newcastle City*, lost for 121 years, has been searched for, located on the seafloor, and positively identified by combining time-honored principals of research with those of modern exploration technology.

With the wreck located and identified, the exploration team's work is finished in one sense and just beginning in another. The wreck is a

Newcastle City helm and author close up
TOM PACKER

perfect nineteenth-century time capsule, providing a window into that narrow period of maritime history when steam was replacing sail and iron was replacing wood in oceangoing ships. There's a great deal more to be learned about the wreck site and the ship. Questions about the finer details of the ship's rigging and machinery, as well as the ship's cargo, remain.

As for those ingots?

After we get back from the first trip to the wreck, we're not really sure what we've got. I've seen lead and tin ingots before on wrecks. Those ingots were a different shape entirely from the ones Pat and I have recovered. One thing for sure is that our ingots are a nonferrous metal of some sort. Silver, of course, is nonferrous.

The first thing I do is call my friend Tom Mulloy, who found a wreck that had seventy-five-pound silver bars on it. Tom has an assayer that he used to analyze his discovery, and I want to get in touch with the guy to get my ingot checked out. Pat Rooney is going to do the same thing with his ingot.

The assayer advises me to drill a small hole and send him shavings or cut off a small section of the ingot. I do both and ship the samples to the assay lab. I want to get it out as soon as possible, because I'm headed back to work on a tugboat in a couple of days.

A week or so later, Pat calls me when I'm on my tug. I'm in Norfolk, Virginia, waiting for tropical storm Hanna to pass.

He says, "Hey, are you sitting down?"

I walk out on deck so I'm alone. "What's up?"

He says he took the ingot to his jeweler. The jeweler did a test on it and said it is silver.

Holy shit!

Pat's pretty fired up, and I'm already starting to think of all the things Lori and I could do with a million dollars.

"I also sent out a sample to an assay lab," he says. "For confirmation."

"Let's hope the lab tell us the same story." I'm trying really hard to not go over the moon with this news just yet, but my mind is beginning to wrestle with the logistics of a salvage job and what it would entail. That pile of ingots is the size of a pickup truck. Everybody on the team is going to be richer than we ever imagined.

About the time we get back from our trip to the wreck in October, Pat and I both get the test results from our separate assayers. Both results come to the same conclusion: The ingots are not silver. They are antimony. It's worth about $3 a pound, not $225.

At the time of the wreck, antimony was mixed with lead to make bullets harder. Today it's alloyed with aluminum and used in semiconductor production. It's also used to make an alloy known as Babbitt for shaft bearings. The ingots have value, but it's a tiny fraction of what we would get for silver. We would probably spend more money on a salvage operation than we would get for the ingots.

It's a funny thing. When I think about the *Newcastle City* today, I should probably be picturing the movie Fool's Gold again. But what come to mind are images of those two crews in the lightship at Christmas joining together over turkey, Yankee pot roast, cranberry sauce, and hard cider. I can almost hear them singing, "God rest ye merry gentlemen. Let nothing you dismay."

CHAPTER ELEVEN

Death by Liner

The SS *Sagaland*

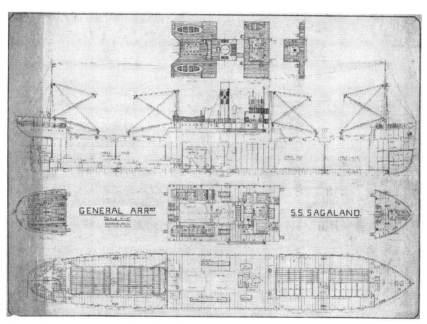

General arrangement outboard profile plan
UK NATIONAL MARITIME MUSEUM

2012

In July 2012 we make a major discovery that garners worldwide media attention. Using two sophisticated side-scan sonar units and Joe Mazraani's dive boat the *Tenacious*, we pinpoint and dive the totally intact wreck of the WWII German submarine *U-550*. It is the last unfound U-boat wreck on America's Atlantic coast that can be dived, and it's a wreck that divers have been trying to find for years. In April 1944, three American destroyer escorts sunk Captain Klaus Hänert's U-boat in 330 feet of water seventy miles south of Nantucket after his torpedo attack on a convoy of ships that were headed for Ireland. On this same trip we find the stern of *U-550*'s victim, the American tanker SS *Pan Pennsylvania*. The full story of these discoveries and the WWII naval battle become the subject of the book *Where Divers Dare: The Hunt for the Last U-boat.*

Finding *U-550* is one of the highpoints of my diving career. It's a wreck I have been researching for two decades. But for me the summer of 2012 is unfolding with extremely mixed emotions, the highest of highs and the lowest of lows. The low comes on May 3, when just after getting back to work on my tug, I read on Facebook that Tim Coleman has died from a heart attack while surf fishing on a beach in Rhode Island. I can't begin to count the number of hours Tim and I spent together researching shipwrecks, going over hang numbers, running search patterns on the ocean, and just plain hanging out. To say I that I'm devastated by his death is an understatement. I miss him terribly.

Tim was a devoted sport fisherman and accomplished writer. A lifelong bachelor, his favorite pastimes were surfcasting for striped bass off the beaches of Southern New England and bottom fishing for cod on wrecks around New England and grouper in the Florida Keys. Tim was the editor of *The New England Fisherman* magazine for twenty-seven years before he retired. Over the years he wrote eight books and hundreds of magazine articles about fishing. He was also a US Army veteran who served in the Vietnam War.

Tim and I go back a long way. The first time we spoke was over the phone, around 1990. I had read his book *Fishable Wrecks and Rockpiles* about bottom fishing sites in Southern New England and decided to call him one day just out of the blue. We hit it off right away over the phone with a common interest in locating lost wrecks and maritime history. I made the suggestion that perhaps we could trade some hang numbers. He agreed, and before we knew it, we were doing that regularly. Whenever one of us would obtain a dragger's hang log, we would make a copy of it and pass it on.

His office in Mystic, Connecticut, was a short distance off I-95 on the way I drove to work on my tug based in New York Harbor. Frequently I would stop to see Tim on the way home from work, and we would talk about different wrecks and where they might be. I really enjoyed Tim's very low key and optimistic manner. He was a guy who always looked forward to the next fishing trip, search mission, or cup of coffee with friends at Dunkin' Donuts.

Even now I can picture him wearing his favorite blue sweatshirt, coffee cup in hand, sitting in the port wheelhouse chair of the *Quest*, and squinting at the sonar display in front of us. He's pointing at the screen and saying in his usual optimistic but soft-spoken voice, "That sure looks like a codfish condo to me, what's the position on that?"

When working with LORAN we always referred to the display as top and bottom, and in that order, the top line being the 13 line and the bottom being the 43 or 44 line. As a sort of shorthand we would record the last three numbers and the decimal point instead of the whole number. So I would reply something like 926.5 and 298.7 and then the depth at the highest point. We would have already noted the water depth we were working in. On a normal day we would try and investigate ten different hang positions, anything more than that we would start to lose focus.

We had lengthy discussions at night over the phone while each of us was looking at our charts and developing search missions for us aboard the *Grey Eagle*, at first, then the *Quest* and Frank Blount's *Lady Francis* out of Point Judith, Rhode Island. We spent more hours than I can count together scouring the bottom of Cape Cod Bay, Massachusetts Bay, Rhode Island Sound, Block Island Sound, and the waters south of Martha's Vineyard and Nantucket. I will never forget the day, during a search mission off Boston, when we actually saw a boat being scuttled.

Tim spotted it first, saying, "Hey look I think they are scuttling that dragger over there. Let's go check it out." We steamed over to get the position, and air bubbles were still coming to the surface from the sunken hull. Talk about being in the right place at the right time to locate a virgin wreck.

The only thing that helps to ease my sadness over his death is getting out on the water to hunt for virgin wrecks the way he and I used to do. But somehow finding U-550 and the stern of the Pan Pennsylvania is not enough. I wonder what Tim would want to search for. Then I know. He always hoped we could find the Norwegian freighter SS *Sagaland*. He used to say it would make a great "codfish condo." We had discussed this freighter at length many times in the past, and I have looked for it on previous trips. It sunk almost instantly during the summer of 1927 after colliding with the liner SS *Veendam II* five miles south of the Nantucket lightship.

Some people believe that when a mariner dies, his soul goes to a place called Fiddler's Green. In his novel, *Billy Budd, Sailor,* Herman Melville describes Fiddler's Green as a seafarers' paradise "providentially set apart for dance-houses, doxies, and tapsters." I like to think that Tim is bound for Fiddler's Green. Finding the *Sagaland* seems like a way to honor him, a way to say, "Farewell, old friend, and fair winds."

In 1927 SS *Sagaland* is a nearly new modern ship. Built of steel and launched in June 1921 by Charles Hill & Sons Ltd., Bristol, England, she's 310 feet in length and 44 feet abeam. Her depth of hold is just over 20 feet, and she has a capacity of 4,350 deadweight tons. In profile *Sagaland* is a classic British-built steamer of the 1920s with a midships bridge and superstructure, two masts, and eight cargo derricks. A triple expansion steam engine, built by Richardsons Westgarth & Company Ltd., of Hartlepool, powers her. She's owned by a Norwegian company (Richard, Amlie & Co), but during the summer of 1927, she's on charter to a West Indies enterprise that specializes in shipping raw sugar to American rum distilleries.

On July 7, 1927, the Sagaland *departs Manzanillo, Cuba, with a cargo of sugar bound for Boston. Captain A. Pederson is in command of a crew of* twenty-five men. It's a sweltering trip. Cuba and the entire East Coast of the United States are suffering from a heat wave. Forty-five people have already died from the heat and humidity in New York City by the time the Sagaland is closing with the American coast on the morning of July 15.

Captain Pederson navigates his ship toward the Nantucket lightship and the inbound lane for Boston ship traffic, but it's not easy. The roiling currents on Nantucket Shoals have done their thing again, churning up a layer of cold air that condenses the humid atmosphere into thick fog.

As the Sagaland plods slowly north at about 8 knots with her bridge crew out on the wings hoping to hear the foghorn of the Nantucket lightship, the Holland American liner SS Veendam II is charging southwest toward the Nantucket lightship at 13 knots from the opposite direction. After leaving Rotterdam on July 8, with stops in Boulogne-sur-Mer and Southampton, she is racing through the fog at nearly 15 knots with more than 170 passengers and 300 crew to make her scheduled arrival at New York on the morning of July 16.

Compared to the Sagaland, the Veendam II is gigantic. Launched in 1922 by Harland & Wolff Limited in Glasgow, Scotland, she is almost 600 feet long with a beam of 67 feet, a draft of 28 feet, and a displacement of 26,000 tons. Two sets of double reduction geared Brown-Curtis steam turbines develop 8,000 shaft horsepower and turn two giant props that are about 18 feet in diameter. Her service speed is 15 knots. She can carry 296 first-class passengers, 396 in second class, and 292 in third class. She will live a long and profitable life, carrying passengers across the Atlantic right until 1953, when she's sold for scrap. In the Veendam II's resumé of more than three decades of service, the events of July 15, 1927, are little more than a footnote. As for the SS Sagaland, they are her epitaph.

In the Roaring Twenties, transatlantic travel has grown into a thriving business, and liners like the Veendam II are the queens of the seas. In 1927 there are eighteen different passenger lines from nine European countries and the United States competing for transatlantic passenger business to New York with approximately ninety different ships. New York is one of the busiest ports in the world, with pier space at a premium. Speed and quality service are the hallmarks of each of these lines. The goal being to carry as many passengers as possible while adhering to strict schedules. It's where the term "liner service" *originates to describe ships departing and arriving on set times and dates. The term is still used today and applied to container ships.*

Liners prize keeping to their schedules above all else, including safety. Their skippers are well-known for driving their ships close to full speed without regard for wind, rain, snow, or fog. At one point the Titanic's *captain, Edward Smith, told a reporter that he could not "imagine any condition which would cause a ship to founder. Modern shipbuilding has gone beyond that."*

In the early morning of July 15, 1927, the Veendam II *is racing for New York. Like the* Sagaland, *she's in thick fog. But she has barely reduced her speed from 15 knots to 13 knots as she skirts the Grand Banks and Georges Bank. By choosing to keep his ship to her schedule, her captain is ignoring the International Rules of the Road that require vessels operating in restricted visibility to proceed at a safe speed adapted to the prevailing circumstances and conditions of restricted visibility.*

Her radio officer has finally picked up the sound of the nondirectional radio beacon on the Nantucket lightship, which will be the liner's first waypoint along her final approach to New York. Because the beacon is nondirectional, the radio officer and bridge crew on the Veendam II *can only approximate the lightship's relative bearing from the liner. Furthermore, nondirectional radio signals of that era are known for bending as they move through changing atmospheric conditions, including fog. Nevertheless, the radio beacon makes the lightship easier to find than just its light, bell, and foghorn.*

At about 4:25 in the morning, the Veendam II *passes the lightship without incident. The liner's bridge crew can see the glow of the lightship's bright beacon through the fog. The ships are that close. Soon Captain Will. Krol and his bridge crew hear the foghorn of another vessel, ahead and to port. They do not know it yet, but she is the* Sagaland. *If the two ships hold their present courses, the northbound freighter is lined up to cross the bow of the southwest-bound liner. It's the* Andrea Doria–Stockholm *situation again, the* Regal Sword–Exxon Chester *scenario. And like the skipper on the* Exxon Chester, *Captain Krol on the liner holds his course because he is the "stand on" vessel as per the Rules of the Road.*

Historical records do not tell us whether Krol signals with one short blast of his horn, his intention to pass the oncoming Sagaland *in a port-to-port situation, but none of his passengers recall it. If he did, the* Sagaland's *bridge crew does not hear it or does not respond. At 4:40 in the morning, with the freighter still heading north, her bridge crew sees the liner emerge from the fog to starboard on a nearly perpendicular course. Spotting the* Sagaland, *the liner fires off five short blasts of her horn, the danger signal, but at this point it's too late for the crew of the lumbering freighter to do anything but brace for impact.*

Within a matter of seconds, the Veendam II *hits* Sagaland *amidships with such force that passengers in the liner wake to a heavy lurch of their ship and sounds of a woman screaming. Rushing on deck, passengers see the* Sagaland *impaled, nearly torn in half, by the bow of the liner. The crewmen of the freighter are leaping to the deck of the liner as the freighter sinks with frightful speed. The liner's passengers count twenty members of the* Sagaland's *crew who manage to scramble to safety aboard the* Veendam II *before the freighter slips beneath the black waters. When the liner finally stops, one of her lifeboats picks up four more shipwrecked sailors. One man is missing.*

The next day reporters meet the Veendam II *when she docks in New York, snap a few photos of the rescued crew of the* Sagaland, *and file stories based on a few comments from passengers and a terse report of the accident by Captain Krol. A short article about the accident makes the front page of the* New York Times *and a few other papers. But it's a "below the fold" story eclipsed by articles about the disappearance of an aviator trying to be the first to fly the Pacific, Bobby Jones winning the British Open golf tournament, riots in Vienna, deaths in New York from the current heat wave, and the execution of three murderers in Illinois. The story garners much more coverage in the Dutch newspapers, even reaching Holland's Far East colonies as front-page news in the* Sumatra Post.

After repairing a five-foot-by-three-foot gash in the liner, Captain Krol takes on a new load of passengers and heads the Veendam II *back to Rotterdam right on schedule. In Holland, the Dutch Council for Shipping finds Krol at fault for the accident because he was traveling too fast in restricted visibility. But within a few months of the collision almost no one remembers the name of the* Sagaland. *Tim Coleman would say she's just another unfortunate sacrifice to the race for speed in transatlantic ocean travel. Not the first and not the last.*

On Friday August 17 we load the *Quest* in Fairhaven and get underway for Nantucket Shoals. On board are Tom Packer, Steve Gatto, Joe

Sagalano crew aboard the *Veendam II* in New York
ERIC TAKAKJIAN, ACME NEWS PICTURES NY

Mazraani, Scott Tomlinson, and me. We have brought along a dual-frequency Klein side-scan sonar that I am borrowing from a friend. I wanted to do some side-scanning east of the former Nantucket lightship ship station (now an automated buoy).

We arrive in the search area late the next morning with perfect sea and sky conditions. The guys waste no time getting the sonar set up and deployed. The first group of hangs we want to scan is the site of what fishermen believe to be the wreck of the trawler F/V *New England*...but I'm not so sure. It's located four miles northeast of the lightship station in about 170 feet of water.

I have set up grid lines in the Noble Tech chart program on the boat's navigation computer ahead of time. Usually when I'm setting up for side-scan, I like to have overlapping lanes laid out on the digital navigation chart so we don't miss anything. We always start mowing the lawn with the boat above our search line and come down to it. When finishing a line, we run well out past the end of the line and make a big, sweeping turn to get lined up for the next line. The whole process takes extra time, but we end up with 100 percent coverage of the ocean floor we are scanning.

Coming down the first line from north to south, we spot a little bit of debris on the port side of the sonar image relayed from the sonar "fish" up a cable to a monitor. We finish the line and make our turn. Coming back along the second line, we see a nice, strong image with a lot of acoustic shadow, indicating the height of a wreck rising off the bottom. We're scanning on the 100 kHz frequency, which is good for longer ranges, but this frequency doesn't give the highest resolution.

On the next line we switch to 400 kHz for higher resolution images. As we reach the area of the target, a clear image of the wreck appears on the screen. It looks to be in two pieces, and it is a lot larger than a fishing boat. The huge propeller's clearly visible in the sonar image. Could this be the *Sagaland?* The fact that it's in two pieces fits with what Tim and I have learned about the crushing blow the *Veendam II* gave *Sagaland* nearly amidships. I hear his familiar counsel in my head. "You won't know until you go down there and knock on the side of it."

That night we anchor near the debris field. The next morning we pull up the anchor and grapple into the wreck. As usual the current is running. Tom and Steve tie in, and Joe follows them down. After they are tied in, we shorten up the scope on the down line. Scott and I jump in after the first team surfaces. Scott has on his closed-circuit rebreather. I'm on my usual open-circuit setup, twin high-pressure 120s with a smaller pony bottle and an aluminum "80" stage bottle.

As we descend, I can see Scott eyeing the heads-up display glowing at the bottom of his mask. It tells him that his closed circuit rebreather unit on his back is delivering him the optimum amount of partial pressure of oxygen for his current depth.

A number of different manufacturers make closed circuit rebreathers (called CCRs) today. The basic principle of operation on all of them is more or less the same. CCRs consist of a breathing loop, small oxygen

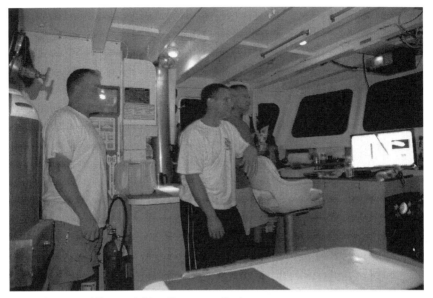

Steve, Scott, and Tom watching the sonar display
ERIC TAKAKJIAN

and diluent gas cylinders (which usually contain trimix), a computer system that drives it, and a chassis to hold all the parts together. The principal of operation is quite simple. The diver breathes in a mixture of diluent gas and oxygen through the inhale counter lung and exhales into the exhale counter lung. The gas expelled by the diver's lungs travels into the CCR's exhale counter lung and then passes through a carbon dioxide scrubber.

The scrubbed gas returns to the inhale counter lung to be breathed again with small amounts of oxygen or diluent gas added as needed. The carbon dioxide (CO_2) scrubber is a canister filled with a CO_2-absorbing material. The capacity or "duration" of a scrubber is based on its size. Typically scrubbers can last four to six hours before needing to be recharged.

Closed circuit rebreathers have many advantages, both from a physiological standpoint and an operational one. The two main physiological advantages are that the CCR delivers the optimum partial pressure of oxygen (PO_2), determined by the diver as a "set point" constantly throughout the dive regardless of depth, and the diver is breathing warm gas from the loop as opposed to cold compressed gas from a tank. Having an optimum PO2 is not possible with open circuit because the diver would have to carry a nearly infinite number of tanks all with a different percentage of oxygen in the mix.

CCRs offer divers extra time to complete their missions and a dramatically reduced consumption of gas. On a typical dive lasting an hour in total, regardless of depth, a diver might use 6 cubic feet of oxygen and 8 cubic feet of diluent gas. The diluent gas is also used to inflate the diver's "wings" or buoyancy compensator. The actual time a diver can spend in the water is more or less the four to six hours the scrubbers can absorb carbon dioxide before being recharged. Should a diver encounter a problem, he or she would have much more time to deal with it on a CCR than an open circuit diver who is steadily consuming the finite amount of gas in his or her tanks. On an offshore dive trip, a diver making four dives on a rebreather might only use 30 to 35 cubic feet of oxygen and about 35 to 40 cubic feet of trimix diluent gas. An open circuit diver doing the same dives might use 400 to 450 cubic feet of trimix and far more oxygen.

Rudimentary rebreathers have been around since the early 1800s, but they got more sophisticated and reliable during WWII when Navy frogmen adopted the technology. Many governments blocked the release of this useful military apparatus until the collapse of the Soviet Union. Since fears of attack by enemy divers have mellowed, Western governments have stop blocking civilian use of rebreather technology, and recreational diving rebreathers are readily available.

In addition to Scott's CCR giving him the safety and convenience of ideal gas mixes and a nearly unlimited supply of breathing gas, the rebreather gives him the ability to talk underwater. Breathing through a regulator with my open circuit set up I can't do much more than grunt, growl, moan, or howl to another diver, but Scott can talk into his rebreather's mouthpiece. Pretty cool and useful. For all these reasons, I'm onboard to buy a CCR of my own. But before this dive I am not quite ready to plunk down ten thousand dollars for a unit like Scott's.

Rebreathers and the sophisticated dive computers we wear on our forearms are among a number of popular new technologies coming to recreation wreck diving in the twenty-first century. On this trip most of the guys have what we call "scooters," DPVs (diver propulsion vehicles). They look like small motorized torpedoes that can pull you through the water. When you are trying to travel distances fast or fight a current, scooters can be a blessing. But sometimes, as I am about to find out, they can be a curse.

Going down the line I can feel the current cranking. Scott and I are kicking and using our scooters to fight the current. It takes a while, but we finally reach the edge of the wreck at around 170 feet. We've touched bottom on the down-current side where the hull meets the clean white sand. Visibility is excellent, at least twenty-five to thirty feet, with plenty of ambient light. Schools of cod and pollock are all around us. The ship appears to be on its side, and we're on the after section. The hull's steel. The rudder and propeller are clearly visible to our right, with one of the propeller blades partially buried in a ridge of sand. The size and shape of the wreck fit the profiles of a classic English freighter of the 1920s.

Would you look at that, a voice says in my brain. Here she is . . . after all these years. *Sagaland.*

Maybe it's me talking to myself. Maybe it's Tim.

I'm about to crank up the speed on my scooter and start to move forward on the wreck when I check my pressure gauge to make sure I have plenty of air left. I can't believe what I'm seeing. The pressure gauge is reading something like 1,600 psi. I left the surface with 3,700 psi. What's going on? Where did all that gas go?

This is exactly the kind of moment—an instant when a diver is surprised at the bottom of the sea by a gear failure and a potential lack of breathing gas—that he can panic, start to hyperventilate, suck up the rest of his breathable air, and die.

But in this particular case I'm not seriously concerned, just really annoyed. We're right next to the anchor line, and I have plenty of gas to get back to the surface safely. What sucks is I don't have enough gas to explore the wreck.

I think for a minute and then realize what has happened. I don't normally dive with a scooter. If anything I use it for digging holes in the sand while looking for artifacts. But today I'm using it as a tool to deal with the current. My particular scooter has handles on the front with the propeller shroud close to my chest. I now realize that as I have been coming down the anchor line, the wash coming off the propeller has been holding the purge button depressed on my backup regulator and dumping gas from my tanks without me knowing it.

I look at my pressure gauge again. It's still reading something like 1,600 psi, nothing is leaking. Scott does a bubble check of my gear. All is good.

I can hear Tim asking, "Can you take a quick look around, confirm a couple of things, and then come back another time?"

I take slow breaths from my regulator to collect myself, to think.

Sure. Why not?

Scott and I swim up to the high point on the wreck and look over the edge. The stern section is on its starboard side and we can see into the aft cargo holds. After a brief look we head back to the anchor line and start up. I feel bad for Scott, having to cut the dive short. But we're dive buddies, so he stands by me even though with his CCR he could stay down here for an hour if he wanted to and still have plenty of gas.

On the way back up the anchor line I think about Tim and how pleased he would be to know we found the *Sagaland*. No doubt he would be planning a cod fishing trip out here as soon as possible with fishing friends out of Point Judith.

I can hear him saying, "Well, my friend, that's one more to check off the list. There will be plenty of codfish on that *Sagaland* for us to catch."

My lungs let a breath out. The gas feels a bit warmer now in my throat before it bubbles away from my regulator, rises, and disappears.

I've heard professional pilots tell me they fly with a ghost in the cockpit. It's the voice of a father, a brother, a mentor, a flight instructor, or pilot friend who has passed on to the wild blue yonder, passed on to Fiddler's Green. It's such a common phenomenon that Hollywood made a WWII movie about it in 1943 called *A Guy Named Joe*. In 1989 there was a Steven Spielberg remake called *Always* with Richard Dreyfus and John Goodman as aerial fire bombers.

My pilot friends say it's that ghost, the voice, that brings them peace and presence of mind just at the moment when all hell is about to break loose in the cockpit. It's the ghost that saves their lives. After this dive to the *Sagaland*, after losing Tim, I get that.

During my watch from 10:00 p.m. to midnight on the nighttime passage home to Fairhaven, I find myself thinking about Tim again. We liked to share stories of shipwrecks with each other. Usually the first thing I would do after getting home and getting the gear stowed and the boat cleaned up was to call Tim and let him know how the trip went and what, if anything, we found. Then a day or so later we would talk in the evenings and go over all the details, checking off the hang numbers in our files that had been investigated. I sure will miss those conversations.

One of the things that always struck us about the *Sagaland*'s story was the cavalier way the *Veendam II*'s skipper kept his ship charging through the blinding fog of the Shoals at the totally unsafe speed of 13 knots . . . until he smacked into the *Sagaland* and sent one of her sailors to Fiddler's Green. I can almost hear Tim asking, "What's a human life worth?"

Here, alone at the helm and squinting between the dark ahead, the chart plotter, and the radar display, I listen to the rumble of the *Quest*'s diesel, punctuated by snores from the rest of the guys, and I try to stay alert. But with the autopilot steering and nothing outside or inside the boat to focus my attention, my mind wanders. Pretty soon I'm thinking about another shipwreck on Nantucket Shoals that Tim and I have researched. During the 1930s the mammoth liner RMS *Olympic*, the *Titanic*'s sister, ran down and sank the Nantucket lightship, killing most of her crew.

On the night of May 14, 1934, the Olympic *is steaming southwest by west on her regular run from Southampton to New York. The next morning the liner is running in thick fog as she approaches the coast of America. Captain John Binks reduces his speed from 16 knots to about 12 knots. Then, a few minutes before 11:00 a.m., Fred Clark, the radio officer aboard the* Olympic *picks up the nondirection radio beacon from the Nantucket lightship LV-117.*

Hearing from Clark that he has identified the lightship's radio beacon and that it lies off the liner's starboard bow, Captain Binks orders his helmsman to alter course ten degrees to port to assure a safe passing. The captain also telegraphs the engine room to reduce speed to 10 knots. Meanwhile, officers on the liner's starboard bridge wing are beginning to hear the foghorn from the lightship ahead and to starboard.

Aboard LV-117 sixty-nine-year-old Captain George Braithwaite is peering into his mug of coffee, pacing in the main saloon, and feeling jittery. It's not just the cheap government coffee that has him on edge. He has barely slept in twenty-four hours. All through the night he has heard the groan of foghorns, the rumble of steam engines, and the whine of propellers of ships passing the lightship in the fog. At about 4:00 this morning the liner SS Paris passed the lightship so close the men on watch could see the dining room staff preparing tables for breakfast in the brightly lit first-class dining room.

No doubt Braithwaite's thinking back to early January when the liner SS Washington sideswiped LV-117 in poor visibility and carried away the radio antennas. Before rotating off his shore leave back to the lightship this May, radioman John Parry tells acquaintances, "Some day we are just going to get it head on, and that will be the finish. One of those big liners will just ride through us."

Even though the lightship is a state-of-the art steel replacement for the old LV-1, which welcomed the shipwrecked crew of the Newcastle City, this nearly new, 135-foot, 630-ton lightship is a flea in comparison to ships like White Star's 882-foot, 45,000-ton RMS Olympic.

At about 11:00 a.m., Binks and his bridge crew spot the shadow of the lightship looming through the fog dead ahead at a range of just a few hundred yards. The captain immediately calls for "left full rudder, engines all astern full." Remembering the disaster that befell the Olympic's sister ship the Titanic, he calls for his crew to activate the automatic system closing the watertight doors throughout the vessel. Then Binks grips the rail of the starboard bridge wing and prays that the liner known as "Old Reliable" can dodge disaster one more time. He has had a superlative career, spanning over four decades in sailing ships, warships, and liners. After over thirty years of service with the White Star Line, he's planning to retire in just six months. But now this.

Aboard the lightship, first mate Cliff Mosher shouts, "The Olympic is upon us!" and starts ringing the bell to warn his shipmates.

Braithwaite spots the Olympic *bearing down on LV-117. He can see the helmsman on the liner's bridge and starts waving his arms as if he's trying like Binks to will the liner off to the east.*

But altering the course of such a monster is impossible, and at 11:06 the Olympic *crashes into the lightship. The liner has slowed to just 3 knots, but her mass and momentum slam LV-117 forward, tear her from her mooring, and drive her down. First mate Mosher remembers, "It was more like a hard push and a terrific shaking, a crunching and grinding. It was not a loud smash as one might expect. The* Olympic *kept coming through . . ." The force of the collision knocks Braithwaite off his feet. Twice. The next thing he knows, he's in the water, and he can't swim.*

What the lightship captain doesn't know yet is that the impact of the liner against the lightship has exploded LV-117's boiler, filling the ship with steam and dooming the men who were belowdecks. The men on watch have just enough time to buckle on their life vests, which they always keep handy, and start to abandon their sinking vessel. John Perry's in the lightship's radio shack and barely has time to get on deck and "swim for my life." Shipmate Robert Laurent will tell the press, "It all happened so quickly, you had no chance to panic. We all had our life preservers and it was a good thing that we did."

Meanwhile aboard the Olympic, *passengers feel the heavy vibrations of the ship as the twin screws churn in reverse. Everyone feels a slight jolt, and the liner shudders for several seconds. Coming out onto the promenade deck to see what is amiss, passengers spot debris floating on the gray waves. The heavy scent of fuel oil clots their noses. It stings their eyes as they watch bleeding men scrambling around on the deck of the stricken lightship before its hull, then its spars, sink out of sight. The water is so cold that the men in the water can swim only a few strokes before they seem to freeze up.*

Even before the liner has fully stopped, her crew starts preparing the portside emergency lifeboat for launching. They light flares to cut through the thick fog while the ship keeps blowing its horn so that multiple lifeboats and motor launches searching for survivors can locate the Olympic *in the fog.*

The liner's boats search in the fog for nearly two hours while many of the passengers line the rails and watch, shouting to the rescuers in the small boats below to go this way or that way to pick up men or bodies in the water. Most of the living are wearing the blue jumpsuits of the lighthouse service. Captain Braithwaite is in plain clothes. When he's fished aboard a lifeboat, his right eye and the right side of his head look bashed in. He's bleeding copious amounts of blood.

Before the Olympic *starts for New York, her lifeboats rescue seven of the lightship's eleven crewmen. Three of the seven die in the liner's infirmary. Captain Braithwaite's in rough shape. With his head heavily bandaged, he's sedated and sleeps almost continuously.*

Upon arrival in New York the next day, Captain Binks, Captain Braithwaite, and the other survivors meet with a flood of reporters and news-reel crews. Outakes from the newsreel interviews aboard the RMS Olympic *will eventually be archived on YouTube. Binks, in full dress–blue uniform, tries to maintain a stiff upper lip, but you can see the smoky glaze of pain and tor-ment in his eyes. He must be thinking about the excruciating accident inquiry that lies ahead and, even more, the souls of seven dead mariners he must now carry on his shoulders for the rest of his life.*

Tim Coleman driving the *Quest* on one of many side scan trips
ERIC TAKAKJIAN

As For Braithwaite, he looks small and broken in ill-fitting clothes with his bandaged head and right eye. He talks slowly, vaguely, like a punch-drunk boxer. A few months later he dies from his wounds.

A survey of the Olympic *at the docks in New York shows that she has suffered only minor damage from the accident. She departs New York on schedule . . . just two days after crushing and sinking* LV-117.

In an out-of-court settlement, the White Star Line pays the US Lighthouse Service three hundred thousand dollars to build a new lightship. As for the dependents of the dead lightship sailors? They receive a few hundred dollars restitution through the US Employees' Compensation Act.

I can hear Tim saying, "The families of those poor guys on the lightship sure got the short end of the deal."

Amen, my friend.

Chapter Twelve

Almost Made It

The SS *Allentown*

SS *Reading, Allentown's* sister ship in ice off Gloucester 1888
R. LOREN GRAHAM COLLECTION, STEAMSHIP HISTORICAL SOCIETY OF AMERICA ARCHIVE, WWW. SSHSA.ORG

2014 TO 2018

OF ALL THE SHIPS I'VE LOOKED FOR OVER THE YEARS, THE ONE THAT has proven most elusive, and quite possibly the most puzzling, is the steam collier SS *Allentown*. I would never have thought it would have taken as long as it did to find.

I first learned of the *Allentown* while looking through the New York *Maritime Register.* I came across an entry for losses in 1888, which read in part,

> Allentown *(steam collier)—is reported lost off Cohasset Mass., she cleared from Philadelphia Nov 21st for Salem Mass with 1660 tons of coal, she was commanded by Capt. Odiorne and had a crew of 18 men.*

In November 1888 a tremendous storm of hurricane strength sweeps the New England coast for four days. Numerous ships are lost, with wreckage strewn all along the coast. Between Boston and Scituate, a distance of less than thirty miles, fifteen ships go to the bottom. Damage to coastal homes and infrastructure is considerable.

According to an account published in the *Boston Globe*, the keeper of Minot's Lighthouse at Hull, Massachusetts, at the southern entrance to Boston Harbor, spots the wreckage of a steamer coming from the direction of Jason Shoal during the height of the storm. Some of the debris that washes ashore has the name *Allentown* marked on it. The lighthouse keeper, Captain M. H. Reamy, surmises that the *Allentown* struck on Jason Shoal and foundered in that vicinity. Over the next few days, wreckage from the *Allentown* continues to wash ashore in Hull, including a lifeboat, considerable cabin furniture, and wood paneling. After the storm subsides, a Ross Towboat tug finds the steamer's medicine chest floating in the Massachusetts Bay.

Archival digging uncovers similar accounts in various newspapers, with some interesting twists. Although the maritime register states Captain Odiorne is aboard the doomed *Allentown*, he, in fact, is not. Odiorne, along with his chief engineer, went ashore in Philadelphia to attend a court hearing. At the time of her loss, the *Allentown* is under the command of her former chief mate, Captain George W. Paul. Former first engineer Benjamin Prichard commands the engine room gang. Another interesting twist I discover is that the *Allentown* grounded earlier that year on Brent's Reef coming into New Bedford, Massachusetts. The ship had to have its cargo lightered in order to be freed from the reef. Then a month after her grounding in the approaches to New Bedford, she struck a submerged wreck near Cape May, New Jersey.

My initial thoughts after this research are that the wreck has to be somewhere northeast of Minot's Light, roughly in the direction of Jason Shoal. This area would be upwind from Minot's Light during the storm. Since the inshore waters in this area have been extensively searched in years past by Bill Carter of Cohasset, who has located a lot of the shallow wrecks in the area—but not *Allentown*—the wreck has to be farther offshore in deeper water. But where?

The *Allentown*'s one of six Reading-class colliers, built at the Philadelphia shipyard of William Cramp & Sons Ship and Engine Building Company, for the Reading Railroad in 1874. Cramp's is known as one of the premier shipyards in the United States at the time. The Delaware River region is often referred to as "America's Clyde," in reference to the River Clyde in Scotland, a region at the heart of iron shipbuilding in Europe during the late nineteenth and early twentieth centuries. Numerous shipyards line the Delaware River during the late 1800s, building all manner of vessels from tugboats to warships. Some of the other famous yards are John Roach & Son and the Neafie & Levey Shipyard located in Wilmington, Delaware. Cramp's is by far the largest yard and has a reputation for turning out first-class vessels.

In 1860 the Reading Railroad begins investing in its own fleet of ships, gradually getting away from chartered vessels to haul its coal mined in the hills of western Pennsylvania. By the early 1870s Reading owns a sizable fleet of ships, including schooners and some new steam colliers. They spare no expense in the construction of their new fleet. In order to receive priority in loading and discharging, Reading also invests in its own port facilities, both at mid-Atlantic coastal loading locations and discharge ports in New England.

In the days before widespread use of petroleum, coal is the main source of heat and fuel for an industrialized nation. Coal from mines in West Virginia and Pennsylvania fueled the industrial revolution in America. Coal-fired boilers provide heat during cold New England winters and supply steam power for machinery in manufacturing plants and factories. Transportation of bituminous (soft) and anthracite (hard) coal from West Virginia and Pennsylvania is the domain of the railroads and independent shipping companies engaged specifically in the coal trade.

Bituminous is widely recognized as superior in its steam-generating qualities. With the development of manufactured gas in the 1840s, demand for bituminous increases. Manufactured gas is the process of heating combustible materials in an oven with an oxygen-lean atmosphere to extract gaseous compounds. Gases generated could be used for a variety of purposes including lighting (gas street lamps), heating, and cooking. Anthracite, with its smokeless properties, is in demand for domestic use between 1873 and 1898. Typically during this era of "King Coal," it's loaded on ships in ports closest to the mines by rail—places like Hampton Roads, Newport News, Norfolk, Philadelphia, and Port Reading (New Jersey). Despite Reading Railroad's early commitment to building steam colliers, the vast majority of coal transportation takes place in large sailing ships, usually immense wooden schooners with four, five, and even six masts. It's not until 1902 that the registered tonnage of steamers exceeds that of sailing vessels.

Moving coal by schooner has its drawbacks. Voyage times and schedules are at the mercy of the weather. Strong tidal currents in Delaware Bay, the mouth of Chesapeake Bay, Vineyard Sound, and Nantucket Sound are factors as well. Often sailing ships must anchor in great numbers at Vineyard Haven, Massachusetts, waiting for a favorable break in the weather or good tidal conditions to head out Pollack Rip Channel and continue their voyage east to Boston or Portland.

Wooden schooners have other limitations. They frequently leak, causing damage to cargo. Due in part to their relatively small hatch size and the presence of spars and rigging, they're difficult and time-consuming to load and unload. By the 1880s the British insurer Lloyds of London begins to discriminate in favor of iron and steel. Insurance premiums are on the rise for wooden ships.

All these drawbacks are incentives for the Reading Railroad to seek a better alternative to the transportation of coal by water. As an extremely wealthy company, the Reading Railroad can well afford to make large investments in the latest technology to improve their bottom line. Reading's management thinks a fleet of six new iron-hulled colliers will be just the ticket to improve service and boost profits. In 1872 the railroad publishes a small book titled, "Specifications for an iron screw collier to carry 1,200 tons of coal for the Philadelphia and Reading Railroad Co." This book of specifications describes all of the details for building new iron ships, from the material to be used for the masts to hatch dimensions and even a description of the ship's bell. Also included are the dimensions and specifications of the ships' engine and boilers. These are details we can use to try to identify the SS *Allentown* . . . if we ever find a likely wreck.

In November 1873, William Cramp & Sons delivers the first large iron steam collier, the SS *Reading*, to the railroad, and the other five ships launch in quick succession. The *Allentown* is the fifth ship in the series and is delivered in October 1874. All six new Reading colliers are named after Pennsylvania towns, the others being *Harrisburg, Lancaster, Williamsport,* and *Pottsville.*

The *Allentown* measures 248 feet in length, 37 feet abeam. It has a depth of hold of about 18 feet. Two water-tube boilers supply steam to a single vertical, direct-acting, independent, compound, surface-condensing engine. She displaces 1,283 gross tons. Her iron hull plates are double riveted below the waterline, and the ship's divided internally by four watertight bulkheads. To Reading Railroad's way of thinking, these safety features make her nearly unsinkable.

The railroad's six new steam colliers are an immediate success, proving themselves reliable, efficient, and seaworthy. Compared to the average coal schooner, they're more expensive to build and operate. Building costs for the new ships is $221 per registered ton, more than four times the cost of a new schooner. Crews are larger, too, twenty to twenty-four men compared to twelve on a sailing schooner. But the payoff comes in the number of reliable voyages each ship can make each year. A round-trip by steam collier from Hampton Roads to Boston and back averages about a week, including loading and discharging at each end. Schooners can take two, three, or even four weeks for the same journey.

On Wednesday, November 21, 1888, the Allentown departs Philadelphia heavily loaded with 1,660 tons of anthracite coal on what's to be her final voyage. She is bound for Salem, Massachusetts. Her crew numbers eighteen men. They're due to arrive on Saturday, November 24. But this is the season of great North Atlantic storms that come one right after another. Sometimes they compound and explode like atmospheric earthquakes such as the swordfisher the Andrea Gail *faced in* The Perfect Storm.

Shortly after clearing the mouth of Delaware Bay, the Allentown *runs into the teeth of a rapidly intensifying nor'easter. As the ship makes her way up the coast, the storm strengthens even more, slowing her progress. By the time the* Allentown's *east of Cape Cod, it's blowing a full hurricane, with wind speeds well in excess of seventy miles an hour.*

The farther north she comes, the worse conditions on the ship get. When fully loaded, the Allentown *and her sister ships do not have much freeboard, something like four to six feet. So now seas are no doubt continually sweeping the decks from bow to stern. Coming up the backside of Cape Cod and then shaping a course for Salem after clearing Highland Light near Provincetown on Cape Cod, the collier finds the howling northeast storm putting the wind and seas on her starboard bow.*

By now it's Tuesday the 27th, and it's almost certain in these storm conditions that hatches and fittings are leaking continuously. Although equipped with the latest in steam pumps, coal dust is no doubt clogging the suction strainers, making it difficult to keep the bilges free of water. Adding to Captain Paul's worries is his concern about the exposed approach to Salem Harbor in the northeast wind. A string of shoals and rock ledges lie just to the west of the channel, directly down wind.

One reef the Allentown *must pass near Gloucester has the ominous name of Norman's Woe. Like just about everyone else of his time, Captain Paul knows that Norman's Woe is the site of the tragedy depicted in Henry Wadsworth Longfellow's immensely popular poem of 1840, "The Wreck of the* Hesperus.*"*

Inspired by stories of shipwrecks during New England's Great Blizzard *of 1839, which destroyed about twenty ships and cost forty lives, Longfellow composed a narrative poem about a schooner coming to grief on Norman's Woe after her overconfident skipper sails into a nor'easter with his young daughter aboard.*

"Colder and louder blew the wind," wrote Longfellow. "The snow fell hissing in the brine...."

> *Down came the storm, and smote amain*
> *The vessel in its strength;*
> *She shuddered and paused, like a frighted steed,*
> *Then leaped her cable's length.*

With all sails gone and the ship at the mercy of the storm, the skipper lashes his daughter to the mainmast so she will not be swept overboard. At daybreak a fisherman finds the captain's daughter "lashed close to a drifting mast."

> *The salt sea was frozen on her breast,*
> *The salt tears in her eyes;*
> *And he saw her hair, like the brown sea-weed,*
> *On the billows fall and rise.*

These are hardly comforting images for Captain Paul to contemplate as he tries to bring his ship to Salem through this nor'easter. He knows making the approach as normal would put the wind and seas directly on the ship's starboard beam and the ledges directly to his leeward. Not a good situation. With daylight fading, the wind-driven spray, and heavy rain, visibility is poor at best, making it difficult if not impossible to spot channel markers in the approach to Salem.

Another nagging concern of Captain Paul's must be the previous summer's incidents. Did the grounding off New Bedford and striking that old wreck off Cape May damage or weaken the hull? The Allentown *has taken a tremendous beating in hurricane force winds and seas. Are previously weakened hull plates being strained beyond their limits? Are the rivets that bind the hull plates together stretching under the constant pounding of the seas?*

Longfellow describes the horror:

> *And fast through the midnight dark and drear,*
> *Through the whistling sleet and snow,*
> *Like a sheeted ghost, the vessel swept*
> *Tow'rds the reef of Norman's Woe.*

> *And ever the fitful gusts between*
> *A sound came from the land;*
> *It was the sound of the trampling surf*
> *On the rocks and the hard sea-sand.*

> *The breakers were right beneath her bows,*
> *She drifted a dreary wreck,*
> *And a whooping billow swept the crew*
> *Like icicles from her deck.*

And so eighteen men vanish into the night, into forgotten history, leaving a space in the lives of all who knew and loved them. A month after the loss, the ship's owners give each crew member's widow two months' pay. So goes the shipping industry. Reading Railroad declares bankruptcy in the 1970s and liquidates all its assets by the start of the twenty-first century.

The *Allentown* fascinates me. She's an early steamer from the same era as the *Newcastle City*. I know if we can find her, she will be a great wreck to dive. Large, iron, and built in one of the finest shipyards in the country, she has a lot to offer divers.

Back in the 1990s Tim Coleman, my dive buddies, and I start looking east and northeast of Minot's Ledge Lighthouse, relatively close to shore. The main source of data that Tim and I are working from is a hang log from a local dragger captain who also has an interest in shipwrecks. We have been slowly working our way through this log and steadily finding wrecks as we go, searching farther and farther northeast from Minot's into deeper water. On one particular day of side-scanning we find six different wrecks east of Boston Light. Going back and diving on these wrecks, we come up with one false alarm after another in our search for the *Allentown*. We find plenty of old wood wrecks and some steel ones mixed in, but no iron-hulled steamship.

One day in 2014, while aboard my good friends Heather Knowles and Dave Caldwell's boat the *Gauntlet*, we decide to check out a hang east of Boston and northeast of Minot's Light in about 245 feet of water. Dave and I jump in first to go down and tie in. We have a lot of scope in the anchor line and touch down on a mud bottom before we get to the hook. Swimming forward along the line, we come to our shot weight and grapple. Visibility's about fifteen feet and dark. As we come to the end of the line, I can see we're hooked into a trawl door. Initially I think we're on a fishing boat wreck. Then I look up and see standing in front of me a two-cylinder, compound steam engine. The rest of the wreck's very low-lying.

My initial thought is, *Jackpot*.

Most all of the scuttled wrecks in the Boston Dumping Ground had their engines removed prior to sinking. I'm sure this is not one of those. But looking at the engine more closely, I begin to have doubts it belongs to *Allentown*. This engine's relatively small, too small to be from a 1,200-ton collier. In comparison it's less than half the size of the *Newcastle City*'s engine. Looking closer, we see a steel plate lying flat on the bottom and then under that wooden framing. This wreck's wood, not iron. After further dives we come to the conclusion that this wreck's a small steamer called the *Pioneer*, which was lost in 1915. She has been on our "to find" list. We can check one more mystery solved . . . but still no *Allentown*.

Dave Caldwell and I have been close friends for many years, going back to the days when Dave owned a dive shop on the North Shore of Massachusetts Bay and I owned the *Grey Eagle*. Since then Dave has moved on from owning a dive shop and is running wreck-diving charters with Heather Knowles. Together they have cofound Northern Atlantic Dive Expeditions (NADE), a company focusing on exploration of shipwrecks in New England. In 2004 they built the *Gauntlet*, a thirty-six-foot boat designed from the keel up specifically for wreck diving.

Heather and Dave first dive from the *Quest* on a joint project with Tim and me to identify a large wreck we have located in 250 feet of water east of Boston. That wreck turns out to be the fishing trawler *Lonely*

Hunter. My first dive from the *Gauntlet*'s on the wreck of the *Talisman*, an ex-Navy subchaser that Heather and Dave find off Marblehead. Since then we've done too many dives together to remember.

Heather has been a member of the National Oceanographic and Atmospheric Administration's (NOAA) Stellwagen Bank National Marine Sanctuary Advisory Council for as long as I can remember. Currently she's chair of the council. The sanctuary consists of a 638-square-nautical mile area north of Cape Cod and east of Boston. It includes all of the shallow water of Stellwagen Bank, Tillies Bank, and part of Jeffreys Ledge, as well as deeper waters to the east and west of the bank. The sanctuary's western boundary extends from a point about three miles southeast of Eastern Point Lighthouse at the entrance to Glouces-ter Harbor to a point eight miles east of Green Harbor south of Scituate. Many shipwrecks lie within the sanctuary, including the side-wheel steamer *Portland*, which was lost with about two hundred passengers and crew in the storm of November 1898.

Part of the NOAA Office of National Marine Sanctuaries's mission is to preserve the cultural heritage sites within the sanctuary's boundaries. The sanctuary has two maritime archeologists assigned to administer this part of their program. The sanctuary archeologists have conducted side-scan sonar surveys of portions of the seafloor within the sanctuary and in so doing identified additional wreck sites. With the sanctuary's lim-ited diving resources and budget, sanctuary archeologist Matt Lawrence sometimes reaches out to Heather for assistance. What has developed is a cooperative research agreement between NOAA's Office of Marine Sanctuaries and NADE to investigate shipwreck sites in the sanctuary beyond the depths of recreational diving. Heather and Dave have hand-picked a group of divers to participate in this program, myself included. Over the past several years we have dived on and provided data in the form of images, observations, and measurements that have assisted in the interpretation of these sites.

During one of the sanctuary's sonar surveys in 2010, the sonar team aboard an NOAA research vessel images a wreck outside the western boundary of the sanctuary. The research vessel has been running east/ west lines and has to make wide sweeping turns at the end of each line due to the size of the sonar tow "fish" and the length of cable deployed. During one of these turns they obtain images of a wreck they were not previously aware of. The image quality is poor, but the wreck appears to be in two sections and substantial in size, with considerable acoustic shadow indicating noticeable relief.

In the course of Matt's research, he has located another wreck in deeper water within the sanctuary, possibly a four-masted schooner. Through a process of elimination, he's hoping to identify it. Given that this wreck is outside the sanctuary's boundary and within state waters, in the spring of 2016, Matt applies to the Massachusetts Board of Underwater Archeological Resources (MBUAR) for a special-use permit to investigate the site. Utilizing the cooperative research agreement, Heather and NADE will conduct the diving investigation of the site for Matt and the folks at Stellwagen Bank National Marine Sanctuary.

In the spring of 2016, Matt e-mails Heather and asks if we have anything at that location. Looking back through my records, I see that we do have a wreck in the area. Tim and I located a wreck there several years back. What appeared on the echo sounder was very low to the bottom and looked to be rather small. The wreck is very close to the location where the fishing vessel *Eve II* reportedly sank, so we have attributed this site to the remains of the F/V *Eve II*. But looking at the sonar image taken during the survey, I can see that the wreck the survey has found is much larger than a fishing vessel.

The first dive to the wreck comes in July 2016. Pulling up to the site, Heather maneuvers the *Gauntlet* to drop the shot line on the target below. Dave and I suit up as the rest of the crew gets everything else ready. By this summer I have fully transitioned over to diving a closed circuit rebreather, a Prism Topaz. Dave is diving a CCR also. With bailout bottles secured and surface checks made, Dave and I jump in as Heather makes a close pass by the shot line buoy. Dave's carrying a GoPro camera in a housing with lights.

After a quick bubble check just below the surface, we start down the line. It's dark going down with not much ambient light coming from the surface. Below 150 feet, it's totally black. Our lights are illuminating just a few feet ahead of us. But at touch down, we land right on top of the wreck. It has been a perfect drop with the shot line. The weight is lying on a lower portion of the wreck, and the shot line's draped across the high part.

From the moment we first land on the wreck, it's clear we're on the deck of an iron or steel ship. A set of mooring bitts are riveted in place inboard of the rail and to the left of our position. Pulling the shot line weight up from below us, Dave and I shackle the chain on the end of the line around the bitts, then send up Styrofoam cups to signal that we are tied in.

The wreck at this point has about 10 feet of relief and a max depth of 210 feet. To our right is a large circular trunk that extends up approximately 30 inches from the deck. It's about 5 feet in diameter and appears to be on the centerline of the hull, which is more or less intact and upright where we are. This trunk is probably what is left of the ship's smoke funnel. The deck appears to be iron or steel.

Visibility is only about five feet, so I clip my wreck reel line around the bitts where we've secured the shot line. Swimming over to the round trunk first and then in one direction along the hull, we come to where the metal decking ends. Exposed metal deck beams extend farther. This section of the wreckage seems to be the middle part of the ship's hull and appears to have broken away from both the bow and the stern. Turning around, we swim back in the other direction past the round trunk. In this direction the metal decking ends abruptly and seems to be more broken down. Descending into the broken lower section of the hull, we see heaps of coal everywhere. The hull plating is riveted to the framing. This indicates to me the wreck is most likely iron and predates WWII construction methods.

As we make our ascent and complete our decompression stops, I'm contemplating what we have just seen. Here's a wreck that's clearly old, probably iron, and most likely a steamship. It has a cargo of coal. All of these details make it a good match for the *Allentown*. There's just one problem: the location. If this is the *Allentown*, why is she here? It just does not make sense to me right now.

We're excited to get back out to the wreck later in the summer, but we're running out of available time. Most of us on the team have a dive

The *Allentown*'s steam gauge panel on the side of the engine
HEATHER KNOWLES

trip to Sardinia scheduled for September. And due to my work schedule captaining a Vane Brothers' tug, it will be October before I can go diving here again. By then the weather patterns are sure to change. It's not likely we can get another dive on the wreck this season.

But all is not lost. Heather, Dave, and I agree that having some high-resolution side-scan images of the wreck would really help us to get a feel for the site. I reach out to my friend Mark Munro in Rhode Island, a very accomplished shipwreck researcher and diver. He owns a survey company specializing in side-scan sonar operations.

Mark side-scans the site for us in early September, resulting in some really high-quality images that make a big difference in our ability to interpret the wreck site. The images show a wreck in three pieces, lying in an east-west arc, with the bow to the west. The bow section is facing southwest. The midships section is oriented east-west, and the stern section lies northwest-southeast. The bow and midships sections are well intact with ten to fifteen feet of relief. The stern section is very broken down and low to the bottom. Looking at the side-scan images, I am growing more and more convinced that what Tim and I thought to be the *Eve II* is, in fact, the stern section of the *Allentown*.

The dive we made in 2016 confirmed the wreck was not the four-masted schooner Matt was looking for, so in the spring of 2017 Matt surrenders the special-use permit for the site held by SBNMS. We are very grateful to Matt and SBNMS for sharing this site with us. Now Heather applies for and receives a new permit, which is granted to NADE with Heather having the role of lead investigator and taking charge of the project.

Heather and Dave schedule wreck charters almost every weekend aboard the *Gauntlet*, so exploration and research trips have to be worked into the schedule in advance. The summer of 2017 proves to be a tough one for weather. Only one exploration trip makes it to what may be the SS *Allentown*. As it turns out, I'm unable to go, but the rest of the team has a great day on the wreck. Conditions are perfect, and the visibility is astounding, on the order of twenty-five to thirty feet. They dive the bow section, and Dave gets some spectacular video of the bow, the anchor windlass, and the two huge anchors. The port anchor's still in the catted position. The starboard anchor has broken loose from its lashings and is hanging from its chain out of the hawse pipe, a testament to the violence of the storm that sunk this ship.

After seeing the video, I am really stoked to get back to the wreck. Unfortunately the weather's not cooperating with our wreck-diving ambitions, and we have to wait another year. Over time I collect a great deal of information about the *Allentown* and her sister ships, including plans, photographs, a copy of the builders specification book, and much more. With Dave's video and the side-scan images, I can compare what I see to the plans and photographs. More and more features start matching up. As I match features on the wreck with historical images and plans, a scenario for the sinking begins to come into focus.

I picture myself on the bridge of the Allentown. *We've been taking a ter-rific beating for the past couple of days. Seas thirty-feet and greater are sweep-*

Foredeck of the *Allentown* with bitts and anchor windlass
HEATHER KNOWLES

ing the deck from bow to stern. The pumps have been running continuously. But the strainers keep clogging with coal dust turned into paste by salt water. Chief engineer Ben Prichard and his gang are constantly fighting to keep the strainers clear.

Our flooding problems are coming from more than water leaking through the hatch covers. Something else is causing the water to rise in the bilges, and the flooding's getting worse. The grounding this summer off New Bedford was a hard one on that rock ledge. Supposedly there was no damage to the hull, but I'm starting to have my doubts. And then there's that wreck that we hit off Cape May later in the summer. But we're deeply loaded with cargo, and there's no way to check those lower hull plates buried under more than 1,600 tons of anthracite coal. We're fighting a losing battle.

The question is, can we keep her afloat just long enough to make port or possibly get into a lee someplace that will lessen the strain on the hull? It's not looking good, but just maybe there's a chance. Having passed Highland Light roughly six hours ago, we should be near the tip of Stellwagen Bank southeast of Gloucester. We've been running at reduced speed to ease the pounding on the hull, and by my estimate we're four hours from the entrance to Salem Harbor. Looking at the chart again, I'm reminded of the rocky shoals between Newcomb Ledge and Baker's Island at the entrance to the channel leading into Salem. We sure don't want to be caught with this northeast wind and sea right on the beam as we make our way up the outer approach to Salem's narrow channel. But we can't hug the coast of Cape Ann too close, which has snares of its own like Misery Island and Norman's goddamn Woe. This isn't a happy coast.

It would be good to put wind and seas astern and try to ease the strain on the hull. So we head the ship in the direction of Eastern Point Lighthouse at the entrance to Gloucester Harbor. When the Allentown *gets close, we can turn downwind and head for a point just below Norman's Woe to make our approach to Salem from the east. It's not a direct course for Salem, but being up under the lee of Cape Ann will lessen the strain on the hull considerably. Facing downwind we might just be able to see better. Right now looking straight into the teeth of this storm, we're steaming blind. If it's not yet sunset, it feels like it. The sky is black as all hell. The clapper in the bell at the bow has come loose and is clanging, ceaselessly clanging. If only we can just find Eastern Point, if only we can get a bearing off the flashing lighthouse, we can turn downwind . . . and stand a good chance of making it.*

The 2018 season gets off to a tough start. Our first two trips scheduled for July are blown out due to weather. The third trip in early August is a go, but I'm unable to make it due to a change in my work schedule. Conditions on the wreck are less than ideal, but the rest of the team is able to get dives in on the bow section, and Dave shoots more video. Meanwhile I'm at work taking delivery of my new 505-foot ATB (articulated tug and barge) for Vane Brothers from a shipyard in Texas. But I'm pacing the decks of tug *Chincoteague* in anticipation of what the dive team might find.

The divers look for bronze letters on the outside of the hull at the bow and search for the bell on the foredeck, all without success. When I get home from Texas on Wednesday, August 15, we have a trip scheduled for that Sunday the 19th. I'm pumped and ready to go. Unfortunately Mother Nature has different plans. As the weekend approaches, so does another strong low-pressure system. By Saturday morning its clear nobody's diving anywhere in the ocean in New England tomorrow. We've been blown out again, and my frustration's mounting. We need some time on the wreck to nail down its identity. But this is hurricane season, and the season of nor'easters looms.

The following weekend is our last scheduled dive trip of the year, Sunday, August 26. As the weekend approaches, things are looking promising. Saturday morning I assemble my CCR in my garage workshop and double-check the rest of my gear. I'm ready to go. All we need is a good day tomorrow. Getting up at 4:00 the next morning, I come down to my kitchen to have a quick breakfast before jumping in my car for the drive to Beverly where the *Gauntlet* is moored. I packed the car with all my gear last night. Sitting down at the island in our kitchen, I look out over Buzzards Bay and the approach to New Bedford harbor. It's flat calm without a breath of wind. It's going to be a good day. Maybe an unforgettable day.

The top of the low pressure cylinder on the *Allentown*'s engine
HEATHER KNOWLES

I pull up in the parking lot at the Beverly town pier around 6:00 a.m. Heather and Dave are already here. Over the next half hour the rest of the crew arrives and loads their gear. We're underway by 7:00 and heading out into Massachusetts Bay. The weather's clear and bright with a slight groundswell from the south. As we near the wreck site, Dave, Feng Zhang, and I suit up. The others get the down line ready. Heather maneuvers the *Gauntlet* over the wreck, and the crew deploys the down line.

Dave, Feng, and I hit the water. We're all diving CCRs, and after a quick bubble and gear check we start down the line. At first the visibility does not look good at all. There's a lot of particulate matter in the water, reducing the visibility to less than ten feet in the upper part of the water column. But once we're below about fifty feet, it starts to clear out in the colder water below the surface layers. It's getting dark real fast as we descend, and before we know it, all we can see is what we illuminate with our dive lights.

We touch down on the bow section of the wreck on the port side and tie into some exposed deck beams. Visibility is a dark ten to twelve feet . . . if we're careful not to stir up too much silt. It's not great, but it's good enough so we don't need to run a line from a safety reel.

Dave has been on the bow section twice before. This is the first for me. We start swimming forward along the port rail. Water depth is 190 feet. A minute or two later the port anchor comes into view resting horizontally in the stowed position. It's a huge stock anchor, probably eight or ten feet high and weighing around five thousand pounds. Moving inboard, we come to the companionway that leads down into the crew's quarters in the fo'c'sle. The wooden covering is gone, but the iron flange on the deck remains with the steps leading down. Immediately forward of the companionway is a slightly raised foredeck and the anchor windlass. Aft of the windlass is a davit used for catting and stowing the anchors. In my mind I hear the clanging of the bow bell. I look around the windlass for it but do not find it. There's only the clanging.

Dave and I drop aft a few feet to a hole in the deck. Passing through the hole we end up in the forward cargo hold. There are iron pillars supporting the deck above, iron cross braces, and big mounds of coal below us. We swim forward to where the iron casing for the companionway stairs meets the forward watertight bulkhead. To our right and to starboard is a hole in the bulkhead. So much for watertight bulkheads.

The hole's big enough to swim through, sort of. I move forward trying to be careful not to disturb too much silt. There is a fine layer of soft mud and silt all over everything. It absorbs light, making everything even darker than it actually is. If stirred up, it can reduce the visibility to zero in a flash.

We need to be able to find our way back out of the wreck's interior, so caution is the word of the day. Moving forward I swim up to the hole and wiggle through. Now I'm in the very forward part of the ship. There is a layer of mud probably about four feet deep in this compartment. It's more mounded up on the port side than the starboard. I can see portholes high up on each side and outboard, three on the starboard side, only two on the port side. I look around for a couple of minutes to get the lay of the compartment. I'm not going to lie. I feel like a man trapped in a sinking ship in here. This is a tomb.

I'm pretty glad to see Dave waiting for me on the outside of the bulkhead. He's my safety spotter in case I get into trouble in here. I join him, and we head aft and then back up through the hole in the deck where Feng's spotting for us.

After coming back up on deck, I look over the starboard rail and see the starboard anchor hanging by its chain coming out of the hawse pipe; it's huge. From there, we swim aft to the first cargo hatch coaming, which is partially distorted but recognizable. Close to the hatch is a long horizontal shaft with gypsy heads on each end. Everything I'm seeing on the wreck—the anchors, windlass, davit, raised foredeck, portholes in the fo'c'sle, companionway, and horizontal capstan arrangement—match perfectly with the photos and plans we have of the *Allentown* and her sister ships.

I swim along the outboard side of the hull just below the rail. I'm feeling my way on the hull plating as I go, hoping to come across a bronze letter bolted in place. Sometimes on older ships the name is attached to either side of the bow and across the transom in raised bronze letters. But no luck today for me with letters.

It's OK. I take a deep breath and hover above that dangling anchor and those heaps of coal . . . that nearly made it to Salem. Safety lies just ten miles to the west of here and Norman's Woe. Without a doubt, I know what I'm looking at now: the *Allentown*. An unlucky ship. A tomb moldering away in the land of broken dreams. A monument to what men will risk even for something as unglamorous as coal.

Once again I'm sailing with a doomed crew in its god-forsaken ship. She's still steaming north, northwest, trying to reach Eastern Point Light by dead reckoning. We don't have far to go, another hour or two at most. But the Allentown's *stern's getting heavier and heavier. The pumps are failing, and the water's rising in the holds aft. That damn bow bell is still clanging away. With the after two holds flooding the stern of the ship is awash. We're losing positive buoyancy. The engine room and boiler room are starting to flood. The engine's losing power as the water laps at the fireboxes.*

I can see a flash of light ahead through the rain and darkness. I think it's Eastern Point Light. It has to be Eastern Point. But the stern is going under. The seas are battering the bridge. I can't feel the throbbing of the engine. The ship is no longer moving forward. She's starting to yawl port, then to starboard, and rolling in a beam sea. Windows are shattering. A torrent of foam is rushing in. Over the helm, over the engine room telegraph pedestal, over the compass. We've got to abandon ship.

Captain Paul shouts, "It's every man for himself now, boys!"

But there's no more time. The weight of the ship and its 1,660 tons of black diamonds are dragging the stern of the Allentown *to the bottom . . . with us in her. The stern of the ship slams into the bottom first. The impact crushes it.*

The bow, with some positive buoyancy left, is still above water, barely. The shrieking wind and those thirty-foot waves from the northeast are slamming against the bow, beginning to rotate the ship around on her stern to face west, down wind.

Iron's a rather brittle metal. The stresses on the hull are causing it to fracture. The Allentown *breaks in two up forward at the number two hold. Then the heaviest part of the ship, with the engine and boiler room, tears away back aft. It sinks like a rock straight down and lands on the bottom upright, level and oriented east to west. As the bow section breaks away, the last of the air trapped inside of it explodes like a geyser above the waves as it veers downwind and sinks. It comes to rest on the seafloor facing southwest a short distance from the midships section. From eighteen dead men. From us. From Norman's Woe. From Longfellow's "Hesperus."*

So ends the voyage, a mere few miles off the coast of Gloucester and safe harbor. So near and yet so far.

For me and the rest of the dive team, finding this wreck is a bittersweet victory. We want to cheer our discovery, but we feel the terror of the *Allentown's* crew. We feel their families' losses. We feel humbled, yet

Allentown exploration team on the *Gauntlet*, left to right, Author, David Caldwell, Heather Knowles, Josh Rackley, Jessica Morrison, Feng Zhang, Tim Maxwell, Scott Tomlinson, John Minigan
HEATHER KNOWLES

again, by the fierce power of the North Atlantic. And we know that we have a duty to the families of those eighteen lost crewmen to say that after almost 130 years, "We know where and how and why your loved ones never came home." We've found them. And we will never forget. That's what divers do.

The Wreck of the Hesperus
by Henry Wadsworth Longfellow

It was the schooner Hesperus,
That sailed the wintry sea;
And the skipper had taken his little daughtèr,
To bear him company.

Blue were her eyes as the fairy-flax,
Her cheeks like the dawn of day,
And her bosom white as the hawthorn buds,
That ope in the month of May.

The skipper he stood beside the helm,
His pipe was in his mouth,
And he watched how the veering flaw did blow
The smoke now West, now South.

Then up and spake an old Sailòr,
Had sailed to the Spanish Main,
"I pray thee, put into yonder port,
For I fear a hurricane.

"Last night, the moon had a golden ring,
And to-night no moon we see!"
The skipper, he blew a whiff from his pipe,
And a scornful laugh laughed he.

Colder and louder blew the wind,
A gale from the Northeast,

The snow fell hissing in the brine,
And the billows frothed like yeast.

Down came the storm, and smote amain
The vessel in its strength;
She shuddered and paused, like a frighted steed,
Then leaped her cable's length.

"Come hither! come hither! my little daughtèr,
And do not tremble so;
For I can weather the roughest gale
That ever wind did blow."

He wrapped her warm in his seaman's coat
Against the stinging blast;
He cut a rope from a broken spar,
And bound her to the mast.

"O father! I hear the church-bells ring,
Oh say, what may it be?"
"'T is a fog-bell on a rock-bound coast!"—
And he steered for the open sea.

"O father! I hear the sound of guns,
Oh say, what may it be?"
"Some ship in distress, that cannot live
In such an angry sea!"

"O father! I see a gleaming light,
Oh say, what may it be?"
But the father answered never a word,
A frozen corpse was he.

Lashed to the helm, all stiff and stark,
With his face turned to the skies,
The lantern gleamed through the gleaming snow
On his fixed and glassy eyes.

Then the maiden clasped her hands and prayed
That savèd she might be;
And she thought of Christ, who stilled the wave
On the Lake of Galilee.

And fast through the midnight dark and drear,
Through the whistling sleet and snow,
Like a sheeted ghost, the vessel swept
Tow'rds the reef of Norman's Woe.

And ever the fitful gusts between
A sound came from the land;
It was the sound of the trampling surf
On the rocks and the hard sea-sand.

The breakers were right beneath her bows,
She drifted a dreary wreck,
And a whooping billow swept the crew
Like icicles from her deck.

She struck where the white and fleecy waves
Looked soft as carded wool,
But the cruel rocks, they gored her side
Like the horns of an angry bull.

Her rattling shrouds, all sheathed in ice,
With the masts went by the board;
Like a vessel of glass, she stove and sank,
Ho! ho! the breakers roared!

At daybreak, on the bleak sea-beach,
A fisherman stood aghast,
To see the form of a maiden fair,
Lashed close to a drifting mast.

The salt sea was frozen on her breast,
The salt tears in her eyes;

And he saw her hair, like the brown sea-weed,
    On the billows fall and rise.

Such was the wreck of the Hesperus,
    In the midnight and the snow!
Christ save us all from a death like this,
    On the reef of Norman's Woe!

EPILOGUE

The SS *Lyonnaise*

SS *Lyonnaise*, painting by Lebreton
UK NATIONAL MARITIME MUSEUM

2019

WHAT'S NEXT FOR OUR TEAM OF DIVERS AND WRECK HUNTERS? How about an actual treasure ship?

Our team of divers and wreck hunters is deep into research on a French passenger ship named the *Lyonnaise*. I first heard about this ship while reading the book *Passenger Liners of the Western Ocean* by Vernon Gibbs. Gibbs dedicates only two pages to the *Lyonnaise*, but those two pages have been more than enough to spark my interest to start digging for more information. She's the first French steamship to cross the Atlantic . . . and she's known to have sunk somewhere off the coast of Southern New England in 1856 with a cargo of gold species (coins) aboard.

On October 30, 1856, the Lyonnaise, *under the command of Captain Deveaux, departs New York bound for Le Harve, France. Built as an iron-hulled passenger steamship for the Compagnie Franco Americaine Line, she has steam-driven side wheels for propulsion. She carries a bark rig for sailing to conserve her limited coal supply, and she's fitted out to transporting high-value cargo. In a number of ways she's similar to the SS* Newcastle City. *Built at Laird's shipyard in Liverpool, England, in 1855 and 1856, her iron hull measures 200 feet long and 34 feet abeam. She displaces 1,655 gross tons and carries three masts for her bark rig. She has one smoke funnel amidships.*

On board are thirty-nine cabin passengers and many more passengers in steerage. Also on board is a mixed cargo of freight and gold species. After dropping the pilot, the Lyonnaise *steers east toward the southern tip of Nantucket Shoals. From there she will take a great circle course toward France.*

The following day the captain's noon sun sight shows that the Lyonnaise *is on course and making good speed. At about 11:00 p.m. that night the bark* Adriatic, *out of Belfast, Maine, bound for Savannah, appears close off the starboard beam of the* Lyonnaise. *There's a thick haze. Visibility is far from ideal, and it's difficult to judge distances at night when there are few reference points except another ship's running lights.*

Captain Durham of the Adriatic *is steering northwest on the wind. After sighting the steamer's running lights and glow of her funnel through the haze steering northeast by east, he endeavors to tack the ship. While her topsails are shaking in the process of coming about,* Adriatic *strikes the* Lyonnaise *abaft her wheelhouse on the starboard side. Durham hails the* Lyonnaise *and asks it to standby, but the* Lyonnaise *disappears in the mist. Taking stock of damage to his bark, Durham decides it best to head for Gloucester. He arrives there on November 4.*

Meanwhile the drama aboard Lyonnaise is just starting to unfold. Struck by the Adriatic *at 11:00 p.m., she has been running more or less with the wind on the quarter. She continues on course for another ten minutes after the collision before the crew realizes she is leaking through damage to iron plating. Water is rising rapidly in the fire room, and the flooding eventually extinguishes the coal fires under the boilers. With the ship filling with water and the loss of steam pressure, the crew must man the manual pumps. Meanwhile a damage-control party attempts to patch the leak with canvas, shoring timber and whatever else the chief and ship's carpenter can come up with. They stem the flow of seawater to some extent, but not enough.*

As dawn breaks the next morning, the ship is still afloat, but barely. It's becoming clear the crew and passengers will have to take to the ship's small boats. Pumping of the ship continues all day until around three in the afternoon. At this point Captain Deveaux decides the time is right to get as many people into the boats as possible while it's still daylight. The Lyonnaise *is dead in the water, beginning to roll heavily in the ocean swells. It may not last the night.*

The crew launches two cutters, each loaded with twenty-five persons. First officer Roussell commands one boat. Two sea captains who have been traveling as passengers take charge of the second boat. The crew also loads two lifeboats, the first with twenty persons and the third mate Dublot. The second lifeboat carries eighteen people and second mate Luguirre. The remaining crew tie a raft and two yawl boats astern for their eventual escape. Each boat is equipped with a sextant, a chronometer, and as much food and water as the crew can gather from the pantry.

At 7:00 the following morning, November 2, Captain Deveaux and his skeleton crew abandon their ship into the yawl boats. The Lyonnaise *wallows with her decks awash for an hour before sinking beneath the waves, presumably with her load of gold coins. All the boats start pulling and sailing to the northwest, toward Cape Cod. Later that day, just before dark, the boats become separated in fog. Then the winds starts to rise, and by 9:00 that evening it's blowing a gale out of the north. The brutal weather patterns of Nantucket Shoals strike again.*

Four days later, on November 6, Luguirre in lifeboat number two sights a ship on the horizon just before nightfall, but it sails on by. The next day the ship Neptune, *bound from New York to Liverpool, spots and recovers a boat from the* Lyonnaise, *but the boat is empty save for a chronometer and spyglass.*

Continuing to steer his boat northwest, Luguirre sights a ship north of his position on November 8, but it too sails on without spotting the castaways. Finally, after being in a small boat for nine days, Luguirre sights the bark Elsie *on the horizon. She's bound from New York to Bremen, Germany. A short while later Captain Nordenblott of the* Elsie *maneuvers his ship alongside lifeboat number two. There are fifteen survivors left out of the eighteen who originally boarded the boat.*

The next day Elsie *transfers thirteen of the survivors, including second mate Luguirre, to a westbound ship, which lands them in New York a few days later. As for the* Lyonnaise, *her cargo of gold, Captain Deveaux, and 130 other human beings who began this transatlantic voyage? They vanish without a trace.*

But maybe not forever. With the help of a new researcher who has joined our team, we hope to uncover clues to the location of the *Lyonnaise*, her gold, and her lost souls. Jennifer Sellitti, a public defender in New Jersey, is using her legal sleuthing skills to unearth evidence that will point us to the final resting place of the *Lyonnaise*. Eventually she aims to write a book about the ship, its treasure, and our search for the wreck.

Perhaps this will be "the one." No doubt it will be another adventure.

A Postscript

The Lost and the Survivors

Over time I have learned that for me hunting shipwrecks is, in the end, about people. First of all it is about sharing these adventures with my wife Lori, friends like Tim Coleman, an amazing group of dive buddies, and the general public.

But it's also about stepping into the shoes of the sea's heroes, its victims, its survivors, and their families. It's about empathy. About coming to terms with the ghosts that can haunt you during a long mid watch (12:00–4:00 a.m.) on a black ocean when there's nothing to keep you from your thoughts but a plodding ship's icon on a GPS display and the circular sweep of a green line on the radar.

At these moments, as well as on deep dives to a wreck and on deco stops, I find myself connecting in indescribable ways to men like Tom Blom as he fights an engine room fire on the *Baleen*. With Bill Kenefick standing his watch on the bridge of the *Exxon Chester*, helpless to stop his massive tanker from slicing through the starboard side of the *Regal Sword*. With Wilma McLean Tucciarone, staring from the promenade deck of the liner *Stephano* and wondering if that German U-boat out there is about to end our lives.

There are lighter moments, though, like when I'm with the crew of the *Newcastle City*, sipping hard cider with the men of the Nantucket lightship and singing English carols on Christmas Eve in the midst of a raging storm. Still sometimes I feel Chief Ben Prichard's do-or-die urgency. I'm down in the bilge of the SS *Allentown* with the chief as he tries every trick he can think of to free coal sludge from the pumps and strainers. But the water keeps rising above his waist. The seas rumbles over the deck above, and he begs his god to watch over those he will leave behind.

During the winter of 2018 to 2019, following the identification of the wreck off Norman's Woe as the SS *Allentown*, my research and writing partner Randy Peffer and I make a concerted effort to find the descendants of the lost crew of the *Allentown* and tell them that after 130 years the final resting place of their families' loved ones has been found. We start with the crew list published by newspapers at the time of the accident. There are eighteen names on that list.

- Captain: George W. Paul, Philadelphia
- First Mate: Joseph Ross, Philadelphia
- Second Mate: Peter Livingston, Boston
- Steward: John Duvall, Philadelphia
- Mess Boy: John Hoolahan, Philadelphia
- Seaman: Franz Maruardt, Philadelphia
- Seaman: Martin Johanson, Philadelphia
- Seaman: John Johansen, Philadelphia
- Seaman: John Samelson, Philadelphia
- Seaman: John Pedering, Philadelphia
- Ordinary: Patrick Emle, Philadelphia
- Chief Engineer: Benjamin Prichard, Penns Grove, New Jersey
- Assistant Engineer: Henry Haywood, Philadelphia
- Fireman: August Tormacio, Philadelphia
- Fireman: Francis McTamany, Philadelphia
- Fireman: Otto Borsun, Philadelphia
- Coal Passer: Harry Adams, Penns Grove, New Jersey
- Coal Passer: James McKeever, Philadelphia

Most of these men and their families prove impossible to find using Internet and ancestry websites, because we know so little about them. We only have a name, an occupation, a death date, and a hometown. And for most of the lost crew, the listing of Philadelphia as a hometown is simply too vague and inaccurate to help us narrow the search.

But in the case of the *Allentown*'s skipper, Captain George W. Paul, we do penetrate that vague hometown reference to Philadelphia and find our man. Using findagrave.com we discover the captain's actual hometown: Belvidere, New Jersey. It's on the upper reaches of the Delaware River.

There's a memorial stone in his honor in the Belvidere Cemetery.

IN MEMORY OF
CAPT. GEORGE W. PAUL
SON OF
THOMAS & SARA T. PAUL
LOST AT SEA NOV 25, 1888
"THE SEA IS HIS"

Next to the memorial stone, a small American flag flutters. It is a veterans' memorial flag. We like seeing that flag. Maybe it has been placed there by someone thinking Paul was in the US Navy . . . and maybe he was in the navy at one point in his life. But maybe the flag has been placed there by some savvy person who knows about the long fight merchant mariners who served in WWII pursued to gain veteran status in 1988.

Being licensed civilian captains, Randy and I take pride in knowing that some of our fellow merchant mariners have won veteran status in the eyes of the government. US merchant mariners suffered the highest rate of casualties of any service in WW II. Almost 4 percent of the 243,000 US merchant mariners who shipped out during WWII never came home. About 9,500 sailors died aboard 1,554 sunken ships.

As for Captain Paul? Our research shows that besides his parents, who likely placed the memorial stone in the cemetery to honor him, he had two sisters. Further research shows those sisters lived together in New Jersey through old age. Neither married or had children. Since the captain of the *Allentown* never married or had children, the story of his close relatives and descendants ends with the deaths of his sisters. There's no family to share our news with here.

But Randy and I don't give up hope. Thinking we might have more luck finding the families of the lost mariners with less generic home-towns than Philadelphia, we turn our attention to the two men in the *Allentown*'s crew from Penns Grove, New Jersey. It's a small town near the head of Delaware Bay in the largely rural area of Salem and Glouces-ter Counties.

Ancestry websites turn up nothing for coal passer Harry Adams, but they do find Chief Engineer Benjamin Prichard and trace his direct ancestors down three generations to the 1940s. Then the trail goes cold. Not giving up, Randy and I turn to archivists in Salem County, New Jersey. They cannot come up with any records, but they refer us to the researchers at the historical society in nearby Gloucester County.

Then one day in early December 2018, we receive an e-mail saying,

We looked into your request to find a living ancestor of Captain Benjamin Prichard. I'm happy to report we had some success.

Researcher Stacey Costantino has pieced together a complete picture of Chief Engineer Benjamin Prichard's direct descendants for us. The pdf file that she sends opens with an article from the *Penns Grove Record* from December 1888. It says that Chief Prichard leaves behind his thirty-three-year-old wife, Ella, and nine-year-old daughter Alma. We cannot imagine the loss that Alma and her mother feel when they learn the *Allentown* has been lost at sea with all hands. It must be devastating. Although a young woman, Ella never remarries. She lives the rest of her life with Alma, Alma's husband Joe Curriden, and the couple's daughter Mildred.

Stacey traces the chief's ancestors down to Prichard's recently deceased great-great-grandson John M. Slovak. Like the chief, he died young, at just age forty-seven. He was a USCG vet, and his obituary picture shows him in his USCG uniform. We're intrigued. What com-pelled the great-great-grandson of Chief Prichard to go to sea, especially to go to sea in a service renowned for its mission to rescue mariners in peril? Was USCG service just a whim or an inherited fascination with seafaring? Did a great-great-grandson hear the lost chief calling to him in his hour of need?

We also learn from his obituary that Slovak shared Chief Prichard's penchant for mechanics. After his stint in the USCG, he became a welding instructor at the Artificial Island Nuclear Generating Facility Training Center in Delaware Bay.

And the story doesn't end here. Slovak and Chief Prichard have living survivors. They are the chief's great-great-great-grandchildren Jennifer and Kevin Slovak. Both are young adults. Jennifer left Southern New Jersey in her late teens to live in British Columbia. But Kevin, his wife April, and young daughters Skylar and Gianna remain living within just a few miles of Chief Prichard's home on the upper reaches of Delaware Bay. And like his father before him, Kevin works at the Artificial Island Nuclear Generating Facility.

In late December 2018, Randy and I send a letter to Kevin, and in early January 2019, he contacts us. As it turns out, until we contact the Slovaks, they know nothing about Chief Prichard or the loss of the SS *Allentown*.

"The only family record I have is an old Bible," Kevin tells me.

We send him copies of our research on the *Allentown* and a pdf of the genealogical research from the Gloucester County Historical Society Library.

"To get this news is, well, mind-blowing," he says. "I'm a history buff, and my first thought is how can I help."

He speaks fondly about his father, who raised him as a single parent from the age of nine after his parents divorced. Kevin says that in his prime John Slovak was a big man, 6 feet 4 inches, 240 pounds, with the appropriate nickname of "Sledge."

"He was a character," says April, "a big teddy bear. He looked like an old biker dude with a full gray beard and a ponytail." He loved to ride all manner of motorcycles, and, of course, he had skull and bones tattoos.

"Every tat had a story," says Kevin. "My dad was definitely a man of the world."

As it turns out, Sledge Slovak was not just an ordinary Coasty. He was a USCG rescue swimmer who served in Alaska, Panama, and the

Bermuda Triangle during his seafaring. Being a Coasty myself, I have always admired rescue swimmers. Their job is possibly the most dangerous job in the service. It takes immense courage to do that work. Sledge Slovak had that.

I can picture him, and in picturing Sledge, I feel like I could be seeing his great-great-grandfather as well. They were men of action, men of courage, men who loved machinery, men with big hearts, men dedicated to their families, men blessed with uncommon determination and resilience.

Life called on Sledge for the same kind of tenacity that the lost chief must have mustered during his final hours aboard the SS *Allentown*. In his early thirties, Sledge developed a rare disease called Alpha One that caused his lungs to crystalize from the inside out. Doctors only gave him six months to live. But he fought Alpha One for sixteen years until he saw his children grown safely to adulthood and launched on their own trajectories.

"My father would have loved to know more about his family," Kevin tells us. "He was a good man and a great dad. He fought very hard his last few years. I tell myself each day that he fought so hard to make sure he put his foot in my butt and make me a better man before he went. Now I'm filling his shoes." Today Kevin operates and maintains a gamma light irradiator at the Artificial Island Nuclear Generating Facility where his dad worked.

Through conversations and e-mails, Randy and I learn remarkable things about Kevin, too. Like his father he shares Ben Prichard's courage, resilience, big heart, and pluck. It turns out that when Kevin was just thirteen years old, his father became too sick to work. Kevin became Sledge's primary caregiver, tending not only to his dad emotionally, but also managing his medications and oxygen equipment.

"It was hard," he says, "but during my dad's last years, April stepped in to help, too."

As for his work operating a nuclear reactor?

"There's a lot to learn about working with radiation, but I am succeeding very well here and doing a lot of schooling on my job," says the chief's great-great-great-grandson. This steely determination and pride in a job well done could very well be the same sentiments the chief felt about his mastery of the engine room and machinery on the *Allentown*, the same pride Sledge Slovak felt about his work as a USCG rescue swimmer.

"It would have made my dad so happy to know that I am doing great in life," says Kevin. "I have two very beautiful little girls, three years and six years of age. I wish he got to meet them."

Kevin's love of family is palpable and compelling. Without question, it's this same love that must have energized Chief Prichard to go above and beyond the call of duty to keep the *Allentown*'s engine and pumps going during those final desperate hours, even as his ship was flooding. The same love kept Sledge Slovak fighting his lung disease for sixteen years so he could shepherd his son and daughter to adulthood.

When Randy and I began searching for Chief Prichard's family, we hoped the discovery of the *Allentown* would bring the family some peace to know the final resting place of Chief Prichard and his shipmates had been found at last. We wanted to share the story with the chief's descendants of how he and the rest of the men in that Reading collier rallied to keep their failing ship afloat off Norman's Woe and tried to bring her to safe harbor in the face of a killer nor'easter, in the heart of a perfect storm.

What we could not have imagined when we reached out to the chief's descendants was that we would find two more compelling stories of courage and indomitable spirit. Sledge Slovak's story of beating the odds, of loving his family, of not laying down and waiting for death is every bit as powerful as the story of Chief Prichard and the men of the *Allentown*. Kevin Slovak's story of becoming his father's caregiver as a young adolescent is equally remarkable.

Sometimes this is how it goes when you hunt for shipwrecks: You end up in the presence of great souls. Bless them all.

Sources & Acknowledgments

A cadre of wreck divers, explorers, commercial fishermen, and professional mariners are at the core of this book. These men and women not only shared the researching, hunting, diving, dangers, and adventures related here, but they shared friendship. None of these projects would have been possible without their dedication and teamwork. Shipwreck projects always have been and always will be a team effort. No one person can do this alone.

This book could never have been written if it were not for my wife Lori. Her love and support over the years during our ups and downs have meant the world to me. She is much more than my wife; she is my soul mate and best friend. Lori is also my partner in maritime and underwater adventures. Lori was with us on many of the adventures described in this book, both as a diver and boat captain on the *Grey Eagle* and the *Quest*. She and I have been shipmates for over thirty years. A veteran of the USCG, she's a licensed professional mariner and a skilled diver.

My dear friend Randy Peffer has been a shipmate in every sense of the word on this project and others afloat and ashore. Most important, Randy has been my writing partner for this book. We have shared numerous adventures together sailing and on boat projects of various sorts. Randy has guided me in the ways of the book publishing community and given me very valuable lessons in writing styles and how to compose and tell a story. His guidance has been of immeasurable help.

A tight brotherhood of wreck enthusiasts have given freely of their time and wisdom to share in the expeditions related in *Dangerous Shallows* and to help this book be thorough, accurate, and enlightening. In no particular order these friends include: Tim Coleman, Mark Stanton, Mike Manfredi, Steve Bielenda, Hank Garvin, Bill Amaru, Brian

Skerry, Butch Amaral, Dave Morton, Pat Morton, Mark Blackwell, Steve Scheuer, Fred Robinson, Leroy Tolentino, Michael Dudas, Tom Packer, Steve Gatto, Bart Malone, Joe Mazraani, Jennifer Sellitti, Tom Mulloy, Pat Rooney, Heather Knowles, Dave Caldwell, John Moyer, Anthony Tedeschi, Harold Moyers, Paul Whittaker, Scott Tomlinson, Moe Ledger, Jessica Morrison, Don Ferrara, John Minigan, Tom and Cathy Murray, and my brother Kyle Takakjian. Many of these people are dive buddies whom I've trusted with my life, and some have helped me weather shadowy and nefarious challenges ashore. You know who you are, and I am in your debt. Enough said.

To help me in my research over the years, I am indebted to Andrew Lizak, Astrid Drew, Ann House, Charles Rochon, and Matthew Schulte of the Steamship Historical Society of America; Bernard F. Cavalcante at the Naval Historical Center Washington Navy Yard; Elaine Killam of the Mariners Museum; Kathy Flynn of the Peabody Essex Museum; Nathan Lipfert of the Maine Maritime Museum; Paul O'Pecko of Mystic Seaport Museum; Ronald Rosie, former crew member and caretaker of the SS *North American*; Donald Nevin, former chief engineer with United States Lines; and Sue and Bill Ewen.

The living survivors of the wrecks described in this book welcomed me and Randy Peffer as the idea for this book about my wreck-hunting experiences began to take shape. These survivors include Wilma McLean Tucciarone, a passenger aboard the liner *Stephano*, and Tom Blom, a deckhand on the tug *Baleen*. William Kenefick, third officer of the tanker *Exxon Chester*, not only shared his story of being on the bridge of the tanker at the time of her collision with the MV *Regal Sword*, he also shared his personal photographs of the accident for inclusion in this volume. I am in his debt. Don Leavitt, owner of Nautiques, gave graciously of his time to talk about the business of nautical collectibles.

Massachusetts has almost sixteen hundred miles of coastline and a large number of shipwrecks. The Massachusetts Board of Underwater Archaeological Resources is the state agency responsible for protecting the historical integrity of Massachusetts shipwrecks. The board issues permits for the exploration and/or excavation of some wrecks under the supervision of a nautical archaeologist. It also maintains a partial list of shipwrecks off the Massachusetts coast. Over the years the board's director, my friend Victor Mastone, has given guidance and oversight to some of the projects covered in this book.

Anyone interested in the shipwrecks of New England, as I am, should become familiar with John Perry Fish's *Unfinished Voyages: A Chronology of Shipwrecks in the Northeastern United States 1606–1956* (Lower Cape Publishing). Another useful resource is Donald Ferris's 754-page volume *Cape Cod's Anthology of Shipwrecks* (DLF Publishing), as well as William Quinn's books *Shipwrecks Around Cape Cod* and *Shipwrecks Around New England* (Lower Cape Publishing Company). The websites www.wreck site.eu and www.wreckhunter.net have a wealth of information.

Jean Boudriot's epic five-volume work, *The Seventy-Four Gun Ship* (Naval Institute Press) provided a wealth of information on French 74 gunships including *Le Magnifique*. My mother Portia Takakjian's *The 32-Gun Frigate Essex* (Phoenix) provided insight into Revolutionary War ship construction. The archives and website of the New England Historical Society offer up multiple short articles related to the loss of *Le Magnifique* and its alleged treasure.

There are a number of excellent books that have offered insights into the wreck of the SS *Andrea Doria*. Chief among these volumes is William Hoffer's *Saved!: The Story of the Andrea Doria—The Greatest Sea Rescue in History* (Summit Books) and Alvin Moscow's *Collision Course: The Classic Story of Collision of the Andrea Doria and the Stockholm* (Lyons Press). Gary Gentile's *Andrea Doria: Dive to an Era* (Gary Gentile Productions) and *Deep Descent: Adventure and Death Diving the Andrea Doria* (Atria Books) by Kevin F. McMurray are accounts of diving on the *Doria* and divers' deaths on the wreck.

The NTSB report as well as articles from the *New York Times* and the *Boston Globe* unveiled the story of the collision between MV *Regal Sword* and the tanker *Exxon Chester*.

Contemporaneous articles from the *Boston Globe* and *Boston Herald* provided details of the fire and sinking of the tug *Baleen*. The Great Lakes Historical Society, as well as Steven Lang and Peter Spectre's definitive work *On The Hawser: A Tugboat Album* (Down East) and

Peter's tugboat photos and research, provided additional information and images of the tug.

Much has been written about *U-853* over the years. Some of the most helpful information for this book came from *The Last Battle of the Atlantic: The Sinking of the U-853* (Thunderfish Publications) by Captain Bill Palmer and *Dive into History: U-boats* (American Merchant Marine Museum Press) by Henry Keatts and George Farr. John Koster's article "Tightrope Walker" in *Military History* magazine and Adam Lynch's article "Kill or Be Killed" in *Naval History* magazine added to the picture.

Der Kapitän: U-boat Ace Hans Rose (Amberley Publishing) by Markus Robinson and Gertrude Robinson provided rare firsthand insight into Hans Rose's personal papers and viewpoints during his mission to America in 1916. *U-53*'s logbook, statements from the captains of the ships that were sunk, deck logs of the destroyers present, and the log of the Nantucket lightship, as well as newspaper articles from 1916, and "The Cruise of U-53" by Wellington Long (US Naval Institute Proceedings), have added greatly to the story of the *U-53* wrecks. "Courtesy During Wartime" published by Fred Zilian in the *Newport Daily News* relates the story of Hans Rose's impromptu visit to Newport in *U-53*.

Sources related to the wreck of the *City of Columbus* include an article from the January 25, 1994 edition of the *Vineyard Gazette*; an article from the January 17, 2012 edition of the *MV Times*; and information from the private collection of Andrew Lizak. While researching the loss of the *City of Columbus*, I turned to *Disaster on Devil's Bridge* George Hough (Globe Pequot Classics). *The Ocean Steamship Company of Savannah: The Savannah Line*, by Edward A. Muller (Steamship Historical Society of America) and *Savannah Line: Seventy Years of the Ocean Steamship Company 1872–1942* (Ships of the Sea Maritime Museum) provide rich background material. *Disaster Off Martha's Vineyard: The Sinking of the City of Columbus* (Arcadia Publishing) gives a valuable narrative of the sinking.

To research the sinking of the liner SS *Stephano*, I found the *New York Times* and *Boston Globe* stories from the era, as well as other newspaper articles, useful. My brother Kyle introduced me to Wilma McLean Tucciarone in North Truro, Massachusetts. Wilma graciously welcomed me in her home and shared her memories of the attack, a large collection of newspaper articles from the period, and her mother Martha E. McLean's memoir of the event with me. The *Cape Cod Times* ran an article about Wilma (November 10, 1996). I also had the help of the US Navy's incident reports filed by the captain of the SS *Stephano*, the captains of the destroyers present during the incident, and the radio operators' logs from the Nantucket lightship. *The Bowring Story* by David Keir (Bodley Head), and *The Newfoundland Fish Boxes* by Roberts & Nowlan (Brunswick Press) added to my knowledge of both the *Stephano* and the Red Cross Line for which she sailed.

To understand the history and sinking of the SS *North American* and SS *Oregon,* I spoke at length several times with Ronald Rosie. He was former crew member aboard the SS *North American* and one of the ship's last caretakers before she was sold. Ronald related to me the possibility that the flap on the vacuum pump might have been left open for the voyage under tow and that this could have been a possible source of the flooding. My friend Donald Nevin sailed a trip as oiler on the SS *South American*, sister ship to the *North American*. Donald explained the engine room operations aboard those ships in detail. My friends Sue and Bill Ewen related the memories of their honeymoon trip aboard the *North American.*

Jack Gruber of Jack Gruber Productions produced two excellent promotional films aboard the *North American* and her sister ship, which I have viewed numerous times to get an understanding of the ships' layout and how they operated. Jack is the uncle of my friend Matt Schulte, executive director of the Steamship Historical Society. I also had the help of John Polacsek at the Dossin Great Lakes Museum in Detroit. The declassified US Navy action report, "The collision between USS *New Mexico* and MV *Oregon*," and the published decision of the Court of Appeals for the Fourth Circuit re. *Pacific-Atlantic SS Co. v United States* aided my research for those two ships. "Foreign Fishing Crippling New England Industry" by John Kifnerjune (*New York Times,* June 16, 1974) proved a good source of information about international trawlers' assault on the fishing stocks of Georges Bank.

Over the years I have found a wealth of material related to the SS *Newcastle City* and her loss. Some of the most enlightening material includes *Furness Withy a Centenary History 1891–1991* by D. Burrell (World Ship Society); *Shipbuilders of the Hartlepools* by Bert Spaldin (Hartlepool Borough Council); *A Newcastle Century 1886–1986: One Hundred Years of Newcastle P & I Association* by Martin Fryer (Newcastle P & I Association); as well as a *Report of Court of Inquiry into the Stranding and Subsequent Loss of the Steamship Newcastle City* by D. Dougan (British Board of Trade). *The Lightships of Cape Cod* by Frederic L. Thompson (Congress Square Press) has narratives and exposition, as well as many contemporary photographs, related to the lightships of Southern New England.

The public relations office of Holland-American Lines provided detailed information about the SS *Vendam II* and her collision with the *Sagaland*, as did the Guildhall Library in London and Martijn Verbon at Stadsarchief Rotterdam. The British National Maritime Museum in Greenwich shared the detailed outboard profile drawing *Sagaland*.

To fill in the story of RMS *Olympic* and her collision with Nantucket Lightship *LV-117*, I consulted *A History of US Lightships* by Willard Flint (USCG); *Guardians of the Sea: History of the United States Coast Guard* by Robert Johnson (Naval Institute Press) an article by Timothy Harrison in *Lighthouse Digest* (March/April 2016); Mark Chirnside's *RMS Olympic: Titanic's Sister* (The History Press); and the YouTube video "RMS *Olympic* Nantucket Collision" (1934).

My thanks go out to Matt Lawrence for his friendship, help, and sharing the SAS-11 sonar contact with us that turned out to be the SS *Allentown*. We are really grateful for Mark Munro's and Larry Lawrence's help in side-scanning the *Allentown* wreck site for us. In researching the *Allentown* over the years, I turned to a great many books and articles in the Steamship Historical Society's quarterly publication *Steamboat Bill*, now *Power Ships*, some of which include *The Great Coal Schooners of New England 1870–1909*, Lt. W. J. Lewis Parker, USCG (The Marine Historical Association); *Schooners and Schooner Barges* by Paul C Morris (Lower Cape Publishing); *A Captain From Cape Cod: The Merchant Fleets of Crowell & Thurlow* by Paul C Morris (Lower Cape Publishing);

Marine Engineering and Shipping Review, May 1937; *Shipbuilding at Cramp & Sons: A History and Guide to the Collections of the William Cramp & Sons Ship and Engine Building Company* (1830–1927) and the *Cramp Shipbuilding Company (1941–46) of Philadelphia* by Gail E. Farr, Brett F. Bostwick, and Merville Willis (Philadelphia Maritime Museum); *Coastal Colliers* by R. Loren Graham; *Steamboat Bill #123*, Fall 1972; *New York Maritime Register*, November 28, 1888; *Specifications for an Iron Screw Collier* (Reading Railroad).

The Salem County Historical Society and researcher Stacey Costantino with her colleagues at the Gloucester County Historical Society in Southern New Jersey helped us trace and find the family of the *Allentown*'s chief engineer Ben Prichard, and they provided us with a copy of an article from the *Penn's Grove Record* (December 1888) about the ship's loss. Kevin Slovak, the great-great-great-grandson of Ben Prichard, chief engineer on the SS *Allentown*, and his wife April shared stories of their family's extraordinary perseverance in the face of adversity.

An essential tool for any shipwreck enthusiast, wreck hunter, and deep-wreck diver is the 790-page volume *Dictionary of Disasters at Sea During the Age of Steam* by Charles Hocking (*Lloyd's Register*).

Randall Peffer's book, *Where Divers Dare: The Hunt for the Last U-boat* (Penguin Random House/Caliber), unfolds the story of the controversial WWII battle that sunk the German submarine *U-550*, as well as the story of our dive team's search, discovery, exploration of the wreck, and interviews with survivors.

For a historical perspective on WWII in the Atlantic, four books are invaluable. Samuel Eliot Morison's *The Battle of the Atlantic* (Little, Brown & Co.); Clay Blair's monumental two-volume set *Hitler's U-boat War* (Random House); Peter Padfield's *War Beneath the Sea Submarine Conflict During World War Two* (John Wiley & Sons); and Dan Van der Vat's *The Atlantic Campaign: World War II's Great Struggle at Sea* (Harper & Row).

Eberhard Rössler's *The U-boat: The Evolution and Technical History of German Submarines* (Cassell & Co) has excellent photos and historical documentation of U-boat development. Lothar-Günther Buchheim is not only the author of the novel *Das Boot*, but also the creator of an amazing volume of photos and narrative called *U-boat War* (Bonanza Books), which documents a patrol on a combat U-boat in 1942 with astonishing photos.

My friend Harry Cooper, president of Sharkhunters International, has been a wealth of information over the years. His organization has a large archive of U-boat- elated material, but more important, Sharkhunters members represent a broad spectrum of people from inside the submarine and intelligence communities worldwide. Many of these people are former German U-boat crewmen themselves. The website uboatarchive.net is a trove of information on battles, submarines, ships, and crew information. Nothing is better at illustrating the strain of life aboard a U-boat than Wolfang Petersen's film version of Lothar-Günther Buchheim's *Das Boot*.

Finally, a book like this one cannot take its final shape without the help of a legion of people. First, my and Randy Peffer's agent, Doug Grad, brought his characteristic enthusiasm to this project. His guidance has been honed by three decades as an editor and agent for some of the best-known authors of military and maritime books. Lyons Press senior editor Gene Brissie brought his gusto and perspicacity to this book to give it a thoughtful massage before publication. He's an editor with a keen sense of effective storytelling. Our production team also included production editor Alex Bordelon, copyeditor Katie Sharp, proofreader Lauren Szalkiewicz, designer Sally Reinhart, indexer Candace Hyatt, and layout artist Wanda Ditch.

To all, my deep and enduring thanks.

INDEX

Italicized page numbers indicate illustrations.

submarine survival statistics, 50–51; German submarine wrecks, 39, 178 (see also *U-853*); merchant mariner deaths and veterans' status, 227; Navy subchaser wrecks, 204; oil tanker wrecks, 79, 178; patrol boat wrecks, 52, 68; war graves, 19, 54–55
WPA (Works Progress Administration), 90–91

"Wreck of the *Hesperus*" (Longfellow), 200–201, 202, 216–19
Wright, Schuyler E., 94–95, 102
Wydah (pirate ship), x

Yarmouth Castle (passenger steamship), 129
Ypsilantis, Ioannis, 17–18, 25–27

Zhang, Feng, 212, *215*